FROM
RUBBLE
TO
ROYALTY

FINDING GOD'S LOVE
IN THE RUINS

By

T. Kennedy, MS

Some names, locations, relationships, and identifying details have been changed in this book to protect the privacy of the individuals.

Dedicated to Nancy Roy LPC, NCC

I saw a show once about how the mother eagle feeds her baby for a few months and when her eaglet is ready to fly she begins making the nest uncomfortable by slowly taking the nest apart. I once wondered what would happen if the original mother never returned to the nest. Would another mother eagle adopt the abandoned eaglet?

That's what happened to me. My original mother was unable to care for me and because she was unable to protect me, I was severely wounded in my nest.

Thankfully, a nurturing eagle flew down from Maine to teach this baby eagle how to fly.

I will never have enough money to pay you for the many hours you spent helping me choose life, choose safety, and choose to face the memories that were destroying me.

As I now fly, looking to help other baby eagles that are wounded in the nest, please know it was your flying lessons that helped me soar!

With love and gratitude,

Tammy

Table of Contents

Foreword

"Then they will rebuild the ancient ruins,

They will raise up the former devastations;

And they will repair the ruined cities,

The desolations of many generations."

- Isaiah 61:4 (NASB)

In my years of working with men and women coming out of pornography, stripping, prostitution, and sex trafficking, I have met the most amazing, brave, resilient, intelligent, hilarious, talented, loyal, and loving people you could ever hope to meet in a lifetime. One of these standouts is Tammy Kennedy.

Tammy is a survivor of childhood sexual abuse, trafficking, eating disorders, self-harm, and shame. But she is so much more than a survivor. She is a faithful friend, a loving sister, a courageous advocate, a compassionate servant, a creative genius, and a precious child of God who knows it. She was one who heard Jesus declare the good news, saw Him bind up her broken heart, and stepped into His glorious freedom. Now, as proclaimed in Isaiah 61, she is rebuilding the ruins, raising up the former devastations, and repairing ruined cities.

I can tell you without hesitation that Tammy has no desire to become a best-selling author or celebrity. She is not in this for personal gain or glory. Her motivation is unshakeable – to praise the God who lifted her from rubble to royalty, and to see you experience the same. You have probably never met Tammy, but she loves you, weeps for you, prays for you, and desires with all of her heart to see you find healing for your soul.

Stepping into Tammy's world is not easy. You will probably grimace, squirm, shout, smile and cry…maybe all at once. You may be deciding right now whether to even read on, or you may be tempted to tuck it away once you begin. But I encourage you to press on. Tammy's is a story that must be told, and more importantly, a story that must be heard. Discussing childhood sexual abuse, incest, trafficking, mental illness and the like is not comfortable. But only when we begin to see these things and understand them can we truly begin to confront them and create safe spaces for the healing process to begin. Tammy's story reflects the very heart of God that we will surely miss out on if we turn away in discomfort.

This book is for the abused, the suicidal, the hopeless, the abandoned, the unloved, the unseen, the neglected, the broken-hearted, the ashamed, and the hurting. In short, it is for all of us.

I was born in Canada, but I live in Atlanta now. Believe it or not, we do experience the occasional cold winter day, even in the steamy south. More times than I can count, I have been underdressed on a frigid day, rubbed my shoulders, and exclaimed, "It is FREEZING out here!" only to hear, "But you're Canadian." My response is always, "Cold is cold, no matter where you're from."

Tammy has experienced significant hurt in her life. You have experienced hurt too. As you read her story, you may find yourself dismissing your hurt because it's nothing like Tammy's. But hurt is hurt, no matter how you experienced it. And the beautiful truth is that Jesus wants to comfort you, whether your hurt looks like the loss of a limb or just a scraped knee. His promise is to restore the years the locusts have eaten. (Joel 2:25) His beautiful plan of redemption awaits you.

Meet my friend, Tammy. I know you will come to love her just as much as I do. But even more than that, I pray that you will fall in love with the Savior King, either for the first time or all over again. His invitation to you is nothing less than Royalty.

Jeff Shaw
Founder, Out of Darkness
A ministry of Atlanta Dream Center

Chapter I

"THAT'S JUST JESUS"

I'll never forget that day at my grandmother's house. I was playing on the carport floor with Stacy, a little girl who lived down the road. We both loved playing there when it was hot outside because the concrete floor remained cool under our little legs. On one especially hot day, it happened. We heard beautiful music so intense that we walked out from under the carport to find the music. We looked around and then up. Looking back, we should have been shocked to see such a glorious sight. As an adult, I certainly would freak out now if I saw a vision such as this. How could she and I approach this apparition so casually?

What we saw almost defies description. We saw the throne of Jesus in the sky with angels all around Him making the most incredible music. The angels were playing golden trumpets, and it was the brightest and most glorious scene one could imagine. I can't convey the beauty we saw, nor can I describe the sound we heard. I would not believe this could have really happened, except that the little girl with me saw and heard it as well. We talked about it on all future play dates and considered it our special secret. I had no idea how valuable this vision would become to my well-being later.

How My Game Began

At three years of age, I knew the smell of death. Have you ever hung out in a funeral home? There's a strange sadness and smell that seems to cling to your body. I knew all about this as a small child. I hated going to the funeral home and especially to the crematorium. Was it the smell or was it something else that happened there? I do know I started playing "my game" at the funeral home owned by Ken, my first stepfather. My game required other participants so I created other children in my mind, gave them each a name, and then instructions on how to play. "Layla, it's your turn to have your picture taken with the bodies," and then "Camie, it's your turn to follow Mr. Green Jeans to the car." I learned to be their director from a safe window in the distance.

Even now, at almost fifty years of age, I'm still terrified of dead bodies! I can still vividly see them lying on the big metal table, if I allow my mind to peek into the "body part" room. That's what I called it when I was three. Sometimes the bodies were naked and sometimes they had on clothes. I hated the naked bodies and their awful stench. I hated the tubes coming in and out. I thought Ken was giving them medicine from a tube like at the hospital, but the people lying there never got better.

Another scene in the window, if I peeked in, would be me sitting on the big table with a naked body beside me. I don't want to imagine the smell in the room or how the body felt when I was forced to touch it. If I think of ice cream really fast, I won't see the frightening scene inside the window. If the pictures taken of me faded, there would be no evidence. No one would ever know the things I did. I wanted God to mess up the camera equipment, and I would've asked Him, but I didn't want to bring it up, just in case He hadn't noticed the sinful things I was doing. Maybe Jesus wasn't looking right then.

The horrific memories I have of being at the funeral home and crematorium still cause me anxiety when I force myself to go back there in my head. For more than three decades, I remained too terrified to tell anyone about the frightening events that occurred there. Even into my adult years, I believed my abusers had the power to hurt me even from the grave.

I was an infant when Ken entered my life; he offered a very confusing fatherly relationship. I have pictures of him holding me as an infant with a proud smile on his face. Though I was only about six months old, I was wearing a beautiful long white dress. In some of the pictures, he was wearing his red Shriner hat and I, about four years old, had on a child-size version. It appears we had just gone to the Shrine circus. He and many of my relatives were very involved in the Masonic organization. This same stepfather had tea parties in the living room with my baby dolls and me. He also bought me a pinto pony when I was three, and he often took my mother and me to the beach in his private plane. However, this was the same man who held my face up to the cremation window until my face burned while threatening to put me in the oven if I told anyone of the secrets that happened there. He terrified me with the rats he trapped at the funeral home. This was the man who raped me, allowed others to hurt me, and who placed me in an empty casket to show me what it felt like to be dead.

Ken knew the cremation part of his job frightened me the most. I rode with him in the hearse to pick up dead bodies at various hospitals. I saw pennies put on their eyes to keep them closed. I saw the dead bodies move when they were put on the conveyor belt into the crematorium oven. The movements weren't simply involuntary twitches; they were the real scary kind of movements telling me, "I'm coming to get you tonight." At least that's what Ken said would happen if I revealed his secrets. His threats to make bad things happen gave me no choice but to remain silent.

Maybe it was monsters kidnapping me at night when I was a small child that caused sleep to be a lifetime battle. Maybe it was monsters that gave me sleeping juice before we got in the car. Certainly it was monsters that took me to a building surrounded by graves. Mr. Green Jeans was always there. I don't know why I called him this, but he worked with Ken. I do know that as a small child, one of my favorite TV programs was *Captain Kangaroo*, and one of the characters on the show was Mr. Green Jeans. There were several other monsters at the crematorium; they had strange faces. Sometimes other kids were there, too, and the monsters played games I did not like! The monsters and I prayed, drank red juice, and they repeated words that made no sense

---

I often wondered, Why is Mother so attracted to abusive men? No one can be this unlucky. Years later I learned this is a very common occurrence when someone has been abused in childhood.

---

to me. Even now, it feels like the monsters will come get me because I'm revealing their secrets. "I'm coming to get you tonight" seemed possible every night for about thirty years. At first, they were monsters coming to steal me right out of my bed. It wasn't until the memories began surfacing, with all the original intense feelings attached, that I realized the monsters I feared were actually safer than the people in my life, even my mother.

My mother once asked, "Do you remember all the jars of body parts Ken kept in a closet where they dress the bodies? He did strange things at times." This comment, among many others, made it very possible that the memory I have of being placed in a coffin could possibly have happened. I often wondered, *Why is Mother so attracted to abusive men? No one can be this unlucky.* Years later I learned this is a very common occurrence when someone has been abused in childhood. I will never know the truth about my mother's childhood experiences; family members said she was spoiled by her older siblings and loved by her parents. Could her lifelong issues with alcohol and depression stem from the loss of her father as a small child? She mentioned missing him a great deal. Other relatives have struggled with addiction to alcohol. Is it some genetic issue? What I do know is my mother had Grand Canyon size needs that could never get satisfied. Sadly, her emotional pain led to a very frightening childhood for her children, an unhappy life for her, and then an early death.

My mother told me on many occasions that she'd been molested a few times during her teens. Actually, she told me about the two times she was abused as a teen every time I tried to tell her about the sexual abuse I was enduring. I vividly remember being her 'on call' therapist in the middle of the night as she cried and drank massive amounts of alcohol after I tried to get her to intervene when one of my abusers brought me back home. The tears were never for my pain.

Mother explained that the attempted rape by one of her cousins when she was seventeen was the reason she left home at eighteen to marry a man much older. Her first divorce occurred about a year later. She then met and fell in love with my father who did not reciprocate the same emotions, but she did became pregnant with me. I was born to an alcoholic, mentally unstable, twenty-one-year-old mother, who was absolutely starved for love and attention, and a father who adamantly wanted nothing to do with me. He, having a two-year-old son already, had no desire for another marriage and another responsibility.

Thankfully, my paternal grandmother insisted he marry mother so that I would not be considered illegitimate. The marriage was extremely brief, so I always wondered, *Does a marriage, just on paper, count enough to make me legitimate?* I heard the word "illegitimate" used referring to me when I was in middle school. I looked it up and the definition included, "Irregular and not in good usage." I thought, *So, everyone knows I'm not like regular people and there is no good "usage" for me?* Due to mother's extreme neediness and my father's attraction to other women, a loving relationship was impossible.

Mother had been dating Ken, my worst abuser and owner of the funeral home, by the time I was born. She used her, "I'm pregnant" tactic again with both Ken and my next stepfather Tony, in hopes of landing a husband. Ken forced her to have an abortion, very uncommon in those days, but when I was four she gave birth to my first sister. I don't remember exactly when mother was married to each husband and where each boyfriend fits into the scene. Pictures of the men who came into and out of my mother's life feel similar to looking at an old scrapbook. The pictures of the faces are very familiar, and pieces of memories are attached to each one. The problem is that looking at each picture brings about so many questions, *Why did I go fishing with this face and where were we? How old was I when this face took me to a motel where I went swimming every day? We stayed there several days so why do I only remember the pool area? Who was that other face with us?* The scrapbook pictures get all jumbled up, cause random and intense feelings to surface, and then I have an extreme desire to shut the confusing book very quickly and never open it again.

Having too many missing pieces can cause a survivor to feel like she's going crazy. To my knowledge, Ken was the first of many pedophiles who would be given access to me. About five years ago, when I began doing volunteer work with a ministry called Out of Darkness, I realized what Mother was doing would be considered child sex trafficking. I was stunned at the thought. However, this explained so much and provided the missing puzzle pieces I needed in order to have a clearer picture of my childhood.

My Mother and Her Empty Cup

From birth, my mother loved me as much as she was capable of loving anyone. She was a successful paralegal, earned a good salary, and bought expensive clothes and toys for her first-born. Her love for me was unfortunately not as large as her "Grand Canyon size needs." As her first-born infant, I naturally met some of Mother's emotional needs, especially when I brought attention from others. Similar to a performing circus animal, mother enjoyed showing me off. For example, Mother often bragged that she taught me to read before my fifth birthday. To avoid the cost of daycare,

Mother wanted me to qualify for kindergarten early. I remembered having reading lessons from a lady in Denton. I also remember the terrifying flashcard sessions with my mother, but I never knew why I was so afraid until she provided the missing puzzle piece. Mother had a new stack of fifty Beginner Reader Flashcards. By age five, I read each one correctly except for two words: *who* and *how*. They had the same letters, but one did not sound like it should. When she flipped to *how*, I said, "Who." I remember feeling the most intense fear as each card flipped because I knew those confusing words would be coming back around. When the word *who* appeared on the card, I

The men who came in and out of my mother's life feel similar to looking at an old scrapbook. The memories get all jumbled up, cause random and intense feelings to surface, and I have an extreme desire to shut the confusing book very quickly and never open it again.

---

stared and stared, too afraid to attempt a guess. She pushed for an answer, and I began crying much harder. Why did I feel terrified? I was on the verge of vomiting, but why? My answer as I sounded it out was "whoa, whoa." The missing puzzle piece was why I remember getting so hysterical when my mother got out the flashcards. Mother was happy to fill in the missing piece! "I gave you the spanking of your life when you missed a word." So, I was not crazy to be wary of flashcards early in life. She proudly pointed out, "It worked; you never missed *who* and *how* again." How can someone be proud of the missing pieces they provide when it makes them look cruel?

Though almost all my memories of our house in Denton include intense fear, I do remember a source of kindness. For the first six years of my life, Mother's best friend, Joyce Berry, came over often to play a card game called Canasta while they drank. Many years later, Joyce provided information about my mother's sometimes cruel parenting style. She told me there was a period of weeks when I screamed for hours at night when I was about twelve months old. Joyce wanted so badly to come pick me up, but Mother insisted I was having temper tantrums because I did not want to go to bed. Joyce, having a daughter of her own, convinced Mother to take me to my pediatrician. Mother discovered I had a severe ear infection. After my tonsils were removed, the "temper tantrums" suddenly disappeared. Joyce cared.

Joyce not only provided valuable information about my mother's parenting practices, she also filled me in on Mother's emotional state during my early years. She told me that Mother was almost successful in killing Ken, but not because he was molesting me. Mother found out he was dating other women, so she went to his apartment with her gun determined to kill him. Ken did not come home that night, so in a state of rage, Mother poured bleach all over everything he owned including his furniture, clothes, and carpeting. Just in case the bleach was not sufficient enough to destroy his expensive suits, Mother also cut them to shreds with sharp scissors. She always said, "If you can't do something right, don't do it at all!"

When Joyce and I reconnected many years later, I asked why she stopped spending time with my mother, which meant me as well. She explained she could no longer be around my mother due to the violence in our home, the neglect my sisters and I experienced, and Mother's alcoholism and erratic behavior. Joyce also explained that she had to protect her own daughter, a concept no one had ever explained to my mother.

There is a family story from when I was about three years old that reveals I did not have the sense that my mother also wanted to "protect her own daughter." Mother used a cream on her lips called Blistex. She kept it in her jewelry box, and I knew I was not to touch it. However, what is one to do when she, her baby doll, and her dog Prissy have chapped lips? How could I let Prissy and my baby suffer so much with those dry lips? Yes, you guessed it. My mother walked in and all three of us had a massive amount of

Blistex on our lips. My mother, like many mothers, set up the usual lie test. "Did you get into my Blistex?" (Why do parents do this when the crime is so apparent?)

I hid the plastic evidence tube behind my back and said, "No, Prissy did it." My thought was, *Mother has no way of knowing which of us did it, so she would obviously believe me.* I knew it was not possible for my baby doll to get up on the dresser, but Prissy was little and could easily jump up on anything. I explained in detail how Prissy opened the jewelry box with her teeth and applied the medicine to our lips with her paws. In my little mind, Mother had two suspects for the crime; would she believe Prissy or me?

This is the first memory I have of feeling emotionally abandoned by my mother. Though my conclusion was unreasonable since I had done the crime, my three-year-old mind was indignant, shocked, and devastated when she picked Prissy as the innocent one. To me, the horrendous spanking I received for my crime was proof that my mother would believe others over me, and that everyone else's wellbeing was more important than mine.

There are many puzzle pieces of my childhood that will always be missing. Why did my mother have a scary lady named Linda living with us for a while? Why did Mother put all of Linda's belongings in the yard and set fire to them? What was the relationship between Linda and Ken? I remember times they were both with me. Why was I afraid of Linda, and why did she force me to watch a show called *Dark Shadows* every day? Those shows really scared me. Also, what is the truth about my mother shooting herself and almost dying? This type of drama, abuse, and constant change can even cause an adult to withdraw from reality. It is similar to Vietnam veterans who returned home after the war with post-traumatic stress disorder whose spouses reported, "He has never been the same."

During these stressful early years, I remember severe headaches that I later learned were called migraines. The strange part of the memory is that when I had these most painful headaches, I was afraid to tell my mother. If I vomited, I'd either quickly clean it up or hide it until I could sit up. I still have no clue why I would be afraid to tell her about my pain. Were the migraines related to Ken's abuse in some way?

I now believe the difficult circumstances in my life occurred because of Mother's mental illness, emotional wounding, and addictions, not because she did not love me. However, there is nothing that can explain my mother's willingness to allow others to have access to me for sexual purposes. The abuse was severe, which is why I have been asked so many times, "How did you remain sane?" In fact, a therapist once told me, "On an abuse scale of one to ten, your abuse was a twenty!"

My reason for sharing this part of my early childhood is to begin illustrating some of the ways I believe God has interceded in my life. As a child, the option to tell a safe adult, as we tell children to do today, felt like certain death. But I needed to be able to put the memories of the funeral home, the crematorium, the sexual abuse, and the intense fear somewhere so that I could function in the world around me. How can a child have fun going to Stone Mountain Park with her cousins the day after horrendous abuse without hiding these overwhelming memories, even from herself?

It was the delightful imagination God bestowed on me that allowed me to assign the memories and feelings to someone else in my mind. Over time, I became so good at separating myself from the pain that I became able to believe it was the characters in my game, such as Lucky, who was placed in the coffin with the dead body at the funeral home. It was Camie who had frantic rats hanging from a trap over her head and tummy. While Beth handled the intense fear, it was Velda who handled the rage I would have felt, but was too scared to express.

Another way I believe God has interceded in my life was to provide a few caring relationships that resulted in a strong enough foundation to allow me to bond emotionally with others. The type of severe abuse and neglect I experienced early in childhood has been proven to cause attachment disorders. This is a serious condition in which an infant/young child is unable to bond with others later in life. It often occurs in orphanages. This disorder can cause developmental delays, permanent changes in brain growth and structure, behavior issues, an inability to express emotions, poor social skills, defiance, the inability to feel guilt, chronic anxiety, and many other negative consequences. The documented causes of attachment disorders include: an emotionally unavailable parent, abuse, neglect, parental substance abuse, and an unstable living environment. Check, check, check, I qualify! Until age seventeen, this sums up much of my life.

Another way I believe God has interceded in my life was to provide a few caring relationships that resulted in a strong enough foundation to allow me to bond emotionally with others.

During these early years, when change was constant, abuse was often, and my own mother was emotionally unavailable, I believe God knew I needed some safe, caring, and stable relationships so that I could learn to attach to others, develop properly, and eventually heal. I have heard it said, "It is through relationships that we are wounded, and it is through relationships that we are healed." If a child develops an attachment disorder, that child's capacity to heal is usually minimal.

"Mom," My Maternal Grandmother and Source of Great Love

My Father in heaven provided the most wonderful grandmother, from whom I learned what it felt like to have a safe and loving bond. Until I was almost five years old, I stayed with her during the day while my mother worked as a paralegal in Ashton. I called this grandmother "Mom" from the time I could speak. From my birth, Mom cared for me each weekday and loved me unconditionally. The stress during this time was intense and I dreaded the evening approaching, but I always knew I would be back at my safe place the next day. Unless Mother went out for drinks after work, she arrived at 6:00 p.m. each evening to pick me up from Mom's house. There were many nights when I cried so hard to remain at Mom's house that I choked, and Mother eventually allowed me to stay. Mom would say, "Sharon, you're just bringing her back in the morning, so let her stay. I already have her pajamas laid out."

It was no family secret that Mom had a very special affection for me, probably due to my mother's alcoholism and my need for stability. I was told Mom once scolded Mother so harshly regarding an incident over dinner that she retaliated and put me in daycare briefly to punish my grandmother. I was about six months old when Mother slapped me very hard in the face because I spit out the baby food she had shoveled in. Apparently, I did not like beets. Thankfully, the fight between them only lasted a week or so, but taught Mom to keep silent about her concerns regarding my care.

During the day, Mom's house was a haven of love and safety. She had an amazing rose garden in the backyard and let me help her grow prize-winning roses. She even created a hybrid rose and named it "Tammy." When Mom won first place at a huge garden show, the Denton newspaper took a picture of Mom letting me smell her prized rose and printed it in the newspaper. One of my favorite memories occurred during our time in her rose garden. As a four-year-old gardener, I was certain that the huge earthworms found in her garden would love sliding down my slide as much as I did. Mom would find the earthworms and place them on the top of my slide. I would then gently flick them down the slide with a stick over and over, so that they experienced the same thrill I felt on my way down. I always imagined they were thanking me in their little heads. My vivid imagination helped me survive!

On the Saturday nights when my mother went out drinking, I spent the night with Mom. She took me to church the next morning, and I helped her cook Sunday dinner. I also enjoyed playing with my cousins and the neighborhood children she kept in her home. There was a routine at Mom's house, with no screaming, no undeserved punishments, and no fear.

Because there were such extremes in my life, times of severe abuse by my stepfather and times of sweet play at Mom's house, I needed to be able to compartmentalize all that was happening around me. "My game" was very necessary for survival! I could not learn how to spell in kindergarten if I was still traumatized by the rape the night before. By assigning that memory, rage, and fear to someone else, I was somehow able to continue functioning during the day as if all were well.

As I got older, my ability to play the game improved. I became able to assign intense physical pain to another child within my game world and separate myself from the actual pain. This is called dissociation, and it's a common survival skill for children when abuse is severe. Everyone dissociates to some extent, and it's natural; our minds focus on something else and we get distracted from current space and time. I learned to mentally leave my body and focus on something else that is comforting. This does not mean the survivor never has to feel the pain, memories, fear, or anger. If healing is to occur, what was once shoved down must rise to the surface. Those who don't eventually face it frequently turn to self-medication, self-harm, or an addiction to get their needs met by someone else, or something equally as destructive in order to hold back the pain. For example, I have met so many women, diagnosed with dissociative identity disorder due to severe abuse as a child, who have an extreme addiction to their therapist.

Mom, my precious grandmother, was the first wonderful relationship the Lord gave to me. She was my favorite and safest person, and I was deeply loved by her, so I was very attached to her emotionally. When she died unexpectedly in her sixties of a heart attack, I was devastated, but I believe Jesus had already interceded in a very real way to lessen my pain.

It was during this time that the first miracle occurred. For the first few years of my life, my grandmother served me a waffle each morning at the same time the children on *Romper Room*, my favorite television show, had their snack. I desperately wanted Mrs. Nancy to say, "I see Tammy," in her magic mirror because I wanted to feel her watching over me. I had already held a lifetime of secrets and just wanted to know someone could see my pain. It was about a month prior to Mom's death that the heavenly throne scene appeared to me. Mrs. Nancy never saw me in her magic mirror, but seeing Jesus on His throne allowed me to know He was watching over me. I believe Jesus revealed Himself to me in a very memorable way because my life was about to get much worse.

It was during this time that the first miracle occurred. Jesus knew I would not be able to sustain my emotional and spiritual foundation without this spectacular encounter.

Jesus knew I would not be able to sustain my emotional and spiritual foundation without this spectacular encounter with Christ. Zephaniah 3:17 (NIV) says, "The Lord your God is with you, the Mighty Warrior who saves. He will take great delight in you; in his love he will no longer rebuke you, but will rejoice over you with singing."

I have never stopped believing in the existence of Christ since I saw Him on that hot, sunny day in 1968. I felt Jesus' love for me. He took "delight" in my friend and me and "rejoiced" over us with singing.

During my many years of recovery, when I was tempted to doubt His existence or that He watched over me, I could go back into my memory vault and retrieve the spectacular picture of Christ on the throne watching me play. Psalms 34:18 (NIV) says, "The LORD is close to the brokenhearted and saves those who are crushed in spirit." When my grandmother died, I was truly "crushed in spirit and brokenhearted." However, Jesus remained very close to me through other special relationships during my childhood!

Everyone Needs an Aunt Alice

Memories are strange and very powerful. Some memories bring huge smiles and a deep sense of being loved. Some memories bring wishes for early death and pain so deep that you truly feel you can't survive it. Some memories never fully present themselves, so you lean on family members to help put the pieces together. When my mother was still a teen, her oldest brother Stephen began dating a precious woman who would become my Aunt Alice, my greatest resource in putting the puzzle pieces of me back together.

Missing pieces feel like craziness and insanity. Missing pieces cause thoughts such as, *I'm just making this all up; nothing bad happened. What kind of movies have I been watching? I have such a sick imagination.* When pieces of our past are missing, it's very hard to ignore the weird pictures that develop in our mind and the intense emotions that manifest with the developing images. The urge to numb oneself using whatever means possible, such as drugs, bingeing, starving, cutting, alcohol, or dissociation from the pain and fear, is almost impossible to fight. Aunt Alice's memories and insight have provided much-needed validation to help me fight my feelings of being crazy.

A puzzle piece such as, "Your mother was a severe alcoholic before you were born and would go to bars with different attorneys after work," helped the strange memories of being left at various places and no one coming to get me finally make sense. It made real the memory of me, at five years old, waiting in the daycare center office with my newborn sister after all the other children had left. The staff grilling me about why my mother was late and who should they call to retrieve us. My grandmother had just died and I already felt abandoned; Mother failing to pick us up from daycare added feelings of guilt and shame as well. It's a strange thing that children can so easily blame themselves for what happens in the world around them. Thankfully, Aunt Alice was faithful to retrieve us each time this happened.

Many clues to my childhood have come from other sources. A few years ago, I met one of my aunt's friends at her 75th birthday party. This friend recognized my name and said she had not seen me since I was a little girl. Her name was familiar, but I have no memory of her. She explained, "I babysat you often when your mother went out, but there is one memory I'll never forget." She explained that my mother drank a lot and rarely returned on the agreed time, so she began telling my mother she couldn't keep me. On this particular day, she stood washing her morning dishes and happened to look out her kitchen window to see me sitting on her curb, next to the trashcan, holding my infant sister. She told me she rushed out to the front yard still in her pajamas and asked, "Why are you sitting out here?" She said my response was simply, "My mother said, 'You stay here until Ms. Pruitt notices you.'" I was almost five years old and already felt capable of caring for my baby sister.

Sadly, there are pieces of my memory that no one will ever be able to explain. Aunt Alice had no idea why I remember sitting alone on the steps of an exclusive Ashton country club to wait for a strange man to come pick me up, and why was I so terrified that I vomited on the steps? Was I afraid because I had been left, or was I afraid of the one coming to get me? Without any other information, I reasoned as an adult, *All children have strange and unfounded fears; maybe I simply had a stomach bug.* My need to manipulate the strange memories into a context of having a safe and happy childhood became more difficult as the missing puzzle pieces started to create a whole picture.

Most of my nighttime puzzle pieces included fear; for example, I was always terrified that something evil was hiding under my bed, even into adulthood. I remember trying to jump onto my bed from about three feet away and sleep in the middle so that no body part was near the edge. Once again, Aunt Alice provided a clue, "You had nightmares as a small child like nothing I'd ever seen. You often woke up screaming and so terrified that you vomited." This missing piece of information regarding my extreme fear at night helped me begin to consider, *Maybe my fears were not the typical "unfounded" kind.* Her memories helped me justify my strange nighttime rituals until I could validate for myself that there was severe trauma to explain the night terror. I was also very afraid of my closet. You never know what horrifying monsters could be living there!

I have very few memories of my childhood home where I lived with my mother until she married her fifth husband when I was almost six years old. I don't remember ever sleeping, eating, or bathing in our house in Denton, so why do I have so many vivid and wonderful memories of my time at Uncle Stephen and Aunt Alice's house? They had four children of their own, so the house was filled with laughter. I was able to relax there because her reactions to mishaps were safe and predictable. Children appreciate and notice the strangest things. I have a wonderful memory of being about five years old and Aunt Alice was taking us to Stone Mountain for the day. One of my cousins asked if we could have Krystal hamburgers for lunch; however, Aunt Alice explained she had already made our picnic lunch that morning. I remembered watching her make our sandwiches; she knew which kid liked which type sandwich. As she created mine, she spread the creamy peanut butter right up to the edge of the crust and then made a smiley face with sprinkled sugar. That sandwich tasted like the best meal I had ever eaten.

She also took us swimming and skating while Uncle Stephen was at work. If I was at her house on Sunday mornings, I went to church with them. The "gum man" was always there, and we had the same Sunday school teacher for many years. I loved singing a song called, "Deep and Wide" while doing the hand motions. Even the pinch by Aunt Alice during church when we whispered, blew bubbles with our gum, or made noise during the service causes me to smile. The memory of her safe and predictable discipline causes me to have the sense that I was loved, just as if I were one of her own children.

Sometimes the memories we do have are clues to the ones that are missing. I have a few detailed memories of my time with my aunt, with the associated feelings attached, that I believe help explain something about my relationship with my own mother. I especially loved bath time at Aunt Alice's house. Every night, my two female cousins and I had a wonderful time playing in the bubbles until our skin pruned. Aunt Alice bathed and dressed the one sitting in the front first, so I always wanted to sit in the back. She had the same routine every time she bathed us; face first, bodice and limbs next, bottom last. I'm not sure why I remember so much detail about our bath time except that it was predictable and provided a time of safe touch. The best part was getting dried off. Aunt Alice would dry us thoroughly and a big hug often followed. Many years later, I discovered why I have absolutely no memories of the bathroom at my own house during this same time. It was Ken who often bathed me at night while my mother was making dinner. I think dissociation was one of the ways God helped me survive.

Another favorite memory of my time at Aunt Alice's house was simply the feeling of being loved. Each night, after being tucked into bed individually, we said our prayers and received a kiss. The best part was not getting tucked in, although I loved that too, it was her second coming that I treasured. Each night, before Aunt Alice went to bed herself, she came back to take a last peek at each of us. Though exhausted after a day of swimming and playing, I was determined to stay awake to see her check on me. I pretended to be asleep, but the act of her checking on me was the best feeling I could imagine. My extreme desire to know someone was watching over me and feel that I was safe is a clue that there must have been many times when I did not feel safe.

Just about every safe memory from early childhood included either my grandmother or Aunt Alice being there. I remember being very afraid of my mother as a small child but only have a few memories that would explain the fear. When I asked Aunt Alice about my fear, she responded, "Your mother had times of instability." I guess setting a roommate's belongings on fire, attempting to murder a boyfriend, and shooting yourself could be considered unstable!

Because of the excessive shame attached to mental illness, families are often tempted to either deny or minimize the reality of what's happening. Mother's "instability" was later called schizophrenia by the medical profession and helps explain the reason I was so afraid of her. I know the reprieve I enjoyed at my aunt Alice's house was essential to my own mental wellness. She and I are still close and I believe the Lord knew how much I needed her during those early years due to the "instability" I experienced with my mother.

My Precious "Little Mama"

Once again, I believe God knew what I needed to remain emotionally stable with the ability to have close relationships later in life. He knew I needed someone praying for me consistently. My biological father refused to marry my mother until his mother, whom I called Little Mama, insisted he marry her so that I would not be born an illegitimate child. He angrily obeyed but had two conditions: the marriage would be brief and he would never be required to pay child support. My father already had a son he adored and did not want a daughter or the obligation of child support payments.

The good part here is that my Little Mama accepted me as her one and only granddaughter and she loved me. She was a "prayer warrior" and filled with the Holy Spirit. She had great faith and was well respected in the Pentecostal community as a teacher, healer, and exhorter in the body of Christ. She went to hospitals and prayed for the sick. She was sent to peoples' houses to cast out demons and pray with people who were suffering. She also taught my mother and me about the Bible and often prayed for us. I know my mother loved Jesus very much. This may seem strange for me to say, but my mother was mentally ill and starving for love and attention, just as I would starve for it later.

There are many precious memories of my time at Little Mama's house. I often had ice cream and coconut cake with my Papa. Little Mama bought an Easy-Bake Oven for me, and we made tons of messes. She loved dolls and bought beautiful porcelain dolls for me to love and care for. She also bought me dolls that I could bottle feed. She may have regretted this. I was a nurturer by nature (remember the earthworms) and would feed those dolls constantly. One time she told me that I fed the dolls so much that I soaked up every towel she owned in one day. I never left her house without a special treat that she bought just for me.

At a very young age, my heavenly Father provided people who loved me, formed a close bond with me, and provided times of safety. All three of my childhood caretakers showed me unconditional love, took me to church, and prayed for me. I believe God formed me in my mother's womb and knew the trauma I would endure on earth because of our fallen world. He knew the enemy (Satan) would try to steal my ability to love and trust others. He knew how difficult it is to have joy and peace in this world even without such a painful childhood. Even if I'd never been sexually abused, God knew my mother had an extreme addiction to alcohol and was mentally ill enough to be dangerous on many occasions. I believe Jesus saw the pain, fear, and abuse I would endure, so He designed a way of escape. His plan for our lives is to be free from the prison of hate, self-pity, rage, guilt, shame, fear, and especially unforgiveness. Even though our difficult circumstances may remain the same for a while, if we follow Him, we'll be led to the destiny He had planned for us all along.

Chapter 2

HIS HEALING HAND

It was a very desperate and frightening night when I had my second encounter with Jesus. The migraine headaches that began when I was four continued almost weekly for many years. On this night, when I was about eight years old, my head hurt more than I can describe. Only someone who also endures migraines would know of this intense pain. I had already thrown up in bed and could barely move. My face was turned toward the wall, where the civil war occurred on the other side. My headache was brutal; I was terrified! All the while Mother was screaming for me to help her, and I felt angry with God. At that moment, the pain and fear seemed too overwhelming to endure. I began an angry prayer, "God, You don't care. You don't really love me. How can I even know You're there?" Suddenly, it felt exactly like someone sat on the bed beside me. I knew my sisters were not in my room that night, and I could hear Mother and Charlie, her fifth husband, fighting in the living room.

During the battle I lay thinking, *Who is that? I never heard the police or neighbors come in. Turn around and see who's there.* As my thoughts went all over the place, I felt a firm hand on my back within five seconds of my question, *How can I even know You're there?* At that very moment, the most peaceful feeling came over me, and my migraine disappeared. I had never had a migraine that simply went away! I could still hear the fighting on the other side of the wall, but it seemed so distant and I was not bothered by it. The hand simply stayed on my back until I fell asleep. This part was also miraculous. I actually fell asleep! I don't think I had ever fallen asleep before waiting to see if Mother was still alive after Charlie left. Even at one, two, or three in the morning, I always listened and waited!

I have found that some of my memories are very strange and sometimes tricky. Pieces get mixed with other pieces, and time seems fragmented. The blank spaces often make me nervous. I don't remember much of the year following my grandmother's death, except that I very much wanted to go to heaven with her, but didn't know how to get there. A few of my memories during this time occurred at Playland Daycare Center.

During recess, due to my crazy imagination, I believed if I could just swing high enough I'd simply be catapulted up to heaven to be with my grandmother. I pumped my little legs as hard as I could each day, much higher than the other children. I knew my precious grandmother had a hard time picking me up before she died, so I was positive Jesus would catch me and hand me over to her. My heart ached to be with her.

Instead of heaven, I find it strange that my other memory at daycare was about hell. Ken and my mother had told me about hell, each with different motives, so I was very curious about this awful place. Feeling extremely sad for all the children burning in the fire while being trapped in hell, I recruited a helper and devised an escape plan. We used at least half of our playtime to work on our rescue mission. We dug a hole behind a tree so our teacher could not foil our efforts. Sometimes my recruit wanted to give up and go swing or slide. I emphatically explained, "We have to help the children 'cuz they're on fire." I was positive this would be the day we got deep enough to break through to hell. We also gathered as many long sticks as possible.

It seemed so simple. The ceiling of hell would break through, and I'd use a long stick for the children to climb out. After a few weeks' time, the hole became quite deep and our teacher scolded us for damaging property. I was so indignant that our teachers had no interest in saving the children in hell!

Little did I know, within a year, I'd be a child living in hell, just the earthly kind. This was the year Charlie entered our world. Let's put this in perspective. The year was 1970 and rules for men and women were very different. The judicial system, law enforcement, and social services were very different as well. As I share this portion of my life, I have no ill feelings against Charlie, just as I have no ill feelings against my mother. I later learned he was beaten severely as a child and never received treatment and healing. His rage needed to go somewhere. No one is all bad or all good. Charlie loved basketball. He took me to Ashton Jumpers' and Harlem Globetrotters' games, and he bought me a huge in-ground basketball goal so that we could play together. Also, Charlie never molested or beat me. For that I am grateful!

One of my first memories of Charlie was when we lived at Tregony West Apartments before Charlie and Mother were married. I'm not sure if I had turned six yet. Mother sold our first house in Denton after my grandmother died. She met Charlie and they bought a lot in a nice neighborhood in Steelwood, Georgia. We lived in an apartment for a year while our new home was being built. In this memory, I was in the living room and heard the loudest screaming and fighting I had ever heard. Charlie owned a Chevron gas station, and three of his mechanics were there during the fight. They often came over after work to get drunk with Mother and Charlie. During my childhood, there was a vast amount of alcohol consumption going on around me.

These guys, whom I knew well, kept telling me to stay with them and not to go down the hall. They explained that Charlie and Mother were "play fighting and wrestling." I begged them to rescue her, but they insisted all was well. Eventually, her screaming sounded so desperate that I knew I had to rescue her myself. I ran to their bedroom; Mother was up against a wall with Charlie's hands around her neck. Her face looked swollen and was a weird purplish color. Her eyes frightened me. I was horrified; especially when I noticed her feet were about a foot off the floor.

I quickly ran back to the living room with this evidence. In hysteria, I explained exactly what I saw. I was sure they would run to Mother's rescue, call the police, and get rid of Charlie. Instead I heard, "Adults like to wrestle like this. It's a game. You didn't see them fighting, just playing." Adults lied to me often back then. There would be many times in my childhood when I sought help and comfort from an adult only to have them lie to me, invalidating my reality. Adults can use drugs or alcohol to numb their pain. Children do not have this option, so the horrible feelings such as intense fear and rage must be placed somewhere. To cope, I continued playing my game and created playmates inside my mind and assigned memories and feelings to them. I would tell them what happened and was able to leave the memories and feelings with them. I eventually played the game so well that I literally was able to forget about the event all together.

Charlie was extremely jealous and possessive of my mother. The horrendous domestic violence lasted until I was twelve years old. Even now, I have a very hard time forcing myself to remember and feel the fear during

Putting Mother "back together" was part of my morning routine after Charlie's rage the night before.

those six years. He beat my mother almost weekly, often to the point of unconsciousness. The violent sounds in the other room were terrifying, yet the periodic silence was even more horrifying. Charlie beat her one night because she put on the wrong dress before they went out to dinner. After this severe beating, I almost did not recognize her face. She was in so much pain that she could not move her arms or legs. She was bleeding from various places and it was always my job to put her back together. Ironically, it was Charlie who bought the "wrong" dress that Mother had put on. It had been a gift to her after a previous beating.

Putting Mother "back together" was part of my morning routine after Charlie's rage the night before. Imagine an eight- or nine-year old child trying to put clothes on a mannequin. I literally dressed her because she was too beaten and battered to move. She winced and complained each time I accidentally caused the slightest movement. Do you remember the dress style in the early seventies? How do you dress someone in panty hose and fitted polyester pants without requiring any movement?

I had two very difficult chores on the mornings after Mother's beatings. The hardest job was trying not to glue mother's eyes shut while attaching fake eyelashes. This task required a very steady hand, and I was functioning on minimal sleep, PTSD, and high anxiety. That tiny line of white glue made me nuts! Yes, my mother was so beaten sometimes that she could not lift her arms. I'm not sure how she typed at work. Next, Mother had several matching polyester suits that Charlie seemed to love ripping off when he got angry. Mother was a very good paralegal for prominent attorneys in Ashton and needed to look nice at work. Hmm, "polyester" and "nice" seem to be antonyms in my mind. The difficult part was the matching process. The pockets on the white jacket were ripped; the light blue pants had a hole at the seam, or the collar to the pink jacket was torn half off. It was very frustrating, so I was just as happy as my mother when Charlie would come home bearing gifts of new matching clothes.

Actually, there were lots of gifts after their fights. Charlie gave Mother diamond rings, roses, a sewing machine (though she had no clue how to use it), and a car. During the many periods of divorce court proceedings, when I was to testify, I too received lavish gifts. At one point, I had a regular bicycle, a five-speed bicycle, a ten-speed bicycle, and two go-carts.

These gifts were hardly compensation for the amount of physical labor required of me as the oldest child. After the storm named Charlie moved in, my household chores included: cleaning up the broken glass and ceramic ashtrays, throwing away dozens of beer bottles, vacuuming up all the ashes, and holding the broken furniture pieces tightly together so Mother could superglue the consequences of the previous night's war. Other household responsibilities increased rapidly as well, such as laundry, dish duty, and primary caregiver for my sisters.

The only wonderful experience during these six years with Charlie was the birth of my youngest sister, Holly. I was nine years old when my mother brought her home and placed her in my arms. I'll never forget my mother's statement, "This is your baby; I can't take care of her." From birth, Holly's crib was in my bedroom, and I was the one responsible for all her night feedings and diaper changes. Though this sounds shocking, and her arrival brought an abundant amount of responsibility, I believe the job of caring for my two sisters is what kept me sane, grounded, and filled with a purpose. I loved them intensely. They needed me, and God knew I needed them!

The domestic violence usually occurred on Friday night. The police would come on the nights I was brave enough to crawl out of my bedroom, get to the phone, and dial 911. The police usually made Charlie leave, but their instruction to him, "Go shake it off," was very confusing. I never knew what that meant; can you shake off rage like a dog shakes off water after swimming? About an hour after Charlie left, the phone calls began, and continued frequently throughout the night. If Mother was conscious, she made me answer the phone and be the messenger. A typical conversation went like this...

Charlie – "Let me talk to your mama!"

Mother – "I don't want to talk to him. Tell him to leave us alone."

Charlie – "Tell her to get her #&**&&^%$% on the phone now!" (His foul mouth was nothing like I had ever heard before.)

Mother – "Tell him I'm going to call the police if he doesn't stop calling."

Charlie – "You tell that cheating *&^%$# that I've cut the brake line on her car."

Sometimes the threat was a bomb in our house or car. Other times, he told me he would be setting our house on fire while we slept. I always believed his threats. Mother's response was almost always, "Good, I want to die!" The problem here is, "Hello, you have children who will be killed as well." I never once heard from my mother, "Don't worry, honey; he won't really hurt us. We'll be safe." My mother was tapped out emotionally and physically; she had nothing more to give! In those six years, he broke her nose at least twice, her ribs a few times, and her arm once. She was almost always covered with multicolored bruises, and I can't count the times he left her unconscious with me to care for her.

I actually assigned the job of bringing my mother back to life after Charlie left to another "self" inside whom I named Angel. Mother always lost the battle and often looked dead when I found her. On the occasions when Charlie thought he had killed her, he paced the floor like a lion in a cage. His fear scared me even further. I vividly remember a night when he said, "If she doesn't wake up by morning, she's dead," and then he left. I applied cold cloths to Mother's head and tried to clean up all the blood while I prayed for God to bring her back to life. On the nights she woke up before I fell asleep, she'd have me fix her a Screwdriver (vodka and orange juice) or Whiskey and 7 (whiskey and 7-Up). I would then find her pills to help the pain.

The threats, loud sounds of furniture being knocked over, Mother's body being slammed around, hideouts at different motels throughout the city, Mother being unconscious, and the massive cleanups after the battles were not the hardest part of the domestic violence. Instead, it was Mother begging for my help all night while she was being beaten to near death that caused the most distress. She begged me to call the police and neighbors. I heard her pleading voice calling my name over and over again.

The sounds of gunfire caused less anxiety than her pleading for me to rescue her. Yes, I said gunfire; they both owned guns. My sisters and I would show the neighborhood kids the latest bullet holes when they came over to play. During Mother's beatings, my anxiety was so intense that my hands itched beyond what I could safely withstand. I rubbed my wrists and hands across the carpet as fast and as hard as I could. My hands looked burned and my wrists were raw. Mother's screams for my help were the beginning of my addiction to self-harm at eight years of age.

My wrists and hands had these same rug burns the night I felt the safe hand of Jesus on my back. The Bible says in Isaiah 41:10 (CEB), "Don't fear, because I am with you; don't be afraid, for I am your God. I will strengthen you, I will surely help you; I will hold you with my righteous strong hand." When I was older and began trying to figure out my beliefs about God's sovereignty, I had a very hard time with this verse. My whole childhood was terrifying. My thoughts to God over the years had been, *Don't fear? What a joke! You did not strengthen me. I lived in and out of mental hospitals. I can't stop cutting and burning myself. Where were You and why did You not rescue me?*

I'm sure most people have asked these same questions about their own traumas. I don't know the answers, but I've been on a journey to discover many of mine. It took hard work and time, but I've learned the promises in Isaiah 41:10 are absolutely true. Was He with me? Yes! Did He strengthen me? Yes! Did He help me? Yes! Did He hold me? Yes! It took many years for my heart and mind to discover that He has restored the years stolen due to the abuse. He has caused everything to work for my good. He did rescue me when I was homeless, and He did meet every financial need in miraculous ways. He really did have great plans for my life, and He did not allow anyone or any evil force to rob me of the joy He set before me.

During my almost fifty years of life, I have been asked numerous times, "How did you stay sane? How did you not have a mental split so severe that you never came back? Why are you not a prostitute living under a bridge? Why are you not strung out on drugs and alcohol? Why have you not been in and out of domestic violence situations or multiple marriages? How do you trust anyone?" The above questions are very valid; statistics would predict that my life would include at least half of these outcomes. My answer is always, "a million miracles along the way."

Although there were many long nights when I could not call for help, when guns were being fired in our home and when bullets pierced our bedroom wall, my sisters and I remained physically unscathed. This alone is a huge miracle. The bravery and wisdom to hide my sisters in the closet when

---

As a child, I could not see God's rescue plan working in my life. I also could not see how His promise to restore my life would be possible. I'll never know all the times He stepped in to help us survive, but I can now recall many such times.

---

things were too frightening, or my hiding them behind the wooden dresser when the gunfire began was also miraculous. How could a seven-, eight-, nine- or ten-year-old child have the wherewithal to listen patiently at the bedroom door for the perfect opportunity to crawl safely to the next room, call the police and then crawl back? Though Charlie screamed, "I'll kill her if you open that %*&$#%^ door," I believe it was God's strength that helped me protect my sisters.

As a child, I could not see God's rescue plan working in my life. I also could not see how His promise to restore my life would be possible. I'll never know all the times He stepped in to help us survive, but I can now recall many such times. For example, my mother was almost always fully intoxicated during our childhood. How is it that she never wrecked the car with us in it, even during the high-speed chases when Charlie tried to force us off the road? I believe Jesus kept us from being killed. I also believe Jesus knew the trauma to come, so He provided the second tangible sign of love when His comforting hand healed my migraine and put me into a peaceful sleep during one of my parents' wars.

It was during this time that Mother required hospitalization on several occasions. When I was eight and my sister Rachael was three, I was told I would be staying with my great uncle Henry for the summer because Mother was sick. I knew he was my mother's favorite uncle, but I didn't know him well. Henry called prior to our vacation and told me all the adventures we would have. His list of fun included: small mini-bikes just my size, a large swimming pool, a boat, a big motorcycle, and horses to ride. Of course, I was simply thrilled just to be away from the violence. During this vacation, Rachael stayed with my aunt Faye all day at the house while I spent the day with my uncle Henry. He explained that Rachael was too little to go on our adventures, which always ended with sexual abuse. Instead of sharing all the horrific details of that summer, I will simply describe our nightly routine.

Instead of allowing my sister and me to stay in the huge living area on the main floor, we were placed in a room under the house. We had to go outdoors and down the back stairs to get to our bedroom. There was a vast lake behind the house with the dock coming up to our bedroom. Every evening, I was to shower with my little sister, get us dressed, and then come up to the main living area. Aunt Faye delighted in fixing Rachael's curly black hair and Uncle Henry insisted I sit on his lap while he slowly blow-dried my long blonde hair. Other than this nightly bathing and sleep routine, I do not remember my sister even being there.

After the blow-drying was over, we were directed outside and back down the stairs to our room. About ten minutes after being sent downstairs, Uncle Henry came down to sit beside me on the bed for our nighttime prayers. All I will say is this was the most painful prayer time anyone could ever have. I tried so hard to pray in a way that my little sister would not know what his hands were doing under the covers. When my voice cracked or I hesitated due to the pain, Uncle Henry would command, "Keep praying; don't stop!" Having a steady and calm voice was also very difficult when he used my hand to "love on him." He said our nightly prayer time would make the adventures during the day much more fun. It did not!

Not only do I have a clear memory of trying to have a calm voice for the sake of my sister, I also remember the stress of trying to keep the prayer going, "God bless Ms. Jackson, my third grade teacher. God bless my friend Haley... God bless..."There are so many events, feelings, and circumstances in my life that I do not remember. It seems so cruel that I would vividly remember the shame I felt, knowing that as long as I was praying, God was seeing the horrible and sinful things I was doing.

Similar to Ken, Uncle Henry seemed to enjoy sharing me with his friends. However, there was one major difference between these two abusers. Uncle Henry was usually very kind and called our time together a "special relationship." It feels cruel that he was so nice. The violent rapes hurt physically, but the gentle "I love you so much" rapes hurt on an entirely different level. Yes, it hurt physically, but for me the shame and guilt caused massive and almost fatal damage to my soul. He made comments such as, "We need to be careful that no one sees us, They won't understand how much we love each other, Don't tell your aunt, but I love you more, Your body is so beautiful, Relax and enjoy it."

I'm guessing at this point you're saying to yourself, *Who are these evil people, and how could so many abusers be in this poor child's life?* I've asked myself these same questions a zillion times. I'm the common denominator in all these dirty activities, so my belief was, *It's my fault.* I believed I had the demons inside me that Mother spoke of when she quoted Bible verses in a mean voice. The word *dirty* floated around in my head most of my life. I don't know if my mother's uncle was part of the same group of child molesters as Ken. They did know each other through their activity at the Masonic

Lodge. My mother's brothers were also Masons, and other female relatives had been in Eastern Star, the wives or children of Free Masons. Some of my cousins and I were Rainbow Girls at some point, but memories are fuzzy.

It seems I need some humor here to break up the intensity of this true story, but nothing comes to my mind. What I do know is that Jesus helped me survive. My memory of His two visitations thus far was always near.

By the time I was ten, my mother felt very comfortable leaving me alone to care for my sisters while she and Charlie went out at night.

I believe it was also He who helped me learn to play the game. I cannot imagine how I would have survived without the ability to pass the intense pain and horrifying memories to another "self" inside my mind.

My mother returned at the end of the summer to collect her children. Once safely back home, I told her what her uncle had done. I was an unusual child in that I kept telling her what happened. With no emotion, no medical attention, no soothing words reflecting that she cared, no proclamation that he would be punished for what he did, and no reassurance that I would never have to see him again, Mother simply responded, "Ok, you won't go back again." Unfortunately, I would be sent back to various abusers many times over the years.

By the time I was ten, my mother felt very comfortable leaving me alone to care for my sisters while she and Charlie went out at night. A family argument broke out once because my mother left us home alone while she and Charlie went to the Daytona 500 in Florida. Rachael was four years old, and Holly was an infant. I thought nothing of my parents' departure, except relief from the constant fear and chaos. However, I felt bored, so I called my cousin to chat. She asked her mom, my Aunt Alice, if we could spend the night with them. Aunt Alice became suspicious because all three of us would be coming. When she got on the phone, her hysteria puzzled me. She immediately came to pick us up. Late Sunday night, Mother arrived home to find a note on the door that said, "They are with me!" Mother was livid for having to retrieve her children late at night. What amazes me now is that she stayed gone for three days and never bothered to call home. She did not know we were gone from our house.

During that same summer, Holly, Rachael, and I were sent to stay with one of Uncle Henry's childhood friends, who we were told to call "Uncle" Robert. Mother knew him well because he came to many of Mother's childhood family gatherings. The abuse by Uncle Robert was less brutal, but the feelings of shame, fear, and hopelessness were the same. I do not know if this "uncle" knew I'd been raped the previous summer by Mother's uncle. The men had grown up on the same block and both had become Masons. I was told we had to stay with him because Mother entered an alcohol treatment center. I remember thinking at night during the abuse, *At least Mother won't be drinking anymore when we get home.* So I resigned myself to endure because some good would ultimately come from Mother's hospitalization. I can't explain the rage I felt when I saw that Mother was drinking vodka on our way back home. I had to pass those feeling directly to Velda who managed most of my anger. I think I would have killed my mother.

In the fall of the year I turned eleven, I bravely told one of my safe family members what had happened during my stay at both uncles' homes. Mother was obviously not going to intervene. My disclosure started a civil war within the family. Each "uncle" told his wife that I was a very manipulative child and had seduced him. In front of my mother, both "aunts," one not being related, scolded me harshly while portraying their husbands as helpless victims of my poor boundaries and sexual desires. I felt like I was being stoned in front of my mother. Because she did nothing to defend me or even say anything, I felt as if my mother was also casting stones. They told my mother I would never be allowed in their homes again. Words cannot reflect the shame and guilt I felt because I had "seduced" two men. I would have preferred actual stones!

One aunt remarked, "What if our children found out what you tried to do with their father?" That day of confrontation was the day my fear was confirmed. Now I knew the truth. I was an evil "sexual whore" who had the power to destroy marriages. I was not positive which behaviors I participated in that classified me as a "sexual whore." I also do not know how that term got created in my mind. I've always hated the word "sex" just as much as others hate the "f" word. My mother was very sensual and seductive throughout my life. Because of the vast amount of alcohol consumed in our home by Mother, Charlie, and their many friends, I saw the act of sex on many occasions. On each occasion, I felt dirty, scared, and embarrassed.

Though the accusations from my aunts felt like stones being thrown at me, I knew Jesus would forgive me just as He forgave Mary Magdalene. Just as her community knew about her evil sins, my family now knew of mine. It is very painful to reflect on my feelings during this time, but because of the two visits from Jesus so far, I knew if I asked, He would forgive me. It took many years to understand the abuse was not my fault and that I was clean, precious, and valuable to my Father in heaven. Unfortunately, because this healing transformation only occurs over time and with treatment, I needed internal help to numb the intense shame I felt.

Mary Mags, one of the characters in the game I played, was assigned the task of being present when my body experienced pleasure during the abuse. Henry, unlike Ken, was very intent on our daily "adventures" ending with my body feeling pleasure. This is a tactic many pedophiles use to provoke enough shame and guilt in their victims that the "don't tell" rule is usually kept. Believing Jesus could forgive me and allow me into heaven was not difficult, but believing He could ever love me like He loved my cousins and friends was impossible. The shame was just too intense!

The two vivid, heavenly encounters, the ability to believe Jesus would forgive me, and the ability to assign my memories and feelings to someone else made holding on to reality possible. God also placed many heroes in my life who went beyond their role to help me survive the horrible years of abuse. Just as Jesus helped me have the ability to attach when I was younger, He also put people in my life to help me remain sane.

Just as God never wanted the children of Israel to be abused in Egypt, I believe He grieved during my abuse as well. God had a plan to rescue me from captivity, carefully lead me through the painful desert journey, and provide miracles along the way. A huge part of His provision during my life included many loving individuals to ensure I made it to the Promised Land. Just as cruel people have the power to hurt us, precious and loving people with good boundaries have the power to help us heal.

There were many neighbors who praised me for taking such good care of my sisters. The pastor's wife and some of the other women at our church, Trinity Cathedral, showed me they cared in various ways. After school, I was often required to walk to the local daycare center to pick up my baby sister. Lucy, the owner, picked me up in the daycare bus on the days she saw me walking in the rain. She also praised me for being such a "good big sister,"

Just as God never wanted the children of Israel to be abused in Egypt, I believe He grieved during my abuse as well.

---

and if I wanted something to eat or drink before the walk back home, all I needed to do was ask. She cared. In addition, there were several loving people who entered my life when I was a child who still remain to this day!

In the fifth grade when life was especially difficult, I had a very special teacher named Mrs. Ellen Barnard. The domestic violence at home was extreme and I was responsible for two little sisters at this point. During the school day, I was exhausted and emotionally drained. Mrs. Barnard knew something was terribly wrong in my home, so she was especially tender towards me throughout the day. I was starving for touch, encouragement, and love.

On the days when I arrived too tired to function, Mrs. Barnard allowed me to sleep for a while in class. The other children called me "teacher's pet," but I did not care. I felt like a baby bird starving in a nest without a mama bird. Mrs. Barnard was able to feed me morsels throughout the day to help me stay alive and emotionally grounded enough to withstand the trauma.

Mrs. Barnard moved away after that school year, but she wrote letters to me occasionally from wherever she lived. She wrote when her children were born and other special occasions. I knew she loved me and I was special in her heart. With new technology, our letters have become e-mails, and I still get the same feeling of being loved when I receive one.

The following is a note from her...

I was Tammy's fifth grade teacher 40 something years ago in the mid-1970s. She was the kind of student who touched your heart. If you can imagine a teacher complaining about such a thing, Tammy was too well behaved. She never talked when she wasn't supposed to, nor did she have conflicts with other students. But Tammy's silence seemed to scream for help. I remember a lovely golden-skinned child with long blond wavy hair that draped her shoulders. I can still see her sitting at her desk with her chin perched on her little clasped hands. Often she would fall asleep in that pose. Even when she was awake, she didn't seem present and connected to the rest of the class. Often she complained of intense headaches and asked to go to the restroom. For that reason, I asked the guidance counselor to meet with her. I left the Ashton area the following year, but Tammy and I continued to correspond. When we reunited a few years ago, she told me of the horrors she had endured as a child. How it amazes me that she was able to function in my class given what she had been going through! I am thrilled to see how hard she's worked and how dedicated she is to helping others heal from scars of abuse.

Ellen Barnard, M.S.

Another sanity saver during this time was the school counselor, Mrs. Diane Brodie. She met with my mother on more than one occasion regarding my late arrival and excessive sleepiness. Mrs. Brodie also addressed my extreme attachment to my sixth grade teacher, Mrs. Rivers. It was during the sixth grade that Mrs. Brodie began taking me out of class about once a week to meet with her. I can honestly say I have been in therapy since age eleven. Wow, that's more than thirty years of counseling; I should be perfect by now!

High school started in the eighth grade but thankfully the building was just next door. I was able to visit with Mrs. Brodie after school whenever I felt the need to connect. She was always willing to sit with me, listen to my pain, and challenge me to work hard in school. Mrs. Brodie cared for me deeply and occasionally gave me tokens of her affection. The Lord knew I needed early therapeutic intervention if I was to remain emotionally stable.

Over the years, Mrs. Brodie has also been able to give me insight into several pieces of the "me puzzle." Due to my ability to dissociate, many of the memories from my school years have been lost or jumbled. Mrs. Brodie was the first person to suspect Mother was getting financial assistance from the men who molested me. She told me she believed this because "your mother lived way beyond her means for a secretary," and because she continued to make me go with these men knowing what would occur. Here is a note from school counselor, Mrs. Diane Brodie, M.S.:

I first met Tammy when she was in the fifth grade. She was referred to me by her classroom teacher because of habitual tardiness, sleeping in class, and being very sad and withdrawn. My first meetings with Tammy were very difficult. She was very guarded and did not want to discuss anything. She simply wanted to get back to class and forget about the issues. After many meetings I found out this was a ten-year-old who was responsible for herself and two younger siblings. Every morning she was responsible for feeding, dressing, and getting her baby sister to the daycare center and her middle sister to school before she came to school. In the evening she also would pick up her sister, get her middle sister to start her homework and then start dinner. Basically this was a ten-year-old who ran a household. School was her second job. Fifth

---

Keeping my own sanity would turn out to be extremely important for my sisters and me.

---

grade was the beginning of a lifetime of involvement with Tammy.

As time went on I discovered that not only was Tammy a child who was raising her younger sisters, but also was a child who has been and was being physically, emotionally and sexually abused.

Through the years I have seen Tammy evolve from a frightened child to an angry teenager to a person who saw herself as an evil person deserving all the bad things that had happened and were happening in her life, to a young woman trying to heal and move forward with her life, to a woman with a passion to help others. The journey has been a long and hard one for her but she has moved past [sic] all this. It is remarkable to see someone who has gone through all she has and come out as a sane, caring person.

I believe this book is her journey from a victim to the role of advocate and helper for others.

Diane Brodie, M.S. – School Counselor

Mrs. Brodie and I have met for lunch many times throughout my adult life. She has helped maintain my sanity by giving meaning to the missing puzzle pieces of my life from grades five to ten. Keeping my own sanity would turn out to be extremely important for my sisters and me because my mother was losing the battle in keeping hers!

Just as Jesus placed his hand on my back during one of Mother and Charlie's fights, I had many people surrounding me throughout childhood who would place their hands on my back to provide comfort and support. I always knew my sisters, my Aunt Alice, and several other precious people living in my community and church loved me. There were a few individuals that I trusted enough to disclose information about some of the stressful oc-currences in our home. I was believed and that felt amazing!

Chapter 3

THE LIVES YOU

WILL IMPACT

I t was Sunday night and the end of our teen revival week. We all stood near the front of the church while the congregation listened to a few of us who had volunteered to give a testimonial about what God had done for us during the week. I was not up for the challenge. Instead of listening to my peers share about the great things God had done in their lives, I was wondering how I could get some much-needed attention from one of my many "mother figures" at the church before going home that night. I had occasionally resorted to putting soap under my fingernails before walking up front for prayer at the end of service. I then managed to get the soap into my eyes as soon as one of the ladies in our church headed my way. Man, did that sting!

After the testimonies, David Cook, our youth pastor, started to end the meeting by praying over each one of us. The congregation was to pray silently as well. I was almost last in line, so standing in front of people for that long was excruciating. It was finally my turn, and I felt his hand hover over my head as usual. He began *praying just about the same words over me as he did the other kids.*

About one minute into the prayer, his voice got much louder and his tone more firm, not at all like the prayers for the other kids. Instead of asking God to do this and do that in my life, he began announcing parts of my future. I felt his hand patting my head really fast, and he began speaking in tongues or "unknown languages," as they called it. Why couldn't he have gotten so excited over some other kid? *The congregation also began moving about and getting more verbally passionate. Pastor Cook then stated very boldly that God would be healing the lives of more people in the world through me than the grains of sand in the ocean. My thoughts*—He is so off tonight; what a joke! *Strangely though, all the other things he said regarding me were true. It was as if God had told him secrets about me that no one else could have known.*

I have found that many well-meaning people sometimes say the dumbest things in an effort to help. Are we listening to what we say to each other? Numerous times throughout my life, I have heard statements such as, "God allowed you to go through the abuse so He can use you later for His glory." That's about the dumbest thing you can ever say to someone to help him or her heal. This statement caused me to feel as if Jesus needed me to get molested so that He could heal me, thus making Him get "the glory."

So many cruel comments, bizarre behaviors, and extreme abuse occurred by people who called themselves "Christians."

So many cruel comments, bizarre behaviors, and extreme abuse occurred by people who called themselves "Christians." I believe I would have healed much quicker if Ken's painful and frightening abuse sessions did not include words such as church, sacrament, sacrifice, sin, and the cross. I would not have felt so much shame and guilt when I thought of Jesus if my uncle had not forced me to pray out loud while he raped me. One of my other abusers kept a Bible on his nightstand. My journey to heal was very stunted until I learned to trust God, understand that He loved me, and realize His plan for me was good. I always knew I would go to heaven, but I believed the lie that Jesus could never actually love me!

The greatest source of extreme spiritual abuse was my own mother. Around age thirty-two, the symptoms of her schizophrenia arrived and most of her delusions, paranoia, and hallucinations were very religious in nature. I was about thirteen and assumed her bizarre behavior was due to her addiction to alcohol. I later learned that many people with mental illness used drugs or alcohol to cope with the symptoms. Understanding this, it's easier to have compassion for Mother now; it was not so easy during childhood. Mother literally terrified us with her religious ideations and behavior.

It's hard to have faith in God when "his angels" keep telling your mother, "It's time for you to bring them to heaven." It's hard to believe Jesus really loves you when your own mother calls you Satan and tries to "cast you out." However, despite the fact that my mother was a Pentecostal believer who was diagnosed with schizophrenia, and despite the fact that almost every person who abused me claimed to be a Christian, the Lord miraculously preserved my faith in Him and eventually proved His deep love for me regardless of the sentiments and behaviors of the so-called Christians around me.

In my heart, I would love to be able to say, "The only reason Mother did not protect me from bad people was because she was mentally ill. She never would have forced me to leave our house with her dates, her relatives, her friends, or some of the neighbors if she had been thinking straight, right?" My mother knew more Bible verses than anyone I have ever met, so her lapse in judgment had to be due to something I just did not understand. I've always had a desperate need to excuse her from being one of the sources of my pain. Was it her insatiable need for attention? Was she abused as a child so she didn't know any better? Was it her mental illness? Was it her "addictive personality" as one therapist explained? Since many of her relatives shared the same unquenchable need for alcohol, maybe all her issues were genetic!

My first memory of Mother's bizarre behavior occurred one Sunday night when I was twelve. She was desperately trying to divorce Charlie and find a way to survive physically, financially, and emotionally. Mother was very intoxicated, even for her, and had been crying all day. My attempts to console her only helped as long as I physically knelt by her chair and stroked her physically and emotionally.

It took much energy and clever thought to battle her endless, negative thought processes. Our typical conversations would proceed like the following:

"I love you, Mother, and we will be okay."

Mother – "I just want to go home (her word for heaven) and be with my mother."

Me – "You can't kill yourself. God gets to decide when it's time for you to go home. I'm sure the attorney will get the motion filed soon."

Mother – "I can't take it anymore. You girls deserve a better mother."

Me – "You're a wonderful mother and we love you so much."

Mother – "You don't love me. You hate me, and you just want my insurance money. That's okay, honey. I've already made out the will, and I expect you to take good care of your sisters."

I still have a file folder with several of her "Last Will and Testaments."

This was the first time we had this dialogue, but it would recur a million times throughout my teen years. Mother would pull out her insurance policy, review it with me, and explain her final wishes as far as her financial circumstances, funeral wishes, and burial needs. It is important to note that one of her instructions was for me to contact Ken as soon as she died. She explained that Ken had already made a "pine box" for her to be buried in, and he was storing it for her. He also knew where she was to be buried. On future occasions when I battled for her to choose life, she often held tightly to the pills she intended to take or her gun. Strangely, she also held her Bible close. She read the verses over and over and prayed out loud for God to heal her. She also cried a lot. Actually, this is a huge understatement.

One time at 3:00 a.m. when I was emotionally exhausted from keeping my mother alive, I was unaware of the unwelcomed guest, at least by me, about to walk through our front door. I had not seen Uncle Henry in a few years, so I was quite surprised at his arrival; though my mother was not. She welcomed him with open arms, knowing he had violently assaulted me a few years prior while he forced me to pray. To Mother, my pain was a pesky memory that needed to be left in the past and she felt no hesitation in saying so. "Therefore do not worry about tomorrow, for tomorrow will worry about its own things. Sufficient for the day is its own trouble (Matt 6:34 NKJV). I heard this verse from the New King James Version a gabillion times. By the way, the New King James is not "new" anymore. The version came out when I was about twelve and my mother started selling Bibles as a side job. She loved this version and we were to memorize from it only.

I also often heard, "Tammy, you're supposed to forgive your trespassers because they don't know what they're doing."

As I walked off to bed, "God forgive me. It's wrong of me to not forgive her uncle, especially since he had come to help us escape."

Unknown to me was the fact that Mother had called him earlier in the day, threatened suicide, and requested he come over to discuss the possibility of our moving to a trailer on his property.

After greeting Mother, Henry rushed over to drown me with affection as if our three-year separation had been traumatic for both of us. He sat beside me on the sofa, gave Mother a beautiful necklace, and began making plans for our relocation. My stomach felt sick with dread; the betrayal around me seemed unbelievable. Mother immediately began asking important questions such as, "Are there good churches in your area?" He began describing his church where he served as a deacon. After listening to their plans and seeing Mother's deep depression move to excitement, I began to panic. My outburst was not planned; it jumped out of my throat before I knew it was there.

"I thought you said you were going to talk to him about what he did to me!"

I so wish I had never brought up the abuse because her lighthearted response did much more damage than the rapes. Mother looked at Uncle Henry and responded, "Oh yeah, why did you do that?"

The tone and attitude in her question was as if he had kept me up past my bedtime. Uncle Henry received no scolding, no punishment, and no legal consequence.

He then explained, "As you know, Sharon, I've always had a very special place in my heart for Tammy. I saw that she was getting older (eight years old) and I wanted her first time to be special with someone who would be gentle and loved her."

This was insane. I expected him to lie, say I made it up, say I exaggerated, or anything else but the truth. If I had had a different mother, one who desired to protect me, the truth would have been amazing. I yearned for someone to scream and yell at all the men who hurt me. I wrote scripts of dialogue in my head where my loving mother came running to my defense, scooped me up, lavished me with love and affection, and then beat the crap out of my abuser. The mother character in my fantasy life changed over the years. The role was originally played by my teachers, but evolved to a much higher standard. Wonder Woman and the Bionic Woman held first place for at least a year.

The longest mother figure role played by a TV character was Kelly Garrett on *Charlie's Angels*. I drifted off to sleep at night writing the scenes and watching them play out. Kelly was my mother and she adored me. We baked, shopped, and traveled together. Every episode included us having fun, lots of affection, and someone raping me. The climax of the episode was always Kelly, my mother, walking in during the rape and annihilating the abuser cast for that role on that night. I had plenty of actors (abusers) to fill the role! Kelly then becomes hysterical. She wants to kill my abuser. She rushes to me, holds me, soothes me with her voice, and then kisses the tears on my cheeks. She cared that I was hurt, she took me to a doctor, and she sometimes applied medicine to my wounds. These "mother-figure" fantasies continued until I was about thirty-six years old. The role was usually cast to the therapist treating me during that time period. Mentally escaping reality was my greatest source of comfort and probably helped me stay sane.

Mother listened to Henry explain why his being my "first" sexual partner was such a great idea. Sadly, he was not the "first" abuser to rape me, and my mother knew this.

She listened calmly to his reasoning and then said, "Well, I don't think you need to do it anymore."

Once again, her tone was very similar to his keeping me up an hour past my bedtime. There was no anger or consequences for him, and of course, there was no concern over my well-being. He never bothered to mention the part about my being required to say our bedtime prayers out loud while

---

By this time, I was already a wonderful bartender; I could concoct many different liquid painkillers. It was the long succession of very strong screwdrivers that eased her pain the most.

---

he raped me. As I left the living room headed for bed, feeling very defeated, I turned and noticed Mother's big black Bible still remained on her lap.

Finding a word or phrase to explain how I felt at that moment seems impossible. It was late, and I was emotionally exhausted. I had doted on Mother all day explaining why we loved her so much and needed her. To ease her deep depression and often hysteria, I quoted many Bible verses and made drinks to calm her. By this time, I was already a wonderful bartender; I could concoct many different liquid painkillers. It was the long succession of very strong screwdrivers that eased her pain the most and shortened the length of her well-deserved self-pity. The focus of the day had been preventing her from suicide, again. I took myself to bed knowing I had succeeded; she would be alive for another day. I would need to pray and ask God to forgive me for not forgiving Uncle Henry yet. Mother insisted I forgive his trespasses so that God would be willing to forgive mine. I had no clue what a trespass was, but I knew it must be something very bad. I had a deep sense that I had done a lot of "trespassing" in my life and needed some major forgiveness.

A child with a different mother would have been surprised when Henry entered her bedroom that night.

About an hour after I had escaped Mother's never-ending need to be stroked, Henry quietly entered my room and stated, "You know your mother is not going to do anything, so you might as well let me."

He also declared, "You know Charlie will eventually kill your mother and maybe even you girls if I don't help. Your mother needs me, so you're moving to my property."

It was as if he was saying, "Come on, be a team player. You can take one for the team, right?"

I knew he was right; no one would be coming to rescue me, and Charlie would eventually be successful in our destruction. He would eventually kill us, or Mother would commit suicide. I retreated to my fantasy world as soon as possible to escape the reality of that moment. This is the point in the story where I first realized something was very wrong with my mother. During my "take-it-for-the-team" sacrifice, Mother walked in to see Henry on top of me. He thought she had gone to bed, but she had only gone to the bathroom. He was so confident in his rights to my body that he had not even bothered to close my bedroom door.

That night, Mother had the first of many meltdowns.

As she began screaming, she looked straight at me and said, "GET OUT OF MY HOUSE AND NEVER COME BACK." Her rage was intense.

Though she was wearing one of her see-through nightgowns with no underclothes, she ran out the front door in hysteria. I'd seen a lot of bizarre behavior over the years due to Charlie and Mother's drinking parties, but this was different. After Mother disappeared in the darkness, at about 4:00 a.m., Henry became very concerned.

He tried to console me by proclaiming, "Don't worry, Tammy, your mother is just jealous of our special relationship. She will eventually get over it, and she still loves you. I'll talk to her; you won't have to move out."

Uncle Henry paced the hall and looked out the windows during the forty-five minutes Mother was gone. It felt as if she were eight years old and had run away from home, and we, as the parents, were horrified something might happen to her, or that she might not come back home. I was not prepared for what occurred when she did return. Mother came in the front door still sobbing loudly, ran straight to her bedroom, and locked the door. Uncle Henry and I stood outside her door begging her to open the door and let us help her. As I write this paragraph, I am stunned at the insanity of what I am describing. A child is raped, the mother runs away from home, and then the abuser and child spend the rest of the night trying to rescue and comfort the mother who is "jealous," according to the abuser. It's too crazy for anyone to believe, yet I remember that night vividly, and various other episodes of craziness occurring throughout my teen years.

Uncle Henry seemed so sad that he had hurt her feelings. Mother was clearly devastated, and her grief was overwhelming. The measure of guilt I felt at that moment was intense. Thankfully, there had been many occasions when I needed to break into her bedroom because she was either passed out drunk or *attempting* suicide again and needed me to talk her out of it. I found one of her bobby pins and easily opened the door. I was frantic to get into her room to take care of her pain which alleviated at least some of my guilt and shame.

Imagine our surprise to find her curled up in the fetal position, on top of her metal shoe rack, in the back of her closet. It felt as if my "affair" with Uncle Henry had caused her to become so emotionally distraught that she regressed to infancy. He kept telling me she would eventually get over it, and that I didn't need to feel guilty about our special relationship. He re-iterated several times that she was simply jealous and all would work out fine, eventually. It took us approximately an hour to coax Mother out of her closet and into bed. Uncle Henry tucked her in as if she were a three-year-old and told her he would take care of everything. At that moment, I wished he could "take care" of the algebra test I would be taking in about four hours! So what's an exponent and why do I need one?

Mother's closet meltdown was my first clue that something was very wrong with her that her drunken state could not explain. The next inkling that Mother was mentally ill occurred when I was in the seventh grade. I had just turned twelve and my two best friends, Melanie and Sheryl, could always talk my mother into anything. They convinced Mother that our full basement was the perfect place for our first boy-girl party. They were a year older and in the eighth grade. Their idea of school friends coming to my house was grave reason for concern. Melanie and Sheryl had been around my mother often. Seeing her drunk and close to nude was usual. They thought of her as the fun mother in the neighborhood. She served us alcohol whenever we wanted, taught us to do the twist when she was inebriated, al-lowed us to be out all night with Sheryl's much older boyfriends, and rarely supervised anything we were doing.

My only stipulation regarding this party was that Mother was not al-lowed to come downstairs. Melanie and Sheryl addressed this with her, and she agreed to the terms as long as one of us came upstairs occasionally to visit with her. Not wanting her downstairs had nothing to do with our wanting to do something wrong, such as drugs or sex. I did not want Mother down there because she would very likely do something extremely embarrassing. Mother agreed, and I reasoned in my mind that she had always followed through with her promises to my friends. She loved the role of the cool mom. It was about this time that they asked to taste Mother's screwdriver. Her response was to get up and make a screwdriver for each of us. Frankly, I hated the taste and smell, so I passed it on for them to share.

My little sisters were ages two and seven at the time and would be sleeping so we were clear to go. We were very excited when the big night had finally arrived. We had spent a few weeks cleaning the basement, hanging curtains, finding area rugs, and setting up tables for punch and snacks. I invited a few friends from my seventh grade class, and they invited friends from their eighth grade class. Almost all of our eleven guests came to the party.

On this night, we felt we were entering a passageway into our teens. The middle school years for us were a time of desperately wanting to be older and allowed to do grownup things, yet unsure how and not quite emotionally ready. Mingling with the opposite sex was a big deal. We were a bundle of nerves yet giddy with the freedom to be unsupervised and in control. Within an hour of our guests' arrival, someone suggested we play spin-the-bottle. This is a game where everyone sits in a circle and takes turn spinning a bottle. In the game, you must kiss the person seated at the location where the bottle stops, unless it lands on a kid of the same sex.

We played for approximately fifteen minutes before noticing my mother had come downstairs to watch. All of a sudden I heard her voice say, "You're not playing it right, that's not how to do it. You have to actually kiss!" Mother, wearing very revealing nightwear, of course, came over and sat down between two other kids. She spun the bottle, demonstrating she wanted to play as well. We were all stunned. Thus far, during our time together, no one had actually kissed. There was always a valid reason why the spin did not require an actual kiss. We just weren't having good luck, it seemed. Sometimes the bottle did not land in the exact location needed for it to be considered a valid spin. Also, either the spinner or the kid to be kissed had various problems with the kiss requirement. It was bizarre; many of us had acquired a cold within ten minutes of arrival to the party. Other issues arose as well; "He's Gemini, and I'm a Libra, so it can't work," or "Where did you say the bathroom is?" Like I said, we were experiencing some bad luck with the kissing game but having a wonderful time. We laughed, talked about other classmates, our parents, our teachers, and life in general.

When Mother spun the bottle, I was horrified. Her slurred speech, non-kid-friendly attire and the smell of her breath was enough to do permanent damage to my self-esteem. Surely, she was not actually going to kiss anyone; I should have known not to trust her. The victim was James Phelts, in my seventh grade class. I'll never forget the look on his face when my mother leaned across the circle to give him what might have been his first French kiss. Was it seeing Mother's nightgown falling down as she leaned across the circle, revealing a clear view of her naked body underneath, or the wet kiss that caused his eyes to bulge, his face to redden, and the terrified expression on his face?

Many people have asked, "Why didn't you tell your teachers or neighbors?"

I was also horrified at seeing the faces of our other friends sitting on her side of the circle. The very close view of mother's backside when she leaned forward on all fours to kiss James was an unexpected field trip on sex education. I was speechless and stunned by what was occurring. The truth is, I don't remember the rest of the night. I know things went from disaster to devastation, so for good reason, I assigned that memory and those feelings to someone else inside.

The reason I've shared two early incidences of Mother's bizarre behavior is to illustrate my reasoning in resigning myself to her control. I was conditioned over years of abuse to believe I had no options. Her religious beliefs, unpredictability, poor coping skills, strange emotionality, and later hallucinations gave me good reason to fear her.

Many people have asked, "Why didn't you tell your teachers or neighbors?"

First, it was very hard to figure out who was trustworthy. There had been so many people in my life that appeared to love me, but they were actually conditioning me to be compliant during the abuse. Second, my mother had all the power. Bringing up the subject of my abuse would sometimes result in another meltdown, which meant she and I would be up all night while she sobbed about her life and her pain. She ignored my pain by setting up suicide *attempts*. Having three hours of guilt heaped upon you would certainly reduce anyone's desire to complain.

Sometimes my disclosures caused her to become very angry.

"WHAT DO YOU WANT ME TO DO, PUT THE PEOPLE I LOVE THE MOST IN JAIL? KEN WAS YOUR FATHER AND HE SPOILED YOU ROTTEN. DON'T YOU REMEMBER THE PINTO PONY HE BOUGHT YOU?"

Actually, her rage at me was also loaded with guilt. I'm not sure my mother knew how to communicate without inflicting blame back onto her victim or anyone she needed attention from. Yet another reaction she would have when I disclosed was a vain attempt to convince me that she would not allow anyone to continue hurting me.

I wish I had a dollar for every time she responded, "Well, you just won't go with him next time."

After my disclosure with the safe family member, this turned into an emotional stoning. I'm shocked I ever shared anything with anybody, but I did.

I eventually told Mrs. Brodie, my school counselor, about some of the sexual abuse that had occurred. She was unable to convince the school principal that I was telling the truth. They held a school conference with Mother to address the allegations. Mother worked for prominent attorneys and was easily able to portray herself as a loving mother who was a victim of domestic violence. She explained that I lie to gain attention because of the fighting in our home. In the administrator's and teacher's defense, they did have strong evidence of the severe domestic violence in our home, so it was reasonable for them to believe what Mother was saying.

This evidence occurred in sixth grade. Mrs. Rivers, whom I adored, assigned us the task of recording different television commercials to find examples of advertising methods; for example, using a doctor to promote medicine or a famous actor to promote a product. We had to listen to television commercials, record them, and then list which method was used to advertise. I used a cassette tape that I thought was blank for recording. We then brought in our tapes so that Mrs. Rivers could play them at a media table where eight children, using headphones, were required to listen to each tape and record their observations.

Unfortunately, I had recorded my commercials over a long dialogue of Charlie beating my mother. When that portion of the recording came on, the kids became loud and called for Mrs. Rivers. She then immediately forced the kids to put down their headsets. She brought in three more teachers to listen. They talked with passion and then brought in the principal and Mrs. Brodie. There was a huge commotion, and I was horrified to discover the tape being played was mine! After the horrifying feeling subsided, I was quite puzzled by everyone's reaction. Why were they making such a big deal about this? To me, the extreme cussing, threats, gunfire, and screams were nothing to get this excited about. After all, this was normal in my home.

The teachers addressed the class and asked over and over, "Who brought in this cassette; it has no writing?" When no one volunteered to take the blame, I hoped the issue was dropped. They talked amongst themselves and then stated, "The owner of this tape has until the end of the day to claim it or they will receive a zero for this assignment."

Making a decision about what to do was traumatizing. I had a huge "mother figure" crush on Mrs. Rivers and wanted nothing more than to please her with good grades. A zero would hurt my GPA. I desperately wanted her to adopt me, and admitting this crime would certainly hurt my chances of becoming her daughter. All the adults seemed so horrified and so angry. It never dawned on me that I was not the one who caused their anger. At the end of the day, I approached Mrs. Rivers' desk with my head down so that I could not see the anger I assumed would be on her face. I admitted the tape was mine, and she slipped it in my hand. I remember the shame and fear I felt standing there, but I do not remember what she said or what happened later. I'm sure the meeting ended with everyone feeling sorry for my mother.

During the conference with my mother, the tape from the advertising assignment was sound evidence that the domestic violence was the real issue, not sexual abuse. And the school conference at which Mother denied I was being sexually abused was also sound evidence that even if I told someone, nothing would change. I would be classified as attention seeking, and then everyone would stroke my mother. Having just gone through this ordeal, it makes perfect sense that I had a good reason not to fight the issue when Mother required I leave the house in the middle of the night with one of her dates or anyone from whom she needed attention and assistance. I had no power; she held all the cards. I was no match for her ability to manipulate others into supplying her endless need for love and attention. When Ken called Mother a year later to request I accompany him on a trip to Kansas, it was a no-brainer that I would be his twelve-year-old escort.

When Mother hung up the phone and told me about Ken's request, the overwhelming panic and terror I felt seemed to come out of nowhere. I had very little memory of the extreme sexual abuse Ken and his circle of friends inflicted on me when I was much younger. The memories and emotions from those horrific assaults had been assigned to "others" inside me, but the feelings associated with him overwhelmed me in that instant. It would be another two weeks before Ken and I left for Kansas, and by the time of our departure I was actually excited about the trip. I had managed to block off any emotion that caused me to be concerned about my safety during the trip. Dissociation is an amazing phenomenon.

To my surprise, Ken began fondling me on the plane before we took off. As we departed toward the runway, the panic in my stomach quickly rose to my throat, and I wanted to scream, "SOMEONE HELP ME," but nothing came out. I desperately looked for an escape route or a friendly face that might notice what he was doing. Abusers are often very cunning with an amazing ability to rationalize and conceal what they are doing. Ken, sitting on the aisle seat, began "innocently" adjusting the window shade next to me. Each time he moved it up or down, he stroked my chest with his thumb. No one could possibly know what was happening, but I now knew what was to come. The same type thing happened with my seat belt, which according to him, needed to be adjusted several times during the flight. We actually flew to Missouri as well in order to meet up with some of his other friends. Most people are unaware of the sickening deeds being done to children by cults who claim to be Christians. I believe if given a chance, I might have jumped off the plane mid-air to avoid the horror ahead.

The thought to call my mother for help once we arrived never even entered my mind. That would be like a prostitute calling her pimp to say, "Come rescue me, this man is about to rape me!" Several of my dates with my mother's dates and the multiple times of abuse by "Uncle" Henry clearly screamed, "Your mother will never rescue you!" Once I resigned myself to this conclusion, I was desperate to find a good reason why she was unable to protect me. Note that I said "unable" instead of "unwilling." I reasoned that Mother's failure to help me was due to her alcoholism. She had explained to me often that her drinking was a disease, and she could not control it. She had been forced into AA meetings after her first commitment into Charter Peachford Behavioral Hospital when I was nine. Sometimes she defended her right to drink alcohol because "Jesus drank wine." I also assigned her failure to protect me as being part her mental illness, which I assumed was caused by the fact that a friend of her father had molested her once when she was fifteen.

There was only one clue during my childhood that Mother was not helpless when it came to my abuse. Prior to this day, it seemed she had no understanding of how to react when I was abused, how to respond lovingly to my emotional distress, or understand the need to press charges against the perpetrator in order to vindicate my pain. It was a hot day in August, and I was now attending the high school. We did not have a middle school. Oak Grove Elementary covered kindergarten through seventh grade and Oak Grove High School, right next door, covered eighth through twelfth grade. I often stopped by the elementary school to visit Mrs. Brodie before the walk home. I missed her and I never wanted to go home.

After the visit, I liked to leave a sweet note on her car. The reason I did this was mostly self-centered. I needed to be sure she thought of me again and again which I hoped would cause her to want me as a daughter. While writing, an older and much bigger boy named Demetrious from my neighborhood approached me. He had flirted with me on many occasions, but I kindly ignored his attempts to gain my affection. I desperately wanted a mother and had no need for a boyfriend. On this occasion, he refused to take no for an answer. He grabbed me by my shirt and hair, dragged me in between two of the trailers beside the school, and put what he said was a knife in my side. The parking lot was deserted because it was close to 5:00 p.m., and most of the teachers and all of the children had gone home.

I screamed until I felt the sharp pain in my side. He easily threw me on the very hot asphalt and completed his deed. I eventually broke away and ran back into the school. Mrs. Brodie was still in the front office and immediately addressed my pain and fear. She had what I considered a very strange reaction. She hugged me, stroked my hair, called the police, called my mother, and called Mrs. Smith, the principal, who immediately came back to the school. I don't think Mrs. Brodie ever let go of my hand, even when she was on the phone. Nothing even close to her reaction had ever occurred when I had been raped previously. The police officers and Mrs. Smith felt the same need for such a strong reaction. I was certainly perplexed by all the attention.

The police officers were taking my statement and talking with Mrs. Brodie when my mother arrived. Mrs. Brodie's strange reaction seemed to be contagious because Mother became very upset as well, but not about her own pain. She actually worried about my safety. The police officers followed us to our house to collect my clothes for evidence. They were so kind. The policewoman asked me more questions while the male officer told my mother to take me to Grady Hospital immediately. He said they were best trained to help a child after rape. I also overheard him say they would be giving me a rape kit. My brain was fascinated that there was a "kit" to go with a rape. I imagined it to be a huge gift basket filled with cute little soaps, fresh smelling lotions, tissues, candy, and other assorted gifts. After I received my "kit," he explained Grady Hospital would set up counseling sessions to help me recover. I was not sure what "recover" meant, and why I needed it this time. I would never get to know what the hospital put in my rape kit.

I dutifully gave my clothes to the female officer. I was very embarrassed and hoped all the wet stuff in my underwear dried before reaching the hospital. I was always extremely ashamed of the wet stuff. Once the officers left, I imagined our arrival at the hospital, my receiving my rape kit, and the opportunity to get the much-needed attention that this particular rape provoked. I even remember thinking, should I tell them about all the other rapes? Not that I could remember the exact number, but they might at least give me a few extra rape kits. I felt entitled to at least ten to fifteen.

As soon as they left, I noted Mother in the kitchen making a screwdriver. Having an alcoholic drink "to go" was the norm, so it was not until she sat down in her recliner that I became concerned. She then turned on the television without a comment. I stood there incredulous.

I said, "Aren't you going to take me to the hospital; the officer said you have to."

Her response was, "Go make dinner" and the tone of her voice changed dramatically the moment the door slammed behind the officers.

She actually sounded mad at me. I thought the day's events should, at the minimum, get me out of dinner duty. The best she offered, after much begging, was granting me permission to shower before starting dinner.

She reminded me that my sisters still needed their bath before bed, so "Hurry up."

I worked so hard in my brain to convince myself that Mother did not have ulterior motives for the abuse I endured. Since Mother was legitimately mentally ill, I worked hard to excuse her on that basis. Since she's an alcoholic, and Mother assured me on many occasions that it was a genetic dis-

---

I said, "Aren't you going to take me to the hospital; the officer said you have to." Her response was, "Go make dinner."

---

ease over which she had no control, I continued to make excuses for her actions or her failure to act. At first, I was willing to acknowledge it was her extreme need for male attention that caused her to look away, pretending not to know what they intended to do to me. I often told her exactly what happened during my time away.

Her response was almost always, "Well, I didn't know he was going to do that. You just won't go with him anymore." Translation: "You can't blame me. I didn't know he was going to rape you. Next time he calls or I go out with him, you just won't go again." I would love to say I was not required to go again, but that would not be the truth.

Later, after more evidence than I would ever want, it became clear that her motives were even more appalling. I discovered she not only received much-needed attention, but received financial benefits as well. I'll never know the details of her transactions with my abusers. Yes, the rapes were very painful, as was the fear that I would be killed. However, the feeling of being expendable to your own mother was excruciating. I didn't find out until my thirties that Mother, at some point, began blackmailing Uncle Henry. She threatened to tell the police and family members if he did not help with her financial needs.

Ken stayed at our house for a few days after we returned from Kansas. During his visit, even after I told Mother about the rapes and that I thought I needed to go to a hospital, Ken slept in Mother's bed. Having a man in her house changed Mother's countenance to that of a blushing bride the day after her wedding. The night after returning home, Ken took the four of us out to dinner at The Colonnade restaurant in Ashton. Before even leaving the house, I pleaded with Mother to allow my sisters and me to stay home. As usual, Mother got her way. I did not want to have dinner with my rapist, and I did not want Ken near my sisters. Her flirting began immediately after she prayed over the food. I was perplexed and wondered if God would really bless this gathering? Watching her attempt to seduce him during dinner made me want to vomit.

He had never met Holly, who was three at the time, and had not seen Rachael since she was about six months old. The rage I felt when he began to dote on my sisters and display affection was almost more than I could endure. My desire to kill him only surfaced when I saw them grinning at him, enjoying his attention, and Mother acting as if we were a happy family. By thirteen, I was almost completely unable to feel or express anger regarding my own safety or needs, but this was not the case regarding my sisters.

My sisters were just that, MY sisters. I felt minimal anger over the abuse done to me, but no one touched them, even innocently, unless I approved. At this point, I was a pro at assigning feelings to other parts of me. In fact, I knew the name and age of the child within who was in charge of my rage. Her name was Velda, and she was nine years old. My childhood would require many more hosts for the rage I was entitled to feel yet too terrified to acknowledge. My ability to remain numb still baffles me. On this night or any other night, when it came to my sisters, there were no holds barred. I could be vicious when it came to protecting them. Fortunately, Mother was skilled at demanding the most attention, and I frequently *needed* to go to the restroom and took my sisters with me.

I felt as if I were up against the world, my mother, men in general, and sometimes even God. Mother and most of my abusers had shown signs of at least a minimal amount of "Christian" faith. She prayed out loud, read her Bible, and took us to church a lot. She was serious about our relationship with Jesus as well. There were times when, of course being very intoxicated, she would wake the three of us up from a sound sleep in the middle of the night and require us to report to the sofa. She would then, while being almost naked, passionately preach sermons to us, yell in her "prayer language," and then require us to speak our heavenly language for a while before being allowed to go back to bed. We simply mimicked the syllables she was saying and endured the ranting.

We actually got very good at playing her religious game. If I tied God into the situation, I could get away with most anything. One night when I was of driving age, I took my sisters with me to visit some friends. We did not want to go back home, so we stayed out way past our curfew to be home. We knew Mother would be furious. We concocted a wonderful story about how there was this woman on the side of the road whose car had broken down. We were concerned for her safety and pulled over to help. Unfortunately, my sisters were not great at staying on script. As Mother became more and more pleased with our "Christ-like behavior," they began adding to the woman's crisis. By the end of the story, the lady had several children in the car, was pregnant and about to go into labor. If I had not shut them up soon, we would have also needed to deliver her baby on the side of the road. Her rage at us for being late turned to praise for being "the hands and feet of Christ."

Her religious and often bizarre behavior continued to get worse and sometimes cruel. For this reason, my love for God is such a miracle. There were times when she became violent, physically abusive, and very frightening. On many nights, when we knew we were not safe, we ran away. There was no need to run far; we simply hid somewhere until she passed out. The Cooley's' carport was an option, or sleeping in Mrs. Henderson's station wagon. Our need to find safety fast might seem horrific. Actually, these nights are some of our fondest memories.

In the summer, when the humidity took your breath and the heat was stifling, we got thirsty often. Drinking cold water from the yard hose on a hot summer night is quite refreshing. Since we needed to drink often, we also needed to empty our bladders often. My imagination being what it is, I came up with a pee-racing game. Our next-door neighbors had a very steep driveway. The three of us lined up, squatted and "ready, set, go." My sister Rachael was especially good at this game.

We jumped on our trampoline until 1:00 in the morning, made up stories about the neighbors, reviewed the frightening events that forced us outdoors, and yet managed to laugh at Mother's bizarre behavior.

Rachael - "Did you see how her eyes bulged out? She said the angels told her it was time for us to go to heaven."

Me – "What kind of angels is she listening to?"

Holly - "When did the serpent lay with the lamb? Can serpents eat lambs? I never saw a snake and lamb hanging out together in our picture Bible."

Me – "I don't know. Why is the antichrist out to get us? What'd we ever do to him? I'm sick of her screaming about him."

Rachael – "Geez! She was angry. Can you sneak back inside and bring out the ice cream?"

Holly – "Yeah, I'm starving. Bring the Oreos and milk."

Me – "I'll go back in, but let me wait a little longer. I'm too scared still. Why does Mother call me a Laodicean witch, and how's she gonna spew me out? She looked like she wanted to kill me with her eyes."

Holly – "I say we spew her to Smurfland. Do we have to go to church tomorrow?"

Me – "If her hangover isn't too bad. She'll probably be the first one praying at the altar."

We felt very safe roaming the neighborhood and only desired to return when absolutely necessary. Being the oldest, I was the appointed spy to assess the safety of returning. Every few hours, I crept back inside to evaluate

---

"I am the Lord your God, who holds your right hand. And I tell you, 'Don't be afraid! I will help you.'" I'm not saying I was never afraid, obviously, but there was always a sense of being held up, strengthened, and helped.

---

the situation. If she was not asleep at the point when we desperately needed sleep, we simply took residence in a neighbor's car until morning. For us to have so much fun during absolute craziness seems miraculous to me. There is a verse in the Bible, Isaiah 41:13 (ERV), which says, "I am the Lord your God, who holds your right hand. And I tell you, 'Don't be afraid! I will help you.'" I'm not saying I was never afraid, obviously, but there was always a sense of being held up, strengthened, and helped.

Most of the punishment Mother assigned was also religious in nature. There might be Bible verses to memorize or extra chores allocated because, "cleanliness is next to godliness." If two of us were arguing, the consequence would require us to kiss "on the lips" one hundred times to help us forgive and love one another again. Poor Rachael got whacked in the back very hard one time because she missed Holly's lips. The whack took her breath away for a moment, and I almost stepped in to defend her. The reason Rachael missed the mark was because they were laughing so hard. That's what we did very frequently. However, the kissing punishment was not so funny when we were forced to do it at Food Giant in front of everyone standing nearby. That will teach you not to argue about what cereal to get!

My sisters and I laughed often through the nightmare we called childhood. Though Mother, and according to her, sometimes God, were against us, we were the three musketeers, and it was us against the world. We had fun despite the horrific manifestations occurring around us. Since it was Mother and her Jesus against us, Pastor Cook's declaration of my anointing and calling to "impact the world" for God seemed especially comical.

Chapter 4

THE HEM OF HIS GARMENT

Though I was in a church service, it felt very much like a prison. I was trapped with no escape route, similar to the prisoners chained to each other in the back of a police patrol wagon. Being only twenty and away from Mother, I had the possibility of a wonderful life ahead. Unfortunately, I was sure all my fortune cookies in life would say, "Sexual whores like you deserve death!" Though I had been out from under my mother's control for four years, I was still in as much pain as I had been while living with her. As I sat there trying to imagine a way to break out from my current and very painful living situation, my first suicidal thought flashed before me.

As I sat there, weighing the pros and cons of making an eternal escape, the only con on my list was the damage it would do to my little sisters. I had protected them as best I could; they were in foster care now; they would be fine. They didn't really need me anymore. As I pondered all these grown-up concerns, I noted Pastor Epps was beginning his summation. I obediently tuned in for his closing remarks to God; it was the least I could do; he lost me somewhere between Cain the murderer and

Cain the father of Enoch.

I heard him begin the final prayer as usual, but then heard him say, "Jesus is walking down the aisle; touch the hem of His garment."

I was astounded he would say such a thing and so clearly. What did the pastor mean? Could there be some type of drama production happening, but why would it be after church? I continued imagining myself looking up, but a sudden reverent feeling came over me that I had never experienced before. I felt myself tremble and I had to force my eyes to open; the option to lift my head was nil. I knew someone was walking down the aisle because I could feel His presence. My body wanted to drop to the floor, partly due to my shame, and partly due to the holiness I felt in the room.

As each moment went by, my heart began pounding faster and the reverent feeling intensified. Then I saw it, the hem of His garment. I could not look up and could not reach out. I held my hand up to make the attempt, but my hand was shaking and the shame was screaming. Then something else happened. I felt the most amazing kiss on the top of my head. The warm feeling throughout my whole being cannot be described.

I cannot overstate the importance of this event in my life and the impact it had on my emotional well-being. The shame I felt was almost debilitating. I had blamed my body for what my abusers did to me for as long as I could remember. My self-harm episodes continued to escalate. Cutting myself was no longer enough; I branched out to burning my skin as well. I craved love, but felt undeserving of it. I wanted safety and acceptance, but didn't know how to obtain it. Even when people attempted to show me love, I could not accept the very thing I craved the most. My ears would hear the compliment or the statement "I love you," but my brain immediately jumped to "You don't know the real me," or "If you knew my sins and how dirty I am, you wouldn't even touch me."

Seeing the hem of His garment that day and feeling His presence once again gave me a sense of safety, and it fortified me with the resilience I would need to endure. In my darkest moments I would try to summon the feelings that enveloped me when He kissed the top of my head.

During my teen years, I simply hated myself. The shame was beyond description, which was one reason I had such a hard time relating to my own peers. Their complaints about their lives seemed so trivial.

"I have the worst life ever. Mom said I can't go to Golden Glide for the next two weeks because I forgot to study for the math test."

They complained about having mean and unreasonable parents. I adored all my friends' parents (mothers actually) and tried to spend as much time with them as possible when I was invited for a sleepover. A friend once told me that she hated her parents. I asked why. She said her parents made her go home with them after church every Sunday for lunch together and then a family activity such as a movie or bowling. I wanted to hit her. I longed for the very thing she hated.

My peers wanted to be grown-up and do grown-up things: cuss, watch R-rated movies, smoke pot, or drink alcohol. I wanted to start over, be an infant, and have a new mom who took care of me. While I dreamed of life with a new mother, they daydreamed about anything other than parents. They wanted to hang out with boys, talk about the latest movies, or focus on who had the best clothes in our grade. Everyone desired shoes called Candies and jeans called Guess, Chic, or Jordache. I did not have those things, but I didn't have the cute figure to wear them anyway. I had begun binging after school by the time I was in the fifth grade, so I was a size twelve husky by the age of fifteen. I hated that my clothes were called "husky," and I hated my body for needing that size. My daily self-harm sessions kept my rage at myself intact.

I ran away at sixteen. The last time Mother delivered me to one of her friends was the last straw, as they say. It was Christmas Eve and Mr. Henry, a neighbor, called to invite us to spend the night at his house. It was already bedtime so the request was odd. On several occasions, he had already put his hands on me and attempted to kiss me. He was from Jamaica and threw lots of huge parties. His parties were a great opportunity for Mother to have an unlimited supply of alcohol for free. I'm not sure why she always made me go with her.

At his previous parties, Mother and Mr. Henry encouraged me to drink alcohol and then pressured me to "dance" with him. Mother would smile, drink her free booze, and watch as Mr. Henry thrust his pelvis hard against me to the point of climax while we "danced." I hated him touching me in front of all the drunken people around us, and I hated how they all laughed and cheered him on. This is why I put up such a fight and initially refused to go with her that Christmas Eve. Mother began to beg and explain that this was an innocent sleepover. We would all be going and it would be fun. Mr. Henry had already made a special pallet in front of his tree for us girls to sleep on. Mother would be sleeping on the sofa, and of course, Mr. Henry would be sleeping with his wife in the back bedroom.

Holly and Rachael were very excited about the invitation after hearing about the bedtime cookies, and Mother was persistent. I finally gave in, but what a huge mistake! Should I have been surprised when Mr. Henry took real estate space on the pallet between Rachael and me? Should I have been surprised when he woke me about an hour after falling asleep? Should I have been surprised when I noticed upon waking that Mother had already gone back home, taking Holly with her? Why did I continue to hope she was trustworthy and cared about my safety?

As I lay there under the tree, I felt like I had become a Christmas present from my mother to Mr. Henry. I was signed, sealed, and delivered. I vowed she would never again be allowed to force me into sexual activity. I also vowed I would never have sexual activity with anyone; I had had enough for a lifetime. No one would ever be allowed to touch me again.

I left home within a month. For the next year, I stayed here and there with friends and different families from our church. By this time, the leaders in our church knew Mother had a serious drinking problem and that I had been molested. Our pastor's wife, Marleen, one of my many "mother figures," and a few other women in the church attempted a very unsuccessful intervention. Mother admitted to drinking a little wine occasionally, but nothing to be concerned about. The night they arrived unexpectedly, she was on her third Screwdriver and was ready for me to make her another one. Mother denied alcohol abuse so it was useless to bring up sexual abuse. The only outcome from their intervention was that Mother became furious with me for telling so many lies.

Even after leaving home, I was still very involved in my sisters' care. Mother had long ago relinquished her parenting role, so I made visits often and called almost daily to check on my sisters. Mother was still drinking heavily and her behavior became more bizarre. I was on a mission to get Rachael and Holly removed from Mother's care, and she was on a mission to make sure the girls didn't want to go. Mother became much more of a friend to them than a parent. She was remarkable at manipulating a situation, so that she was either "the good guy" or the "victim."

For example, Mother called me once to tell me Holly had started refusing to go to school, but she partied all weekend. Mother asked me what to do. I told her that Holly should not be allowed to have fun on the weekend if she does not attend school all five days of the week.

Mother literally relayed the message, "Tammy says, 'You're not allowed to go out on the weekend if you don't go to school.'"

Holly called me immediately and was, of course, furious with me.

The worst part of this setup by my mother was that Holly called me back later in the week to report, "Mom says I can still go out this weekend, but not to tell you."

This was the precious baby who had been placed in my arms when I was ten years old and was told by my mom, "This is your baby; I can't take care of her."

I became the enemy on many occasions.

My life had revolved around my sisters for as long as I could remember. I had not been a typical teen. There were times I skipped school for no apparent reason; oh, I was quite the hoodlum! Was it drugs I longed for, sex with multiple partners, drinking binges, or hanging out with friends at the local pizza place? Nope! I skipped to hang out with my younger sister, Rachael. This is an example of how enmeshed we had become. When I was fifteen and sixteen years old, Rachael was ten and eleven years old. We lived within walking distance of our school. I waltzed right into the elementary school, explained that Rachael had a dental or doctor appointment, and I needed to pick her up early. The school was so accustomed to my being the primary caretaker for my sisters that no one questioned it.

I often asked God to rescue us and then, once I left home, I prayed He would rescue my sisters. There was a close call when Rachael was about ten and arrived at school with long welts on her legs and back. Mrs. Brodie, the school counselor, called the Department of Family and Children's Services (DFCS) after questioning Rachael about the wounds and discovering Mother had beaten her with an extension cord that morning for not cleaning her room. Sadly, Rachael was the target of most of the physical abuse in our home.

Mother openly acknowledged this to be true and stated, "I think it's because Rachael looks the most like me and I hate myself. I guess I'm beating myself when I hit her."

I often asked God to rescue us and then, once I left home, I prayed He would rescue my sisters.

This, however, was not Mother's explanation to the DFCS investigator. She put on a performance deserving of an Oscar, playing the role of Mother of the Year. Most anyone having a conversation with Mother would walk away believing she was a victim, a saint, and an awesome mother who had sacrificed her own life for the sake of her children. The DFCS case manager instructed Mother to use more appropriate forms of punishment and recommended parenting classes. Case closed. I would later learn that DFCS had been called several times by neighbors and the school system, but the outcome was always the same. It was confusing, frustrating, and discouraging that the authorities could not protect us, but I was determined to find a safe place for my sisters, away from Mother's craziness even if I had to kidnap my sisters and flee the state!

Thankfully, it was Mother's own behavior that provided a way to safety for my sisters and a respite of sorts for me. The night police officers finally rescued my sisters began innocently. Mother invited family friends, Anne and Kurt, over for barbecue on the grill and lots of alcohol. My sisters were thrilled that Anne and Kurt would be bringing Jason, their six-month-old son. Anne had been our babysitter during the early Charlie years starting when she was fifteen years old. I was about seven when Anne entered our lives, and Rachael was about two. Sadly, even though Anne was underage for alcohol consumption, Mother loved having friends to drink with, so she supplied alcohol to Anne and her friends for many years. Anne had never tasted alcohol prior to meeting my mother; she never quit afterward. Ten years later, the night Rachael and Holly were finally rescued, was no different than many other nights, except this was the beginning of our long and frustrating history with DFCS.

As the night progressed, Mother not only became more intoxicated, but also more belligerent. I later learned that she grabbed baby Jacob, refused to give him back, and actually left the house attempting to run away with him. Anne wrestled with Mother to get Jacob back and Kurt called 911. When the police arrived, they found my terrified sisters hiding in the floorboard of Kurt's truck. Rachael and Holly would finally be safe, or so I thought.

At the time of my sisters' rescue, I was seventeen and had just become employed as a live-in nanny. I had been living with Aunt Alice for the summer when I answered the newspaper ad. I was desperate to find a job and place to live because Aunt Alice would be moving in August. The job required full-time care for Adrienne, a precious ten-month-old, house-cleaning, laundry, cooking, grocery shopping, and whatever else came up.

Ms. Miller, my new employer, had just moved to Ashton and was beginning a new career. As they say, it was a match made in heaven. I asked her once why she felt comfortable hiring a teenager, especially since she had an applicant in her twenties who had been in the Peace Corps. She replied, "Your references from your previous babysitting jobs and the owner of the daycare center where you worked last summer gave such amazing accolades that I took a chance." Thankfully, Mother had trained me well to care for babies, clean house, do all the grocery shopping, cooking, laundry, etc.

I was able to do such a great job that firing me was never a thought, even when I needed to dash off to rescue my family. In fact, I brought much family drama into all my living arrangements. There were many times when Mother called me throughout the night, while extremely drunk, to either tell me she was about to commit suicide, or tell me how I had ruined her life. Ms. Miller taught me a life-changing lesson during one of those nights.

I was still getting debilitating migraines, which had begun when I was four years old. One particular night, I had been vomiting so much during the evening that I remained on the bathroom floor until almost 1:00 a.m. when Mother started calling. Ms. Miller got on the phone and blasted my mother about her self-centeredness and emotional abuse. First, I had never had anyone stand up to my mother like that to protect me, and second, the idea of not meeting her needs during her meltdowns had never seemed to be an option.

Mother initially got off the phone after being confronted but called back about an hour later. I got on the phone at that point, but I was so sick that I literally could not hold my head up.

Mother began her hysterics about wanting to die, "Tammy, I already took the pills. I made out my will, take care of your sisters," and on and on.

I kept telling her about my pain and she knew firsthand how severe my migraines could be.

"Mother, I can't come this time, I can't drive!"

She heard nothing I said but pressed me to get her much-needed fix, a heavy dose of, "Poor you. You've had such a hard life. I love you more than I love anyone else. You're such a wonderful mother. Rachael and Holly adore you. You have so much to live for. I never said you were a bad mother. ..."

Even after I pleaded, I heard a sound that resembled Mother dropping the phone, and then I heard the dial tone. I became hysterical myself. Mother had attempted suicide way more times than I could count, but this would be the first time I was unable to rescue her. I tried calling her back throughout the rest of the night. The pain in my head was almost unbearable. Mother called the next morning while I was preparing Adrienne's breakfast. I had wanted to call her all morning, but I was afraid to face the fact that Mother was probably dead, and it was my fault. I was a wreck. I was absolutely sure she would not answer the phone; I had envisioned all night the scene of her being dead in the living room floor. Would my sisters blame me?

When I answered the phone, Mother said, "I'm sorry, Tammy."

I replied, "For what?"

She sassed, "I'm sorry I didn't die like you had hoped. The pills just made me sick."

This was the first time I remember ever being so mad at her that I actually wished she had died! I had suffered so much all night emotionally and physically due to the migraine, and she called to elicit more pity from me and inflict more guilt. I was livid!

I roared back, "You don't really want to die. You own a gun; if you wanted to die, you would shoot yourself. You live near a bridge constructed over Highway 288; you could jump during rush hour. There are a million ways you could commit suicide, and you play these games instead."

The next words came out of my mouth before I had a chance to censor them, "Mother, I can't stop you from killing yourself. If you want to do it, then just do it!"

I expected her to begin sobbing and say something like, "How can you say such a thing? I've done so much for you girls. Haven't you always had good Christmases? Didn't I buy you a trampoline and go-carts?"

Instead, Mother simply said, "I guess you're right," and then she changed the subject as if none of the night's drama had occurred.

The fact that Ms. Miller put up with so much drama was quite a miracle. She even allowed me to bring my sisters over occasionally. Ms. Miller was the first person to begin telling me I had a right to take care of myself. To me this idea was so foreign. There were other great emotional benefits to my new living arrangement. Not only did I enjoy caring for Adrienne, but also the job required me to minimize my self-harm episodes. Mother rarely mentioned the scars and fresh cuts on my arms; Ms. Miller was not so oblivious.

Mother's suicide game the night of my migraine occurred a few days after my sisters were rescued from Kurt's truck. Rebecca Rhodes, MSW, a social worker with DeKalb County DFCS, called me the day after Rachael and Holly were taken into care. If I had not been over an hour away, in Bethelwood, and on duty caring for Adrienne, I would have made a beeline for her office to demand I see my sisters. It was a great day and an awful day at the same time. I had been praying for someone to rescue my sisters, but I was not prepared to let them go permanently into someone else's care. I was certainly not prepared to have no control over what they ate, where they lived, if they did their homework, and especially not prepared to have any control over when I was or was not allowed to see them.

Being separated from my sisters was a very new trauma, and I did not know if I could survive it. I had never had to live a day without access to them; my intense craving for them seemed similar to what a drug user feels without their drug. Without them, I had no purpose to live, no access to feelings of being loved, and my need to control their care kept my terrifying memories and feelings at a distance. Focusing on them was a great way to dissociate from what was going on inside me.

DFCS stepped in, but the removal would be temporary if there was not sufficient evidence presented to the judge to require more intensive treatment for Mother. The state would need detailed information about our abuse in order to maintain custody for more than a few weeks. Rebecca was able to collect substantial evidence from the school system and our neighbors in order to require parenting classes and treatment for alcohol abuse. She would need my testimony about Mother's psychosis, delusions, and dangerous behavior in order to require psychological treatment for Mother. A few AA meetings and a couple of parenting classes were not going to fix what was broken in our family!

The first week after Rachael and Holly had locked themselves in Kurt's truck to hide from Mother, not only did Rebecca need me to tell her about

---

I had no clue at that point the incredible role Rebecca would play in my survival.

---

the abuse in our home, but I was also required to tell several attorneys and other related juvenile court workers. Rebecca soon began meeting with me weekly, partially because she cared, but also to gain information about Mother's current behavior and progress in treatment. Mother was allowed weekly visits with my sisters, and I would make every effort to be with them during these visits. The role of "official tattletale" caused me substantial stress, and I became the target of my family's verbal abuse and rejection on many occasions. Making changes by establishing new boundaries was difficult and often unwelcome by family members!

I had no clue at that point the incredible role Rebecca would play in my survival. Though she was never actually considered my case manager because I was close to eighteen and already living away from home, she worked very hard to watch over me. As the story of our life unfolded over time, Rebecca became very aware that I had lived through a phenomenal amount of sexual abuse. She strongly tried to convince me to get counseling, but I was seventeen with very little money and no health insurance. Besides, I was becoming attached to Rebecca fast, so the idea of seeing someone else was out of the question. Once I began sharing evidence of Mother's neglect and the abuse of my sisters, the floodgate opened much bigger than I had wanted or knew possible. I'm not sure Rebecca was prepared for the flood, but with a master of social work degree, many years of experience, and the help of coworkers, she helped me start my own long journey towards healing and wholeness.

After meeting with me for several weeks, Rebecca found an urgent need to get professional help with my care. I began showing up for my sessions claiming to have different names and ages. I had never heard of multiple personality disorder, now called dissociative identity disorder, and had no clue what she was talking about. I knew it must be related to my game but unsure why this was being called a "disorder." I knew time played tricks on me, but I chalked it up to being extremely forgetful and "not too bright." Rebecca took me to a psychiatrist who gave me the official diagnosis. I now knew I was mentally ill, just like my mother. Ouch!

For about the next five years, Rachael and Holly remained in and out of DFCS custody. I would continue to monitor their safety and assess Mother's ability to care for herself and for them. Thankfully, I was only a phone call away. There were many times I arrived just in time. On one occasion, during a trial reunification with Mother, Rachael called to report Mother had "gone crazy." Mother's behavior had to be extremely horrific for any of us to become as frightened as Rachael sounded.

Rachael reported Mother was talking crazy and she could not understand what she was saying. I first thought, *Ok, take Holly over to Mrs. Cooper's house and stay there until I come get you.* I asked about Mother's current delusion. Are the angels telling Mother that we all have to go to heaven today, or is Mom saying she's going to heaven today? Big difference!

Rachael replied, "This is way different. Mother wrote Bible verses all over the living room walls with permanent black marker. She's almost naked, and she put all her Kenneth Copeland, Jim Bakker, Kenneth Hagin, and Fred Price cassette tapes in the middle of the living room floor. The battle of Armageddon is today and she will be the Antichrist. Tammy, what do I do?"

Truly, Mother was behaving differently than her usual bizarre and often scary self. I arrived to find my sisters frantically trying to figure out how to stay safe while also trying to keep Mother from harming herself or destroying the house. Rachael's hysteria that day was valid. Thankfully, I had had at least four years prior to this day dealing with mother's delusions when she was fully intoxicated. I also had a lot of experience communicating with her when she was in one of her "religious" hysterics. Trying to convince Mother to stop listening to the angels took a lot of creativity and required the ability to use Bible verses to challenge her thought processes.

I began trying to reason with Mother and figure out what to do. Reasoning with a person who is having a full-blown psychotic episode is quite challenging. She began talking out of the side of her mouth and was making very bizarre hand motions. I did see the mountain of cassette tapes piled on the floor as if she were making a bonfire. Actually, by this time, Mother had also put all her Bibles, concordances, and various other religious books there as well. I studied all the scriptures Mother had chosen for the new wall decorations and realized this was not her typical ranting about the book of Revelation. My sisters and I had suffered through many long nights listening as Mother preached to us about the book of Revelation. To this day, I still don't read or listen to anything related to that book in the Bible. I believe God understands!

Realizing her delusion was related to the mark of the beast, and the second coming of Christ, I was better able to battle her beliefs. I called Dr. Vincent, her psychiatrist, and told him what was happening.

I was positive he would say, "Take her to the ER," which I had done several times for various reasons.

Instead, he said, "Bring her to my office for an assessment."

His office was almost an hour away and he could easily hear her strange babble and bizarre voices in the background. Why in the world would he need to actually see her? Just getting Mother to put clothes on that actually covered her body and get her into the car was a major ordeal.

Once I told Mother we needed to go see Dr. Vincent, she became insistent that I understand what she was trying to tell me.

In a very bizarre manner, Mother explained she couldn't use her mouth to communicate because "Jesus is stepping on my face."

She seemed very distressed and used exaggerated hand and body motions to relay what seemed to her to be very important for me to know. First, she began acting as if she were placing a crown on her head. Next, she pointed to her chest and began rubbing all over. Her hands then went lower to pat and rub her abdomen area frantically. Mother became more and more frustrated with me when I was unable to understand what she was trying to say. I was baffled and even more so when she began pointing to the floor and placing imaginary socks on her feet. Mother finally picked up a Bible, turned to Ephesians 6:13-17 (NKJV) and thrust it in my face.

> *Therefore take up the whole armor of God, that you may be able to withstand in the evil day, and having done all, to stand. Stand therefore, having girded your waist with truth, having put on the breastplate of righteousness, and having shod your feet with the preparation of the gospel of peace; above all, taking the shield of faith with which you will be able to quench all the fiery darts of the wicked one. And take the helmet of salvation, and the sword of the Spirit, which is the word of God.*

After reading the Bible verses out loud, I thought, *Oh, now I understand, duh!*

Why didn't she just show me the Scripture forty-five minutes ago? It seemed my life would always consist of chaos, uncertainty, episodes of danger, and mental illness! After acknowledging the verses and agreeing with her that the battle of Armageddon would be occurring today, I was able to get Mother into more clothes and into the car. I was a pro at getting her to comply, at least eventually. The trick was to agree with her delusion and use her strange beliefs to your advantage.

"Mom, it's time for you pray with Dr. Vincent. He may not know that the Antichrist is coming today, or that we all need to gird our waist with truth. You must tell him!"

If that didn't work, then I'd try again. "Mom, the fiery darts of the wicked one will kill Dr. Vincent if we don't go save him."

After Dr. Vincent did his assessment, he said, "Your mom is having a psychotic episode."

After agreeing with her that the battle of Armageddon would be occurring today, I was able to get Mother into more clothes and into the car.

Oh, thanks for telling me; I had no clue anything was wrong.

He then instructed me to take her to Southside Hospital where he reserved a bed for her.

Once we arrived, I was thinking, *Ok, someone come help me get her back out of the car; it was hard enough getting her in.*

Rachael and Holly were in the backseat and it would sound realistic to say, "They were scared to death." The truth is, they were not. Once I arrived, they felt safe, Mother's bizarre behavior was nothing new, and the event became quite funny. We had dealt with her craziness for so long that it had become the norm. Having a mother who is severely addicted to alcohol is a great prelude to prepare you for a mother who would be diagnosed with schizophrenia. The three of us dealt with this day just like all the other days—we laughed and made jokes about the situation. On that very day, Dr. Vincent had scolded us harshly when we busted out laughing during her assessment.

When Mother made the statement, "I think I cut my daddy's thing off," the three of us could no longer hold in the laughter.

It came out so forcefully that we had tears in our eyes, and he dismissed us from her session. He must have thought we were extremely insensitive and cruel.

It may seem disrespectful or mean, but we always laughed. The laughter might come after the fear, but we always eventually laughed over the incident.

Psalms 30:5b (CEB) says, "Weeping may stay all night, but by morning, joy."

My sisters rarely knew the extent of my pain and fear; yet, God knew. That night turned out to be one of our favorite memories.

There were many times that our situation seemed bleak, but our heavenly Father provided help. For example, on one of the many nights that we had to escape from Mother quickly, I drove my sisters and me to a close friend's house to stay the night. It was very late, but we were close enough that I felt sure she would not mind.

To my surprise, she would not let us in, stating, "You mean you kidnapped your sisters? I can't be a part of this," and then she shut the door in my face.

I had no place to take my sisters. I was very anxious, but I always tried to put on a fun and calm exterior. They rarely knew the extent of my pain and fear; yet, God knew. That night turned out to be one of our favorite memories. I took them to a Hilton Hotel on Central Avenue in Oak Park. We slipped in the gate to the pool area to sleep on the lounge chairs. We ended up meeting an employee who gave us permission to swim, as long as we were quiet, and he provided fresh towels. Even though it was about 2:00 a.m., we had such a wonderful time playing in the pool. I believe God gave us enough creativity and humor to survive the chaos and remain able to experience His joy.

Unfortunately, there were several occasions when it took quite a while to find something funny about one of Mother's episodes. One very cold winter night, when Mother was on a drinking binge, we endured enough fear that it would be weeks before we could laugh about the events that had occurred. It was a school night, so my sisters and I had gone to bed. Around one in the morning, we heard a horrible noise that woke us instantly. It was a very loud roar which seemed to be coming from downstairs. Our full basement was partially a garage. We slowly descended the stairs to find Mother inside her *Chevrolet* Chevette with the car running, and her foot pressing the gas pedal to the floor. The horrible sound coming from the car and the strong smell of gasoline was very frightening.

Once I got Mother to roll her window down, she explained she was trying to blow up the house. The furnace, with the pilot light lit, was about a foot from the front of the car. I panicked. Knowing it would take me forever to convince Mother to get out of the car because it was not "our time to go to heaven," I quickly escorted my sisters upstairs to the back outside deck. We had a two-story home and unfortunately the deck was covered with a thick sheet of ice. I hated leaving them out in the cold, and, even more, I hated the fact that I needed to go back inside to get our clothes. It would not be fun to roam the neighborhood in a T-shirt and panties. I was so afraid to go back inside that I only went in each time long enough to just grab shoes, then just grab pants, and then our coats. I imagined if the house did blow up, Rachael and Holly would be thrown from the deck and maybe break a few bones, but it shouldn't be fatal. If they were inside when the house blew up, we would all burn to death.

I was about fourteen during this event and especially hated that I was the oldest. After my sisters and I at least had some clothes on, we stood on the deck shivering. At some point, I realized Mother was not going to stop her mission to "blow up the house" without some manipulating on my part. I would have to go back downstairs, but the noise and my fear were overwhelming. I had convinced Mother so many times to remain on earth, at least for one more day. This occasion was different because she couldn't hear me over the sound of the racing engine. I was too terrified to think straight. The gas fumes had already drifted upstairs which was already causing me to have a headache. It seemed the decision to go back downstairs was similar to my attempting suicide.

I don't remember how long it took me to get Mother out of the car. Actually, I don't remember anything after making the decision to go back downstairs. I certainly deserved to "check out" and play the game at that point. Thankfully, we did survive and were able to laugh about the incident, after much time had passed.

On the day I had to deliver Mother to Southside Hospital, after meeting with Dr. Vincent, I was frustrated with Mother and the situation, but not scared. This time, getting Mother out of the car was not life threatening. Once again, I used her reality to manipulate the situation.

"Mother, Kenneth Copeland and Jimmy Swaggert are inside praying for the people. Jim Bakker is on the way. They need you to pray over the people."

Rachael was great at adding to my lies, "Yeah Mom, none of the sick people are saved. They'll all go to hell if you don't pray with them."

When I went to visit her the next day to bring her clothes, the nurse told me, "Your mother slithered out of her room last night, on her belly, completely naked."

Mother told them that she needed to show the world how the Antichrist would look when he arrived on earth. The day before, on the ride to Southside, Mother had the same delusion, but additionally, we were told TV cameras were filming her. Clearly, Mother's meds were not working yet!

••••

Rachael and Holly spent several years in and out of foster care. I feel so sad for Mother now. She worked very hard each time to regain custody. She was required to refrain from alcohol use, attend AA meetings, take her antipsychotic meds daily, maintain employment, and meet with her mental health counselor monthly. It would take six months to a year to regain custody, but then she'd manage to lose them within only a few months. The removal from Mother's custody usually occurred because I told Rebecca or the new caseworker what was happening in the home. For instance, Mother managed to fake sobriety when no one lived with her. The moment Rachael called to tell me she found a gallon of vodka hidden in Mother's bedroom closet and another one in the trunk of her car, I immediately called DFCS.

I discovered Mother was great at hiding lots of things. After a phone conversation with Mrs. Sanders, Mother's county mental health worker, I discovered why long-term sobriety would probably never be in my mother's future. I called her in regards to Mother's prescription refill. During the conversation, Mrs. Sanders asked about Mother's progress during her inpatient treatment. I reported the latest events and told her about our last family counseling session at Charter Peachford Hospital where Mother was receiving inpatient services. I shared my regret about bringing up the sexual abuse in the session because Mother began sobbing so hysterically that we could not continue. Once again, Mother's ability to demand center stage, avoid confrontation, and elicit massive amounts of attention came shining through. After Mother was successfully consoled,

I left to go home without anyone acknowledging how the abuse or the session affected me. Mrs. Sanders's response to my account of the session was extremely illuminating. She had been treating my mother for over two years by the time of this phone call.

Mrs. Sanders replied, "I didn't know you had been sexually abused."

I was completely astonished. I began telling Mrs. Sanders the truth about our life thus far. She was completely in the dark about most of Mother's life. She didn't even know Mother had been married five times, and that the last marriage included a lot of domestic violence. I blurted out, "What in the h___ do you talk about?"

There was one great thing I learned during this conversation. Mother's behavior and addiction would never change as long as she did not tell the truth, the whole truth. I knew at that moment, telling the truth about my abuse, my emotions, and my own poor choices would be necessary if I ever wanted to enjoy life.

When my sisters got older, they began hiding Mother's secrets from me. What American kid would want to enter another foster home, leaving all friends behind, where there would be rules, an actual bedtime, consequences for misbehaving, and where school attendance was required? They hated having to see the county-appointed therapist. They were especially embarrassed when the DFCS caseworker showed up at their school for the monthly check-in. To remain with Mother meant freedom to stay out all night, drink alcohol whenever, skip school, have boyfriends over with no supervision, and basically have no responsibility.

Mother and I competed for the role of "parent" for several years. Rachael and Holly wanted me when they needed to feel safe or needed me to rescue them when Mother was scarier than usual. They also needed me for crises, such as the beginning of menstruation, an illness, or difficulties with the consequences of living with Mother. Other than that, they wanted their actual mother, who required very little of them and allowed most anything.

I was always in the doghouse with either Mother or my sisters. Mother called me to tell on them, and they called me to tell on Mother. In fact, my enmeshment was so severe that their DFCS caseworker had to set limits with me about many things whenever they were in state custody. I was not allowed to buy their clothes or actually anything. I was limited in when I could see them or call. The restrictions began when I started calling Mrs. Noble, their first foster mother, to tell her how to care for my sisters. I actually had the nerve to get angry with the Nobles because they weren't "properly meeting my sisters' needs," though James and Cheri Noble had three precious and well-adjusted children of their own and had already fostered at least fifty children.

God's emotional, physical, and spiritual provision sustained me through many very difficult circumstances, and sometimes it came from unexpected places. It was Mrs. Noble who bought me much-needed clothes, out of her own money, when I entered college at Georgia State University (GSU). She also nurtured me as if I were one of her foster children. She set clear boundaries to help me begin focusing on my own needs. It was also very helpful to meet a family who went to church weekly, loved God and prayed, yet no one was hurt, even verbally. Mr. Noble loved Cheri deeply and they had a very playful marriage.

Their behavior at home and in the community reflected the truth about their home life. This was a huge shock to me. The Nobles loved their children: no one was sent off to get hurt, no one drank alcohol, both parents were clothed all the time, and no one had to kiss on the lips, and on and on. They allowed me to spend the night often, and I continued to feel their emotional support as I entered college.

The best part of being around the Nobles was the playful atmosphere. They cracked jokes until we could barely laugh anymore. This couple played fun tricks on us and on each other. Jimmy often tickled the kids, but it was innocent and precious. I had never seen my sisters enjoy a male father figure as much as they enjoyed him. I kept my distance, of course, but I stored the information in my head. *Maybe men can be safe.* Once again, the Lord placed us in a situation where humor and playfulness were used to help us cope with the pain.

I remember all of us skipping through the house singing the Boy George song, *Karma Chameleon.* Cheri loved Boy George; yet, she also loved God. I thought listening to this type of music was very sinful.

I've lived in many different homes since our Noble days, but I have never found a family who laughed as much or found so much peace in the midst of chaos. God knew this was exactly what the three of us needed to get through the years to come and to begin learning how a healthy family operates.

There were many other ways my heavenly Father showed his presence in my life. He comforted me through so many people and kept me safe despite my self-destructive behavior. Father blessed me with the ability to laugh, enjoy parts of my life, and remain creative. The day I sat in the church service, when Jesus walked by and kissed my head, I sensed His love once again. I sensed His joy fill me yet again. It had been about four years since Pastor Cook announced that God had an amazing purpose for my life. I still thought he was way off in singling me out as someone with an anointing to help others heal. There had been so many rapes and terrifying moments since that day, how could I ever help anyone? I wanted to be dead myself.

The Bible says over and over that we will suffer on earth and have "tribulation." Yet, in Jeremiah 31, it says the women and men of Israel will dance and be happy because God will change their sadness into happiness. As I look at the details of my childhood, I easily acknowledge mine and my sisters' lives vacillating between times of turbulence, fear, and pain to gut-wrenching laughter, times of secret adventures, and the feeling of being loved. My sisters and I might endure horrendous abuse one evening and then spend the next day skipping school, playing in a creek, climbing Stone Mountain, and singing as if we owned the world. I believe God sustained our ability to use humor and play to overcome our difficulties and nourished our inner sense of joy despite the trauma.

Chapter 5

⟶◦⟋⟍◦⟵

THE PRINCESS'S
WINTER COAT

*H*ave you ever felt so undeserving that receiving anything from anybody seemed overwhelming? My self-worth, I had none, and I mean none! I carried the shame of Mary Magdalene around with me wherever I went. By the time God sent me the winter coat, I had already sinned more than anyone in the world, or so I thought!

At about age twenty, I was still babysitting Adrienne on the weekends for additional cash while attending Georgia State University. It was winter, and most of my clothes were more suited for warmer weather. I desperately needed a winter coat but had learned to do without. At this time in my life, having warm clothes was the least of what I needed. However, the Lord enjoys providing for his children even when we don't ask for or think we deserve it.

One Saturday night, Gina, Ms. Miller's best friend, came over to pick her up for ladies night out. She entered the front door carrying a beautiful new coat and *handed it to me. I had never heard the name Norma Kamali and did not know it was a designer coat. What I did know—I desperately needed a coat, Gina barely knew me; she had no way of knowing how much I needed a coat, and only God knew how much I complained in my head about not having a coat. Only He knew how often I slept in my car at night when I felt too afraid to be "home," wherever that might be at the time.*

I asked Gina why she gave me such a beautiful and warm coat.

She said, "I don't know. I loved the coat when I bought it, but then didn't like it when I got home. I thought I should give it to you."

It would be many years before I discovered the princess inside me, or began to feel my value according to the King who created me. All I knew was I felt special every time I wore my "Princess Coat."

Boundaries—I pretty much hated all of them—especially if someone was trying to put them on me! I had none myself, so why should others be allowed to have them? If I loved someone, I did not want an inch of emotional space between us. I was starving for love and attention. If you had a picture of my need for emotional nourishment, similar to the pictures we see of starving children in other countries, instead of a protruding belly, you would see me with a big empty cavern in the center of my being.

God gave me a mental picture once of a starving little girl named Amanda, a character in my game who had dozens of people standing in line to feed her. Due to her ravenous hunger, which had built up over time, Amanda was willing to swallow absolutely anything put near her mouth. Outwardly, the people in line all looked safe and caring. Only God was able to see that some of the people had deep caverns of their own and had nothing to give. In fact, some of these "safe" people had ulterior motives, i.e. satisfying their own appetite. They sought to feed on the starving child, taking what little food she had been given.

The people standing in line that were fully nourished and had plenty to share, only gave small morsels during irregular time periods. Sadly, Amanda had no way of discerning which people were starving and which people were nourished and able to give. There were times when the food tasted bitter and caused severe pain, but if one is starving enough, even poison will be ingested. Amanda had no ability to feed herself due to her incredible weakness, so she was forced to rely on what was given to her. She had been born healthy, but was raised by a mother who had no nourishment to share due to her own empty cavern. From birth, Amanda was forced to give her mother any nourishment that she managed to contain. The starving mother was never willing to feed herself or allow others to teach her how to get her own nourishment. She relied on her child and others to fill her own ocean-sized cavern.

God has brought many friends into my life to fill my empty love tank, as I call it. The problem was that my tank was seriously damaged, so I could not store any amount of love and attention poured into me. Not only did I have

---

Rebecca worked hard to teach me about boundaries, so that I could protect myself emotionally and physically. There were times I was very difficult to teach because I was so "hungry," and because a person must acknowledge at least the smallest amount of value in something before they will protect it.

---

a serious leak, I also allowed my mother and others to feed on me, thus draining anything I did store. Over time, I came to realize that I was the one causing most of the damage to my love tank, and because I was starving, allowed others to damage it as well.

I lived at a minimum of twelve different locations from ages sixteen to twenty-four. Many of those living arrangements were at least unhealthy and some included sexual abuse. I'm not sure how I would have survived those years without Rebecca. Even after my sisters aged out of DFCS custody, she remained a huge part of my life. She worked hard to teach me about boundaries, so that I could protect myself emotionally and physically. There were times I was very difficult to teach because I was so "hungry," and because a person must acknowledge at least the smallest amount of value in something before they will protect it. No one protects "filthy whores." I'm quite sure I'm the cause of her hair turning gray.

There must have been a sensor inside me that attracted abusers, similar to how alcoholics say, "If I were in a room with one hundred people, I would end up meeting the one person who was also an alcoholic."

Though I had vowed to never be touched sexually for the rest of my life, I left home and walked right into several abusive relationships. I can call it abusive now, but at the time I, of course, blamed myself. One of the issues was my desperate desire for a mother and for maternal affection. Appropriate touch and boundaries were a mystery to me.

My mother, during periods of significant intoxication or due to her bizarre religious beliefs at times, had very poor boundaries when it came to affection. This made recognizing signs of inappropriate touch very difficult for me. Even when I finally acknowledged something might be inappropriate in a relationship or living arrangement, I was often willing to put up with the sexual part in order to have the feeling of being mothered.

At nineteen, during my first quarter at Georgia State University, I saw George Williams in my first psychology class. I had worked for him a few years earlier when I lived with Aunt Alice for the summer. Bernetta had to put Adrienne into daycare when I entered college. Though I remained a part of their family, babysat Adrienne most every weekend, and would live with them off and on for many more years, I was at this point basically homeless. As George and I got reacquainted, he told me about his wife and two teenaged daughters, Carrie and Lisa. I was invited to dinner and then invited to live with them.

I was very happy there! Susan, George's wife, was very nurturing and very protective of me almost immediately. I could barely wait for her to get home each evening after work. I was starving for her to hug me or give the slightest amount of attention. She too, like all the previous people I had lived with, became aware of Mother's manipulation and emotional abuse. During a phone conversation, when Mother had me close to the point of crying "real tears," a physical reaction that I had lost the ability to do as a small child, Susan took the phone from me and attacked my mother.

She basically said, "You had nineteen years to take care of Tammy, and you failed. She's mine now."

At the moment I heard Susan claim me as her daughter, she could have done just about anything to me, and I would have never complained and never left!

It only took a few weeks for me to become infatuated with Susan and long to be her actual daughter. I hated the fact that I had already turned nineteen, so we could not make the adoption legal. I enjoyed spending time with her daughters from a previous marriage, but also felt very jealous of them. When they complained about chores or rules, I was incredulous.

"You mean you think your mom is horrible because you have to do the dishes and start dinner before she comes home? Are you nuts?"

One of the types of complaints that really angered me was when they said that their mother was too protective.

I might hear, "I can't believe I have to call her when I get there and call again when I'm on my way home!"

Seriously! If they only knew!

Over a brief period of time, she began getting more affectionate. I absolutely loved it. It was subtle and the best feeling I ever remembered having. One Friday night when Carrie and Lisa were out for the night, Susan invited me to watch a movie with her in the bedroom, just like other moms would do. She had me sit close, and she put her arm around my shoulder; no alarms went off for me. She then began kissing my cheeks and telling me she loved me. My mother did that occasionally except my mother often insisted we kiss on the lips. There were no warning flags for me, but Rebecca was becoming more concerned, especially after I told her about Susan and George's strange marriage arrangement.

Even though George was the adult Sunday school teacher at their church we attended every week, he and Susan had an "open marriage." I had never previously heard this term but was very curious about it. I found a beautiful art book on her shelf that had pictures of naked people, mostly women. I knew what pornography was because Uncle Henry showed me those kinds of pictures. Susan's book was nothing like that; it was art. The women were graceful and the scenery was gorgeous. Pasted in the front of the book was a single photo of Susan holding hands with another woman sitting near a stream. It was signed, "With Love, Suzanne." I felt jealous of the woman because I knew Susan must love her very much. I later learned Suzanne came to Ashton often from New York and was a third party in Susan and George's open marriage.

Rebecca continued asking me questions, and I relayed all that I was experiencing.

It was Susan's foot rubbing on my bottom that really caused Rebecca to say, "You need to move now."

On the night that Susan and I watched a movie together, I moved to lie across the bottom of the bed by the middle of the movie. Susan was still leaning up against the headboard. We were fully clothed, but she began rubbing my backside with her foot. I loved every minute of it and thought it was sweet. Emotionally, I was probably a four-year-old, because that's how I felt. She was my mother and mothers rub their child's little bum all the time. Once again, no flags and nothing more than my mother would do.

Susan was also motherly in other ways. During much of my life, I suffered from what is called night terror. I would wake up screaming, and the fear would be so intense that I could not calm myself down. Susan would often hear me cry out or scream and, even though my room in their home had only a twin-sized bed, she came into my bed each time to hold me. What four-year-old would not welcome a mother crawling into her bed for comfort and safe arms? My mother had never, not even once, come in my room at night to comfort me. She never, not even once, hugged or held me after knowing I had just been raped. She also never let me share any details of what happened when I was sent away. She immediately brought up her own pain and expected me to stifle mine.

It's hard to admit, but after Susan came in a few times legitimately, there were occasions when I cried out hoping she would come in, even though there had been no nightmare. In order to do this, I had to keep myself awake for a few hours to pull it off, but it was well worth it. In the meantime, while I was busy discovering new ways to acquire Susan's attention and affection, Rebecca was frantically looking for alternate places for me to live. Though I loved Rebecca deeply, I was not willing to move at that point.

If a person has a strong addiction to cocaine, what is the likelihood of the person moving away from their sole source of the drug if they have nothing with which to replace the high? If a person has a strong addiction to alcohol, what are the chances he or she would give up the substance without severe consequences, such as DUI, loss of job, family, or financial security? The emotional deprivation I experienced in childhood created in me such an intense longing for love that it would almost require a near-death experience to keep me from my drug called "love." So, it wasn't until the "severe consequence" occurred that I became willing to leave, but even then reluctantly.

After a few more months of living with George and Susan, and after enjoying a wonderful family vacation to Minnesota for the Christmas holidays, something began to change. Susan began treating me differently from the way she treated Carrie and Lisa. She actually treated me better. I was favored in a strange way, and she seemed protective over me when there was no danger in sight. She actually got angry with me if I spoke with my mother when she called. She also did not like it when I spoke with Rebecca or allowed Rebecca to help me make decisions. Susan became more possessive of my time and affection. Part of me loved it, and part of me feared it. All of a sudden, something felt eerily familiar, but I would not have been able to explain it. She told me no one would ever love me the way she did. She assigned negative motives to Rebecca or anyone else that was a part of my life. As Susan began to spend more time with me, she spent less time with her girls and George. He, on the other hand, began asking strange questions about my past and flirting with me.

Alas, the night of the huge consequence arrived. I had a horrible chest cold, no health insurance, and no money for a doctor's visit. Though I was in college and Mother could have easily left me on her medical insurance plan, she opted to drop me at least two years earlier. When Susan arrived home that night from work, she seemed very concerned about my cold. After giv-

---

I walked into their bedroom to find them sitting on the bed and smoking marijuana. Susan patted the bed for me to sit beside her. I felt a little stunned but still believed her love for me was 100% maternal.

---

ing me medicine from a prescription bottle, she created a hot bath for me and put eucalyptus and something else in the water. The bath was wonderful and extremely relaxing, except for the fact that she stayed in the bathroom with me and watched.

Even though I had lost a lot of weight the year prior in order to gain my father's love and acceptance, I was still a few pounds overweight. I had a horrible body image, so having Susan watch me lie naked in the tub was terribly embarrassing. I did not feel I had the right to tell her to leave. I actually never felt like I had the right to ask or expect anything from anyone, especially not the right to protect my body or have privacy.

After about thirty minutes in the bath, she said, "After you put your pajamas on, come to our bedroom."

I thought she wanted to watch a movie together; I certainly did not feel up to doing anything that night except go to bed."

I walked into their bedroom to find them sitting on the bed in their nightclothes and smoking marijuana. I knew they smoked this but had never seen them do it. Susan patted the bed for me to sit beside her. I felt a little stunned but still believed her love for me was 100% maternal.

I thought, *Maybe there are medicinal purposes*; I had heard of that.

I felt clean and safe with her and trusted her completely.

She said, "This will help you feel and sleep better tonight."

I had never even smoked cigarettes, so learning to smoke marijuana was not easy. The first thing I noticed was that she handed the joint to me, and I handed it to George, who then insisted on passing it back to me instead of her. I was getting a much higher dose than they were, but once again, I thought it was because I was sick.

I choked a lot and hated how the smoke felt in my lungs.

At first, I kept thinking, *Why do people do this? I don't feel anything.*

Then it happened, I could not feel my arms. I was almost completely numb. I don't think that's a common reaction to the drug. Was it the cold medicine causing this reaction or was the pot laced with something stronger? They certainly did not go numb when they smoked the marijuana, but they took in considerably less than I had been encouraged to do. I remember vividly the point at which I could barely sit up, thus it only took a small nudge from Susan to have me slump backwards on the bed. I could hear her sweet voice telling me to relax and rest. I still thought the extra attention had to do with my cold, and the drugs were to help me sleep.

It was not until I felt Susan's hands under my nightgown, then pulling down my panties, that I realized *something was wrong*! I was wearing a flannel nightgown with little flowers on it, and I still had on the fuzzy slippers with little frogs. Is this not the attire for a four-year-old?

Don't you understand, I want to be your baby, not this, not sex, please not this!

My head was screaming, but words were not coming out of my mouth.

What is she doing to me down there? I thought.

George watched intently and kept repeating, "Relax your legs, you're ok."

He put his hand on my inner thigh to force my legs open more. Resisting was not an option because I could barely feel my legs. I looked down at the top of Susan's head and began playing my game.

This is not really happening to me; Mary Mags, it's your turn to take the window.

Mary Mags complied dutifully until George decided to join in. During this time, he was holding himself and getting ready to join the "fun." My thoughts and feelings were similar to the reaction of a four-year-old child. It seemed as if he were holding a huge monster in his hand that was growing to a very dangerous size.

As he began moving the monster closer to my mouth, I heard a scream, "NO!"

Did that come out of my mouth or Susan's? I was so confused.

At some point, Susan looked up and gave me a sweet smile as if she were proud of me. George was signaling her for something, but what?

Oh no, the monster's coming to get me!

Susan moved from between my legs and George moved into her place. The hysteria in my head had been manageable up until this point except for maybe the "NO," depending on who said it. As long as I was able to play my game, I had become efficient in dealing with being raped. Unfortunately, though my own biological mother had given me the experience of being set up, I had not become efficient in dealing with the pain of betrayal.

George began trying to get that huge monster inside me.

I heard Mary Mags screaming, "STOP! STOP!"

Susan was trying to help "her" calm down. George continued trying to force himself into "her" over and over. I couldn't watch any longer, I had to leave. The next thing I remember is waking up, and Susan was screaming at George with venom in her tone. She sounded as if she hated him. It was so bizarre and so wonderful; she was protecting me! My mother had never stepped in to rescue me, even when she walked in while someone was raping me. Susan began hitting him and pushed him out of the bedroom.

She screamed several times, "GET OUT AND DON'T COME BACK."

He looked confused and actually afraid of her. It was awesome. I now loved her even more.

I slept in Susan's arms that night and willed myself to stay awake.

I knew Rebecca would insist I move out immediately, so I reasoned, *This will be the last night I'll ever have a mother, so let's feel it as long as possible.*

I knew I had the option to keep that night a secret from Rebecca, but for some reason, I felt very guilty when I lied to her. She had protected me from my mother, helped me in practical ways, and spent many hours of her time counseling me. I sensed Rebecca's love for me might become the forever kind if I eventually twisted myself into something lovable. Also, I thankfully sensed Susan's love for me was not the permanent kind and had the potential for disastrous pain.

I wish I could say my time with this family was the only time during my adult years that I needed Mary Mags or one of the other characters in my game to take over. I had not yet learned that my intense emotional need to be loved and cared for could not be filled through other people, except temporarily. In order for my deep cavern to be filled, I would have to become willing to submit to the One who has "living water." I would be required to give up my sometimes-dangerous coping skills and exchange them with His resources to help me cope. Having a full cavern would require hard emotional work in therapy, complete honesty regarding my own poor choices, and a growing trust in Jesus. It would be years before I was ready to submit long enough for Him to pour His living water into my dusty cavern, so that I would never thirst again.

Until I was able to trust God enough and feel His love enough, I continued to enter into the same type of scenario as I had with Susan and George. The painful living arrangement or relationship did not always have a sexual component attached, but always included allowing others to treat me poorly in order to feel a temporary sense of being loved.

I once lived with a couple, Mr. and Mrs. Harrison, who had some similar religious beliefs to my mother's. The most difficult part of this living arrangement was the fact that they had no understanding of how twelve years of sexual abuse would affect a teen. Most every sign of my emotional illness was assumed to be spiritual in nature. In many ways, they were very good to me, and I knew they cared. I loved them very much, too, so I endured long hours at "table time" where I was told that I had a spirit of lust or spirit of rebellion that needed to be cast out.

After they found the journal hidden in my bedroom, where many of the characters in my game wrote about their thoughts, memories, feelings and adventures, the Holy Spirit in Mr. and Mrs. Harrison sensed even more spirits, the not-so-good kind, in me! I was in my first year at Georgia State University, majoring in psychology (no surprise), when I came home not only to discover that they had found the journal, but had read it as well. I was horrified, humiliated, and felt extreme guilt. I was confronted immediately with the evidence. Because there were several journal entries with different handwriting styles, and many signed by other characters in my game there was now proof that I was filled with demons that needed to be cast out. Not again! I was told to renounce each name that had written in the journal. To my horror, they lit the fireplace and threw my journal into the flames. Death by fire—I deserved it. I was more disgusted with myself than they could ever be. I was so filled with hate for myself that nothing would be cruel enough for me to endure. With enough punishment and pain, could I be at least a little bit clean again? I bet the woman with the issue of blood in the Bible never felt as disgusting as I felt!

It was a few months after this exorcism, while still living with this couple, that I heard our pastor say, "Jesus is walking down the aisle, touch the hem of His garment."

Why did I not insist the people in my life, including some family members, respect my needs and not continue to expect that I be the one to meet their needs? Children growing up in households where parents are alcoholics often have a very hard time setting boundaries, often hang onto relationships that aren't healthy and even abusive, feel a need to rescue others, judge themselves very harshly, have difficulties with intimate relationships, often have to guess at what is "normal," constantly seek approval, feel different from other people, are either overly responsible or super irresponsible, and are extremely loyal even when there is much evidence that it is undeserved. Is this why I allowed my schoolteacher, whom I loved as a mother, to engage in a sexual relationship with one of the very young characters in my game? This teacher began "breast feeding" baby Camie, but over time began initiating activities that would require Mary Mags to take over the window.

Another unexpected person with whom I was unable to set boundaries was one of my Sunday school teachers at a well-known Baptist church. She was much older than I, and she knew I had been diagnosed with a serious dissociative disorder. However, because of her own deep cavern, her need to be "loved" trumped my need to be safe and have a healthy relationship.

Instincts would easily have people think, *those teachers, especially the Sunday school teacher, should burn in hell for what they did!*

I have discovered there are a zillion wounded people in the world; wounded people almost always wound other people! Unfortunately, this means I have wounded many others in my lifetime, maybe not sexually but in many other ways. Without Christ, I have no ability to do only what is best for another person. I am unable to expect nothing from others while simply living my life to serve and love all people in a pure and unselfish manner.

Most people don't walk right into one relationship after another where the line between healthy and unhealthy gets so drastically crossed. Why did I not recognize these people had empty caverns themselves and had nothing to give? Why did I not recognize that sometimes I was in a very dangerous situation? The fact that my mother was an alcoholic, had varying degrees of mental illness, and we had lived in a household for six years with extreme domestic violence made identifying emotionally empty people even more difficult. There had been so much chaos and sometimes danger in my childhood that detecting when a circumstance was not safe seemed relative. Bullets flying through the house do not actually mean anyone gets shot, and most times don't even require police intervention. Being raped really doesn't require a doctor's visit or even counseling. Besides, I'm not sure why, but sometimes I even sought dangerous situations.

By the age of five, I was already able to put "someone else in the window" when an abuser initiated contact. Certainly by adulthood, the "switch" during my game was automatic and unconscious. The vulnerability that caused the most damage to my emotional health was the deep cavern longing to be filled with a mother's love. Having this need caused me more

---

I've heard many people question, "Why would a person subject themselves to the life of prostitution if they didn't like it? They must like sex."

---

shame, guilt, and self-hatred than I could express in words. I needed to express these feelings on my skin by cutting or burning myself, sometimes severely. I needed to express it through what I ingested, such as large volumes of carbohydrates, followed by doses of syrup of ipecac or laxatives. I needed to express the pain of my shame and guilt through what I refused to eat, such as periods of dangerous fasting while also engaging in a rigorous exercise program. I lost twenty to thirty pounds in one month on several occasions and was essentially evicted from an exercise center. Actually, the staff at the Druid Hills gym where I had my membership told me not to return until I had a doctor's note verifying it was safe for me to exercise. I had passed out a few times on the treadmill. For some reason, they got nervous about it. Go figure.

I hated having "needs." As a child, I was punished for having needs and for expressing my needs. If I chose to reveal my need, I walked away in much more pain. Which scenario hurts more—getting a third-degree burn on your hand while home alone or getting a third-degree burn while your mother watches, but says nothing and makes no attempt to comfort you or address your wound? Instead, your mother brings up the pain of her first-degree burn that she endured at seventeen and expects you to comfort and hold her. Mother was the only one in our family allowed to have needs and allowed to express them. What we were allowed to do was meet those needs.

I actually hated having just about any feeling. Feelings and needs were a setup and often got me in trouble. Unfortunately, my attempts to punish myself for "feeling" never kept the emotions down for very long and continued to require more drastic forms of self-punishment.

I've heard many people question, "Why would a person subject themselves to the life of prostitution if they didn't like it? They must like sex."

I long to slap the people who are this ignorant, but I must acknowledge my own ignorance in many areas. If a child is raped over and over, what would be the greatest punishment she could do to herself? Sometimes the self-hate is intense enough that you subject yourself to the very thing you hate the most.

I never had a pimp during my adult years. I never lived in seedy motels where I would be beaten for not bringing in enough money. Food and other basic, physical needs were never withheld from me by someone who controlled every aspect of my day. Therefore, I was "required" to do it myself. The degree of self-hate I felt was so intense that I'd inflict as much physical pain to my body as possible without getting myself in the emergency room or a behavioral hospital. I crossed the line many times and ended up in both on several occasions.

Self-harm often requires creativity and careful planning, and it serves many purposes. I hated men and desperately wanted a mother. This saved me from the life of a "typical prostitute," but the cycle was the same. If I needed punishment for having a "wrong" feeling or for allowing myself to enter into a sexual situation in order to feel the maternal portion of the intimacy, the self-harm required intense pain in hidden places. I might be required to cut the skin on my inner thighs so that it inflicted pain all day when I walked. Unfortunately, the other players in my game also needed the outlet of self-harm, so preparation and planning for any given day was very necessary. Just as a mother carries a diaper bag for emergencies, I too had to be prepared. A common crisis, such as being in class at college, looking down and discovering your inner thigh area is wet with fresh blood, required a sweater and/or fresh clothing nearby. Another necessity needed for my "diaper bag" was razor blades in case an unwanted feeling or unacceptable behavior occurred.

The worst and most unacceptable feeling was neediness or anything similar. Relying on anyone for anything was a setup for which I needed to be punished if the feeling showed its ugly head. If I acted on the feeling, the punishment was much more severe. If I saw Susan take her girls out for new school clothes, I felt jealous that I did not have that type of relationship with a female. I did not desire to have that type or any type of relationship with my own mother, but wanted it with someone. The jealous feeling would require punishment, such as a few cuts on my inner thighs. However, if I acted on the feeling by doing or saying something to get the attention, the punishment might be cuts on thighs and breasts.

My self-harm and eating disorder had become an addiction, very similar to my mother's need for alcohol, and had the same numbing results. Acknowledging this fact would be the very thing that helped me forgive my mother. Why would God send me a beautiful princess coat when I was so dirty, so sinful, and so ugly? I saw nothing of value within me. I was a "sexual whore" who dared to have needs, who should be punished daily and severely. I wonder if my mother had the same estimation of herself.

Not only did God send the coat, he met many other needs during this time, even though I was engaged in some very wrong activities and had pulled away from Him almost completely. For example, I went to church most Sundays, but I argued in my head with just about everything the pastor said. I almost always left church feeling worse than when I walked in the door.

For example, the pastor says, "God died for your sins." My response, *Maybe for the people who read their Bible every day, do good things, give tithes, and go on mission trips. Maybe He died for those people over there that raise their hands in church and serve in the choir. Me? Not possible. Maybe He died for the little sins of everyone else, but I'm like Mary Magdalene times a hundred. I think people are supposed to run from me, and wasn't there something about shaking the sand off their sandals?*

The pastor says, "The Spirit who lives in you is greater than the spirit who lives in the world." My response, *Hmm, that reminds me of the man Mother invited to our house to cast all the demons out of us. I guess it was a mistake to lock my little sisters and myself in the bedroom. By now, the spirits who live in the world must have invited seventy times seven more of their little demon friends to live in me. Mary only needed seven demons cast out of her.*

The pastor says, "Jesus says 'He has removed our sins as far away from us as the east is from the west.'"(Ps 103:12 TLB) My response, *Pastor, you don't know my sins! I'm the most disgusting person on earth; my mother even called me Satan.*

Mother often said, *"Get thee behind me, Satan,"* whenever I disagreed with her religious beliefs, argued with her about something, or confronted her with an issue such as her drinking. If my mom looked at me and sometimes saw Satan, then my sins in the east must have gotten so numerous that they merged with my sins in the west.

During prayer, someone says, "And with his stripes we are healed" (Isaiah 53:5c KJV). My response, *Are you kidding me? Children are being raped and hurt all over the world. Why doesn't God keep them safe now instead of telling us He will heal them later?*

The Sunday school teacher says, "For we do not wrestle against flesh and blood, but against the rulers... over this present darkness, against the spiritual forces of evil..." (Ephesians 6:12 ESV).

My response, *George's huge penis sure didn't look like the spiritual forces of darkness! In the Bible, Luke reports that Jesus saw Satan fall from heaven like lightning; does this mean he fell directly into my bedroom?*

In my Sunday school classroom someone read, "But the Lord is faithful, and he will strengthen you and protect you from the evil one" (2 Thessalonians 3:3 NIV).

My response, *Ok, now I'm getting mad. God never protected me from the "evil one" and I've met many. This is a bunch of bull crap! Let's leave.*

Today's message, written on the board in our Sunday school classroom is titled, "You have already won the victory."

My response, *I'll feel victory when I get enough nerve to end my life altogether. Living SUCKS!*

Though this was my attitude, the miracles continued. For example, I had a bad case of strep throat once while working at a daycare center where

I was paid for the hours worked. Having no insurance, I didn't go to the doctor until it had progressed to be almost unbearable. I did not deserve comfort anyway so no need to cut and burn myself when the intense throat pain covered the issue. I was living with Bernetta and Adrienne again after leaving yet another living arrangement that ended in intense emotional pain. While staring at the ceiling and begging myself not to produce any spit that might need to be swallowed, I calculated how much financial trouble I was in for missing so much work. I would need $350 to pay my car note and car insurance by the end of next week and had no clue how to come up with the money.

I have prayed to God every day for as long as I can remember. I tell Him how I feel, I pray for those I love, and I often pray for strangers I see who appear to be suffering. My own personal needs were something I almost never prayed for, because to do so would be the hugest setup in the world!

In the mail on the following day, I received another "tiny bit of hope that God might love me." There was a $350 check from my friend Debbie with the notation, "a gift from God."

Just as I quit asking my mother to rescue me and stop the pain, I quit asking God for anything regarding myself. If He chose not to help someone that I prayed for then no skin off my back, as they say. I was obedient and prayed; that's all I was responsible to do. Besides, we rarely know if or how God will be meeting someone's needs, so my feelings were never hurt if it seemed the prayer was not answered.

During my strep throat prayer, I mentioned the $350 deficit, but was very careful not to ask for the money. What a huge mistake that would be! When my car got repossessed, I'd have to acknowledge the fact that God doesn't care about me any more than my mother cared about me. I'm positive I could not have survived if I didn't have at least a tiny bit of hope that God <u>might</u> love me. In the mail on the following day, I received another "tiny bit of hope that God might love me." There was a $350 check from my friend Debbie with the notation, "a gift from God." No one knew about my $350 deficit, and I was reluctant to even tell God! As soon as I was able to talk again, I called her because I was so confused. The check was in the mailbox the following day and could have arrived even prior to that. Bernetta was not great at getting the mail every day. How did Debbie know I needed that exact amount? She stated, "I knew you were sick and might need medicine or something. I asked God how much and this was the figure He gave me."

Princesses get designer coats and random money in the mail, not "sexual whores." Is it possible that God loves "whores" too?

Chapter6

THE "A"

I NEVER EARNED

I t was the class I most dreaded in my postgraduate counseling program at Georgia State University, Psychological Appraisal. I just wanted to help people feel better. Why did I need to know if I should be using a Trait-Based Test versus a Type Indicator Test in my counseling practice? Who needs psychometric testing? I can look at someone's face and examine their beliefs and behaviors to know if they are sad. Is it really that important to know whether my client scored a "28" versus a "35" on the Beck Depression Inventory? Wouldn't my client already know if he or she were sad? I signed up for this course at the very end of my program...it was required!

I had miraculously achieved an "A" in every class thus far except one, and that fascist professor proudly announced on the first day that an "A" was rare in her class. She also stated that she wanted to break us of our "perfectionist personalities" now before we started seeing clients. How can punishing us with a "B" break my desperate need to be perfect? I'm still mad at her!

When I walked into Dr. Richards's Appraisal class, I could immediately sense failure in my future. The writing on the board from his previous class had not been erased. There were symbols I had never seen and terms that looked like another language. Even the word "psychometric" scared me. The metric system was called New Math when I was in the seventh grade, and they began teaching it to the class one year behind mine. In all the hubbub of life at the time, I simply had not had time to go back and figure out the difference between a kilometer and a mile. *Now I'm in trouble,* or so I thought!

I was happy to see my friend Heather walk into the classroom. We had several classes together over the last two years, but I had not seen her for a few quarters. Dr. Richards began explaining the syllabus, and the measurements we would be studying. He paused then stated something that shocked the whole class; it appeared to shock him as well.

He said, "I'm going to try something new this semester. I've decided to have this class take their exams in pairs."

He just said what? Are you serious?

I looked up, and Heather had a huge smile on her face. She motioned for us to be partners. My feelings were so mixed for a few moments.

Oh no, she'll fail because I'm going to fail.

We met briefly after class, and she was excited, "This class will be so easy."

I quickly needed to share the bad news with her. We had both gotten an "A" in the classes we had previously taken together, so I knew I needed to tell her the truth.

"I will study hard, but I can't comprehend the material."

I knew this because I still had the textbook. I had attempted the class about a year prior, but dropped it because I found the material impossible to learn. I told her I would understand if she wanted a different test partner.

To my surprise, she said, "Don't be silly," and then explained, "My graduate program is School Counseling, and I've started my internship. I've been giving these tests in the schools for several months, and I love it."

Throughout the course, she tried to help me learn the math portion that went with each assessment. We planned to take the tests separately and then compare our work. On our first test, not even one of my calculations was the same as her results. She eventually gave up trying to teach me the extremely complex math that required an IQ of 274 with no standard deviations!

We turned in all her tests and I "earned" an "A." On the last day of class, I asked Professor Richards what he had learned from allowing us to take exams in pairs.

He confessed, "I have no idea why I did that, and I'll never do it again."

I sensed something divine had occurred but wondered, *Why would God care whether or not I had a master's degree?*

I still didn't think I would live long enough to actually help anyone!

••••

I have had "mother figures" as long as I can remember. Since elementary school, with every new schoolteacher came a new chance to earn a mother. But nothing could have prepared me for the obsession and pain I would have with one of my therapists, Dr. Wilson.

I met Dr. Wilson, the clinical psychologist assigned to me while I was an inpatient at Oak Pines Hospital, in August of 1993. I was twenty-nine years old and worked as a weekend houseparent at a residential facility for pregnant teenagers in Clarksville called The Hope Home. I graduated with a BS in psychology when I was twenty-five and began working for The Department of Family and Children's Services (DFCS) at that time. Working as a case manager for DFCS kept me very busy during the week, but it did not provide structure for the weekend. For the previous decade, I thrived on a manic lifestyle. I did not understand why I needed to do at least three things at one time, work at least two jobs at the same time, and hated even one minute of silence. Due to my fear of silence and being alone, I spent many a night studying at the Waffle House to get my degree.

Many of my fears seemed strange, unrealistic, and disconnected. For example, it would be many years before I knew why I either lost time or became confused when passing funeral homes or entrances to subdivisions with lots of flowers. I was not sure if I was afraid of something external or internal. There's a big difference between the two, requiring very different solutions. I eventually discovered the cause of my crazy symptoms: severe insomnia for years, brutal sessions of self-harm, bouts of violent diarrhea, migraine headaches, an insane need to be busy, an eating disorder where I obsessed over every bite of food I put into my mouth, bizarre phobias, confusion, memory loss, and many more epically crazy behaviors.

God showed me a picture of myself at an arcade with bright neon lights everywhere and deafening noise. I was standing in front of the Whack-a-Mole game holding the heavy mallet. In the vision, I frantically began bopping the little moles back down their holes, as if it meant the difference between life and death. I knew immediately that the moles were my feelings and memories popping up, and I was desperately trying to stuff them back in before I was forced to feel the feeling or see the memory. At that time, I thought I knew everything that had happened to me. I did not understand

---

I eventually discovered the cause of my crazy symptoms: severe insomnia for years, brutal sessions of self-harm, bouts of violent diarrhea, migraine headaches, an insane need to be busy, an eating disorder where I obsessed over every bite of food I put into my mouth, bizarre phobias, confusion, memory loss, and many more epically crazy behaviors.

---

that the game had taken over to keep much of my past hidden from me. I spent a lot of time punishing myself for every feeling that popped up, believing if I just punished myself enough ...

One of the problems was that I did not know what I should be "allowed" to feel. During those last ten years prior to working at The Hope Home, I was extremely enmeshed with my mother and sisters who were trying to keep their own moles under control as well. If one of my moles popped up its ugly head in their presence, it meant one of their moles popped up as well, and they were desperate to "leave the past in the past." If I mentioned anything about my feelings or memories, Mother would say, "Give it to the Lord," followed by the recitation of multiple Bible verses that shamed me into even more self-punishment. My sisters accused me for years of being "attention seeking" just like Mother. Ouch! We knew the most painful statement we could ever make to each other was to insinuate we had an ounce of likeness to our mother.

Although my sisters were unable to be emotionally available to me, they were still emotionally attached to Mother. We certainly all loved her, but each had a very different relationship with her. Also, my sisters desperately needed to keep our childhood under the covers and very distant from the present time. It's not that memories from childhood did not pop up, but the manner in which they needed to discuss them was through laughter. I was verbally and emotionally punished if I attached "real" feelings to the memories.

A typical example of how the dynamics worked in our family occurred in 1991 on Mother's Day. Mother had sold our house in Bentwood and bought a trailer in Carrington. Holly was still living with Mother at the time. Mother was still drinking heavily and had been even more emotionally draining during this time. The Mother's Day plan was to take her out to lunch. Rachael would be meeting us at the restaurant, and Holly would drive Mother and me. When I walked into their trailer and saw Mother's level of intoxication, I should have refused to go. I had the thought to leave, but the option to actually do that seemed impossible. If I refused, there would be a severe verbal and emotional lashing from my sisters.

The nightmare began on the ride to Ryan's, one of Mother's favorite restaurants. Unfortunately, since I rode with Mother and Holly, the option to escape was unavailable. Mother lay down in the backseat immediately and turned on her cassette recorder. She was listening to her favorite TV evangelist, Kenneth Copeland. Mother's car was a small *Chevy* Chevette, so the backseat was only about a foot from the front seat. Due to the dynamics of Holly and Mother's relationship, Holly could get away with absolutely anything. She was fearless and had no problem cussing Mother out if the need arose. I, on the other hand, was terrified of our mother. My childhood experiences with her created a lasting fear that I could not shake. By the time Holly was five years old, Mother had lost interest in the role of being a parent, had stopped dating, and had become emotionally helpless.

This partly explains the reason for the Mother's Day nightmare. Holly was driving and listening to her favorite music, rap. As Mother turned up her religious music, Holly fought back and turned up her rap music. Then Mother fought back, and this continued until both had their choice of music, "noise" to me, turned up at full volume. At the point when Holly's rap music was more deafening than Mother's tapes, her screaming began.

"Turn that Satan music off right now," but she was screaming and addressing me.

I responded, "It's not my music. You know I don't listen to rap."

She continued getting angrier and angrier with me.

At one point she commanded Holly, "Put her out of the car right now."

Mother actually commanded Holly to put me out of the car and leave me stranded on the freeway!

I had numerous emotions at that moment, but mostly fear. I forgot that Holly had no fear of Mother and rarely complied with anything Mother told her to do.

I began begging Mother, "Please don't put me out, please. It's not my music; Holly, please turn it down."

I tried turning it down myself, but Holly turned it back up. I looked at Holly and pleaded for her to keep driving and not pull over.

She responded, "I'm not putting you out," and she laughed.

Mother was getting angrier by the moment because Holly would not evict me. Meanwhile, Holly thought the whole scenario was hysterical. The ride to Ryan's was only about fifteen minutes from Mother's trailer, but it felt like a drive to China.

Mother chose to punish me for something she knew Holly was doing.

When we arrived at Ryan's, Mother began crying. Rachael met us there and wanted to know what was wrong with Mother. We explained the dramatic ride to Ryan's.

I said, "I think we need to take Mother back home. She's too drunk for us to do this."

Both Rachael and Holly insisted we needed to do something for Mother, "IT'S MOTHER'S DAY, TAMMY!"

We walked in to discover we were not the only family attempting to bless their mother on this special day; however, I doubt their ride to Ryan's included the mother insisting someone be put out of the car and left on the freeway. Once in the very long line, Mother began crying a little louder. Rachael, being the peacemaker in the family, started soothing Mother and trying to make her laugh.

Mother then exclaimed, "I won't stop crying until Tammy says she loves me."

In the past, I would have simply complied immediately. At this point, I had taken some classes at my church and was learning about a strange concept called *boundaries*. I hated the feeling of being manipulated and punished. For about ten minutes, I refused. Mother, being the master manipulator, increased the pressure. She began crying even louder and then even louder. She became so hysterical that people from the very back of the restaurant came up to the entrance to see what was happening. My sisters were not mad at my mother in the least. They were furious with me!

"Just tell her you love her!"

They loved on her and tried to reason with her.

Instead of saying, "I love you," I said, "Mother, I want to buy you the kind of steak you most like. You can pick out any steak you want."

She responded in a very loud cry, "I won't eat until you tell me you love me!"

This was the kind of cry a three-year-old has when a toy is taken away. Her volume and hysteria evolved to the point that my sisters' anger at me and the embarrassment of over a hundred people staring at us, was stronger than my need to set a boundary.

Feeling powerless and humiliated, I blurted out, "I love you, Mother."

Her crying immediately stopped almost as if she had never begun. She ordered her steak, a rare rib eye, and I quickly paid the bill. We found a seat in the back of the crowded restaurant. I was relieved the ordeal was over, or so I thought. All of a sudden, Mother became very distraught again. Both of my sisters had invited their boyfriends to join us, so the six of us sat at a rectangular table. Mother and I sat at opposite ends of the table. When the waitress came to take our drink orders, Mother was crying so hard that the waitress could not understand anything Mother was saying.

Rachael patted Mother's hand and explained to the waitress, "Mother gets so sentimental when all her girls are with her."

Holly ordered her some sweet tea and asked Mother what else she needed.

Once the waitress left, Mother exclaimed "I WILL NOT EAT UNTIL TAMMY GIVES ME A KISS!"

Are you serious? I'm expected to kiss her on demand just because she wants it right now and in front of all these people?

I adamantly refused! Our power struggle continued until the food came. By that time, Rachael and Holly were furious with me. Mother was asking for such a small token of my love, and I had the nerve to refuse, and on Mother's Day no less! I was told I was being selfish and self-centered. I was told I was trying to create drama. Seriously, I'm the one causing the drama? This scene was not unusual, though. Mother created a mess, and somehow it became my fault.

Once the food arrived and the peer pressure became unbearable, I got up and carefully stood behind her. As she sat waiting for the kiss, I intentionally kept my body as far as possible from her chair in order to "control" the kiss. I leaned around to kiss her cheek knowing her intent was to kiss me on the lips. As I leaned around her side, trying to give a quick cheek kiss, she roughly grabbed the hair on the back of my head and pulled me forward. Mother planted a wet and disgusting kiss on my lips. I know this is strange, but I felt raped and violated! Again, I lost the battle. Mother fights dirty; I almost always lost the battle with her. I turned and looked at her as I made my way back to the other end of the table. She had a huge smile on her face, with no sign of the recent distress. She began cutting the most expensive steak on the menu and chatting it up with everyone. My sisters were now happy as well. I said almost nothing throughout the rest of the meal. No one noticed.

In my journal entry dated 8/14/93, while I was a patient at Oak Pines Behavioral Hospital, I wrote,

> I'm not sure why self-destructive behavior is on my mind so much today. Is the desire due to my actual pain and the memories attached, or is it a power struggle between me and the helping professionals? I feel powerless but if I cut, I have my power back and staff cannot force me to comply. I need power over my feelings and actions. I need power over everything about my life. Mother has been stealing my power and my choices since my birth. I don't know how to feel about her.

Should I hate her or love her? Do I help her or evict her from my life? I wish someone would tell me how to feel and then I could pull out those acceptable feelings like a magician pulls a rabbit from a hat. Unfortunately, Mother is no rabbit! On some days, she is a cobra and I am her prey. She will squeeze me to death if I get too close and then consume me so that I become a part of her. Other days, she's as helpless as a wounded lamb, her needs are all consuming, and she insists she has sacrificed her life for me. Because I caused all her pain, I owe her my life, which includes my feelings and decisions.

At the point in my life where I was living at The Hope Home, the moles popping up were constant and vicious. I was terrified of each one and was losing the battle in trying to keep them down. Anger was one of the moles I was trying so hard to keep under control. The methods I used to whack the feelings back down only helped temporarily. For example, a friend of mine gave me a seventy-six-piece dinner set of Corelle dishes, plus a lot of the matching serving pieces. I dropped a plate one night and it did not break.

I was intrigued and thought, *I wonder how hard I need to "drop" it before it breaks*.

I remember that thought, but the truth is I did not remember much of the "Crash Parties" until years later. Velda was the character in my game that handled much of my anger. She and some of the other characters rescued me from having to remember and feel the associated anger; they all took turns "crashing" the plates and accessories on the kitchen floor. About ten pieces of dishes were crashed each night and the broken pieces were left on the floor. I even convinced my friend Julie to break a dish, so that she could feel the rush.

Julie was the primary therapist at The Hope Home. Her approach and success in counseling the girls amazed me and elicited my own longing to be a therapist as well.

My career goal was not possible having only a BS in psychology. Also, the fact that I was functioning only through the efforts of over twenty separate "characters" probably put a damper on my ability to be an effective therapist as well!

At The Hope Home, the house we lived in on the property was divided into two separate smaller units with only a wall and door in between. Although Julie did not experience the same rush as I did when she broke her dish, she knew the dynamics of my family and understood the reason for my desire to break things. It wasn't until my insomnia got so severe causing me

---

There were many sleepless nights when I could hear the scratching noise and some strange thumping in the wall.

---

to hallucinate that she realized I was in crisis. I had a lifetime of practice in keeping the game, the self-harm, and the addictive behaviors a secret, sometimes even from myself.

The final crisis that caused my emotional break was due to a squirrel! This demonic creature was living inside the walls on my side of the house. We didn't know for over a week that it was a squirrel rather than a rat. I've always been terrified of rodents, and for good reason. I'm not sure if it was bad luck that a squirrel decided to move in with me or if it was divine intervention. There were many sleepless nights when I could hear the scratching noise and some strange thumping in the wall. When I did manage to fall asleep, the nightmares were horrific and confusing. I didn't have most of my memories, which included rats, from when I was very little and abused by Ken, so when I dreamed about it, I often thought I was crazy.

Even after we discovered that my new roommate was a squirrel rather than a rat, I was already playing my game most of the time and still unable to sleep for very long. Thankfully, Julie allowed me to sleep on her sofa when my exhaustion began causing migraines, and my driving skills declined to a dangerous level.

As much as I longed for sleep, I was equally terrified of it. Nightmares of rats raping me or crawling all over me were so intense that I literally believed it was happening in the present time. I began taking massive amounts of sleeping pills on the nights when I did not have to go to work the next day. I was barely functioning at my DFCS job because I had a limited ability to concentrate, remember, or organize my thoughts. Documenting a home visit or conversation with a client required so much more brainpower than I had, and the ability to keep my eyes open during the interview, as well as follow the conversation, became almost impossible.

I'm not sure what had occurred the night Julie decided to take me to Oak Pines Behavioral Hospital. She must have had a good reason. Possible options could have been the huge pile of broken dishes on my kitchen floor; the cuts on my feet because one of us thought it was fun to master the art of walking on broken glass; the screams she heard in the night due to my nightmares; or my declining ability to think rationally. What I do remember is the long ride to the hospital and my acknowledging the final verification that yes, I was mentally ill, just like my mother!

I spent about five weeks at Oak Pines. This is where I met my absolute dream mother figure of all time—Dr. Wilson! Just as there is a Mr. Right for a husband, she was the Mrs. Right for all my maternal needs, which were massive. Unfortunately, she and I had very different goals. She was interested in helping me lay down my poor coping skills, such as cutting and dissociation, and exchanging them for setting clear boundaries with my family, choosing healthier ways to cope with the feelings and memories that surfaced, and becoming able to handle life without the need of her support. What nerve!

I had an intense fear of boundaries because even the tiniest bit of a boundary meant rejection, which hurt immensely. My goal was to become her child, just short of literally being nursed as her infant! Thankfully, I was aware that nursing me was impossible, but taking me home with her and filing for a legal adoption was not too much to ask. I just wanted her to let me sit beside her on her sofa when she was home and tuck me into bed at night and pray over me. It wasn't like I was requiring her to quit work or anything; that would be over the top. She could simply take me to work with her, and I would be very good in the waiting room. I felt like I was three or four years old whenever I was near her, so I imagined I would color inside the lines really well while she saw her clients.

It was the character in my game named Amanda who most wanted Dr. Wilson to be her mother. My self-assigned job was to earn the money we needed in order to pay the bills. This meant I had to be able to work every day which would require me to be separate from all the intense pain. The greatest source of intense pain was not the memories of being abused; it was the requirement to leave Dr. Wilson's office. It was the fact that I could not go home with her. It was the fact that she had two children, and I could never be one of them. It was the fact that every slight boundary she set caused me so much hurt and rage that I barely survived between sessions. It took hours of self-harm each week and often dangerous behavior to cope with the separation. Therefore, Amanda was the main character who carried the intensity of the "need" I felt for Dr. Wilson. She was also the one who at four-years-old grieved the loss of my grandmother when she died.

I spent more hours fantasizing about Dr. Wilson being my mother than all my other mother figures put together. The amount of time I spent imagining mother/daughter scenarios of Dr. Wilson being my mother probably surpassed Kelly Garrett, one of TV's *Charlie's Angels*, within a month! I fully understand why so many women remain in an abusive relationship. I also understand why a woman would allow her body to be sold in order to keep her pimp in her life. Dr. Wilson had intense power over me. I would have done just about anything for her. She could have severely beaten me during every counseling session, and I still would have run back each week for more. I thought I deserved horrendous punishment anyway; therefore my need for her love was much stronger than my need for safety.

When I met Dr. Wilson, I finally knew I had met the mother who would not try to seduce me in exchange for maternal love. I knew it was against therapeutic rules for her to touch me inappropriately, so I was safe at last! I think the intense infatuation began from the very first session. It seems like I was hiding under a desk when we met. So many of my game characters were popping in and out of "the window," that my "age" varied from three to twenty-nine-years old.

A facemask is the best way to describe the window. My face was the mask and each of my personalities took turns looking out the mask or window. If a four-year-old was using the window, then I sounded four, had the perspective of being four, and held the memories of my life at four years old.

Each character had a different purpose. Some were in charge of specific emotions while some were responsible to hold certain memories. My emotional and sometimes physical well-being depended on it. For example, there were times in childhood when a situation would evoke rage in me, and for good reason. As my mother's child, I was expected to please, comfort, obey, and adore her. If I had been filled with rage and showed signs of rejection, it would not have gone well! I needed Velda, age nine, to be in charge of my rage. Amanda, age four, held much of my intense need to be loved, and Breanna, a teen, held many memories and expressed the rebellion that was too dangerous for me to act on.

I discovered later that it was Amanda hiding under the desk in our room and using our window the day I met Dr. Wilson at Oak Pines. I vaguely remember her kind tone and loving eyes as she tried to convince "me" to come out from under the desk. Actually, I don't remember anything else about our sessions at Oak Pines, or even if she came to see me there again. The plan was for me to see her on an outpatient basis as soon as I could escape the prison called inpatient services. The part I do remember is the intense love I felt for her almost immediately.

Transference is a very powerful issue between client and counselor. My symptoms of this cruel occurrence included excessive thoughts about Dr. Wilson between sessions; an intense fear of her disapproval or rejection; acting-out behavior that could be positive or negative; an obsession with her to the point that complete honesty was almost impossible because I sought her love more than anything else; and lastly, my desire for her to be my mother was so intense that the pain I experienced in therapy seemed to have nothing to do with my past abuse, but was due to the boundaries she needed to set.

My infatuation with Dr. Wilson led to what I thought was "crazy" behavior for which I deserved horrendous punishment. Therapists usually call it "acting-out" behavior similar to a child's temper tantrums. I wanted a maternal relationship with Dr. Wilson. She basically said no, we need boundaries which I loathed, so I did the adult version of kicking and screaming. Some of my acting-out behavior included self-mutilation, overdosing on sleeping pills, binging and purging, and running away. Yes, I actually ran away similar to a child who runs away to punish her parents. I also followed Dr. Wilson home one night to discover where she lived. I would then sleep in my car on many nights in front of her house. My stalking behavior went beyond her house to her other work places such as a school and a hospital. My brain seemed to have unconsciously transferred the love and intense need I should have felt for my mother onto Dr. Wilson. Sadly, I also transferred what I thought my mother felt for me onto Dr. Wilson. The intensity of the emotions I felt seemed worse than any pain I had ever felt, but also swung to the highest high I had ever experienced. It felt as if I had a serious and dangerous addiction to my therapist. I would have done anything for my "drug" contact with her and any morsel of love and attention she was willing to give.

During the five years of seeing Dr. Wilson, my self-harm was intense. Sometimes I needed the pain to distract me from the pain I felt from her "rejection." Though she cared about me as much as she did her other clients, my emotional state was similar to someone covered with third-degree burns. My emotions were extremely sensitive, so bumping up against a boundary felt emotionally similar to the excruciating pain of someone pressing on burned skin. Unfortunately, therapy is one huge boundary! Other times, I cut or burned myself in order to control my emotions! If I could just be punished enough for the feelings that surfaced, I could control which feelings to have, the intensity of them, and even have the choice to feel or remain numb.

I hate to admit this, but I also cut and burned at times to either gain her attention or make her angry. Much of my life was shared with Dr. Wilson through the characters in my game. This was partly due to my actually not remembering major incidences of abuse; remembering them and feeling it

I saw myself as even more sinful and more disgusting than I deemed my perpetrators to be. I blamed myself mostly. It took many years for me to understand that I had projected the feelings I should have had for the people who hurt me onto myself.

would jeopardize my ability to work—and I was too ashamed to look at the abuse or have her see it. Remembering and sharing the events of my exploitation with Dr. Wilson felt similar to what a prostitute might feel if she were forced to show her favorite priest the porn movies she had starred in, as well as all the other sins she had committed. So humiliating!

I saw myself as even more sinful and more disgusting than I deemed my perpetrators to be. I blamed myself mostly. It took many years for me to understand that I had projected the feelings I should have had for the people who hurt me onto myself. It was certainly not safe to feel or express these emotions when I was a child. I now also understand that I projected many of my feelings onto Dr. Wilson. This means I often assumed she had the same feelings towards me as I had for myself.

I also had a very difficult time trusting people and believing what they said. Dr. Wilson could tell me a thousand times that she cared about me which might create a moment of warm fuzziness, but then my brain quickly needed to remove any good feelings and exchange them with either numbness, suspicion, or even contempt. As soon as the session was over and I got into my car, especially when I saw her greet her next client, I became furious, hurt, jealous, and often suicidal! My thoughts turned to negativity:

She doesn't care about me.

She loves all her other clients, but not me.

She only sees me because I have good insurance.

Why would she care about me? I'm disgusting and gross.

Why didn't she sit beside me on the sofa this time? She knows how sinful I am.

No one loves prostitutes!

As these thoughts scrolled across my brain continuously, I experienced a rage so intense that I literally could not keep myself safe. I turned into the female version of the Incredible Hulk. Typical behaviors after my sessions included severe cutting, extremely dangerous driving, burning myself on the stove, lots of alcohol before going home, excessive laxatives, binging, and sometimes a dangerous dose of sleeping medicine.

One night after a painful session, I got drunk and then had the desire to drive very fast. Note, I did not remember what happened in the session. Someone else inside me usually attended and spilled the beans, so to speak. What I "knew" at the point of consciousness was that Dr. Wilson was mad at me, did not care about me, and regretted taking me on as a client.

On this night, after a few margaritas, I drove into Ashton to "hurt my car." I desperately wanted to be in my car, driving very fast, while scraping the driver's side on the concrete median. I imagined massive sparks and a loud scraping sound. Just imagining the scene felt wonderful. I also wanted to tempt death.

Thankfully, the Lord intervened every time I tempted fate. That night, there was an accident on I-35, so police officers were everywhere. I also attempted to flip my car in vacant lots on several occasions. It's not as easy as it looks on TV. Not only did God intervene in physical ways such as police officers being in the area where I wanted to cheat death, but he also provided many friends to help me stop the war inside my mind.

Cathy Gates was my primary source of support and love, though there were many others. I was twenty-two years old when we met. I can't imagine how I would have survived my journey of healing without her. We both attended the same Baptist church and became close friends very quickly. That was twenty-seven years ago, and we are still very close. Cathy is about ten years older than me and is the first Christian I had ever met who actually lived what she believed. She worked at a Christian ministry. Her love for Jesus does not show so much in what she says or feels; it's her commitment to Christ that exudes her love for Him in just about every choice she makes. She is the exact opposite of my mother. Cathy actually drives the speed limit, won't say a bad word, always tithes, and often helps people without the need to let others know about her good deeds.

There were many times when Breanna, a teen character in my game, showed up at Cathy's work, knocked on her window, and requested time together. Cathy often spent more of her allotted lunchtime with Breanna, but was faithful to work the extra thirty minutes at the end of the day even though no one would notice or keep up with her hours. These small signs of faithfulness to God helped me trust her regarding bigger issues. She read her Bible, memorized verses, attended church faithfully, tithed, and often helped others, but so did my mother! Finding safe friends was very difficult.

One of the major ways God used her to help me heal was by challenging my perceptions and beliefs.

Me – "Dr. Wilson hates me!"

Cathy – "Didn't she meet you at her office on Saturday when you were in crisis? I don't think she hates you, but she might be frustrated."

Me – "Dr. Wilson didn't even call me back yet."

Cathy – "She probably has three or four patients back to back and can't call you right now. This does not mean she doesn't care about you."

Me – "Why would she care about me anyway? I'm too needy. I'm not working hard enough, and my feelings are all messed up."

Cathy – "You are very easy to love. You went through incredible pain during childhood, but you will heal. Tammy, I love you and I'm sure Dr. Wilson loves you and more importantly, Jesus loves you!"

After five years of counseling, I was still not willing to accept or face most of the memories and feelings that my characters held. As we continued to meet, Dr. Wilson began expecting me, Tammy, to attend my sessions rather than doing my work through the "others." This felt impossible and extremely more painful. What I discovered was that she knew things about my

---

Not only did God intervene in physical ways such as police officers being in the area where I wanted to cheat death, but He also provided many friends to help me stop the war inside my mind.

---

past that I didn't even know. Some of the things she knew about me were hard to believe, so I felt like I must be lying to her. One of the ways my characters communicated with Dr. Wilson was through journaling. They wrote in a journal, had her read it, and then they talked about it. I was strongly encouraged to read the journals but my thought, *Thanks, but no thanks.* Why would they tell her such awful things? I was so confused and when I did read an entry in the journal, I had a very hard time believing the words could be true. Naked——that's exactly how I felt when I made myself look out the "window" during our sessions. As they told her about the gross and sinful things that went on in my childhood, it felt like the scenes of the events literally went through her mind. She could see me lying there while I was with all those awful men doing awful things. I was completely exposed.

Another frightening issue that I tried not to admit was the fact that I knew some of the pieces they were telling Dr. Wilson were true, but the puzzle pieces of me had huge gaps. During one of my final sessions, Dr. Wilson asked me to tell her everything I remembered about being thirteen.

Weird question but okay, I can do that. "Well, I was in eighth grade and starting my first year next door at the high school. Mother was still drinking like a fish. I already told you about Darryl and all the other abusers."

I began searching my memories and a funny story came to mind that I thought, *Maybe I've never told her the Ricky story.*

So I began, "I had a funny pregnancy scare at that time."

She asked more questions so I explained what happened.

This is when I had my first childhood boyfriend, Ricky. It was a little late for my age to have a first boyfriend, but I guess I'd been a little busy. Ricky went to my church, and we began hanging out with each other. Over time, the hanging out began to include some kissing and touching, but none of his parts came anywhere near my parts. I discovered I was not "gay," which was one of my many concerns at the time, but I also discovered that I did not like male body parts!

In the early fall of that year, I began missing my menstrual cycles. I was so worried the first month, but then became undone the second month. I had started on my tenth birthday and was regular by that point. I told Ricky because he was the only one who had gotten anywhere close to affectionate with me. He freaked out as much as I did.

He called me every day after school and blurted out, "Did you start yet?"

Over and over we reviewed every intimate activity that had occurred late that summer and none of it seemed to have the possibility of causing pregnancy. We were stumped, and I was terrified.

Mother would kill me! God must really hate me now!

As I shared this story with Dr. Wilson, I thought she would be as amused and entertained as everyone else who had heard the story. Strangely, she did not look amused, but even more serious. I continued hoping she would see the funny part at the end.

So, then Ricky called one day frantic and asked, "Do you remember the day I showered at your house before I went home? I was sweaty because we jumped on the trampoline all day, but I was going somewhere with my dad that night?"

I thought about it and remembered the day but responded, "Ricky, we didn't shower together!"

He sounded like he was about to have a panic attack and said, "I know, but I used a white wash cloth that was already in the shower. You showered after me. Did you use that washcloth on your parts?"

I told Ricky I didn't remember, but if it was hanging in there, I most likely used it!

He said, "Oh crap! Oh no! I washed with it. I washed down there with it. Did you wash your parts with it, too?"

"Of course, but so what?"

"Tammy, think about it! If one of my guys got on you down there, then that's how you got pregnant!"

Both of us thought this was very possible, so we believed I had gotten pregnant by a shared washcloth. Funny, huh?

Dr. Wilson looked at me without the smile I expected. I loved entertaining her, but this must not have been a funny story. The next statement out of her mouth almost took my breath away. She told me I had gotten pregnant, but it was not due to Ricky and a washcloth. I remember staring at her face in silence. I did not know what to say, but I knew how I felt—sheer panic! It seemed like the moles from the Whack-a-Mole game were about to come up, and I needed to do anything possible to keep them down. I had no clue what memory or feeling was about to surface, but I knew, or thought, there was no way I would survive if it popped out.

I calmly looked at Dr. Wilson and asked, "Can I leave now?"

I don't think I had ever requested to leave early before, but she said, "Yes."

I guess she had no clue the degree of crisis I was in at that point. In fact, that was one of the worst nights of my entire life, apart from the abuse, of course. I was absolutely terrified of the memory attached to getting pregnant and the feelings that would go with the memory. I got in my car and do not remember how I got home. The next thing I remember was sitting on the sofa with my roommate watching a TV show called *Mad About You*. I was counting in my head the exact number of Trazodone, my sleeping medication pills, I would need to take to sleep just until my tennis lesson the next night. I was desperate to fall asleep immediately and wake up exactly thirty minutes prior to my lesson. I was even calculating the amount of time it would take for me to tie my shoes and grab a water bottle.

I just have to sleep until my tennis lesson.

I seriously was not thinking straight.

I'm not sure how the events occurred that night, but basically I miscalculated and ended up in the ER. I do remember that when I was still not sleepy after the next rerun of *Mad About You*, I panicked even more. My brain was going a mile a minute and no cutting or burning would keep this memory down. I would need very drastic measures to survive the volcano about to erupt. I survived the abuse, but I seriously doubted I would survive the therapy and the memories I would need to face.

After my stomach was pumped, a rather barbaric and inhumane procedure, I was told I had taken a very deadly dose of Trazodone and would be transferred to Charter Peachford Hospital.

Here we go again, inpatient services, and this time without Dr. Wilson's assistance. She was angry with me, but not nearly as angry as I was with myself. I only have one memory from that hospitalization, but it shook me to the core. I was sitting in an AA-type class about addictions which I was required to attend, especially since they did not have enough survivors of sexual abuse at that time to have a survivors' group. While sitting there somewhat bored, my lower abdomen started cramping more than I can describe. It was intense and came in waves.

I was barely able to walk out of group and had to stop a few times while walking down the hallway to my room. I knew I had not taken laxatives; this

---

It was the memory of how I got pregnant that my spirit, soul, and flesh fought drastically to keep buried.... I was an emotional wreck when I returned home from the hospital.

---

pain was different anyway. Once I got near my doorway, I literally dropped to the floor and crawled the rest of the way to the toilet. The pain felt similar to needing the toilet really badly, but still different. I crawled up and felt a huge need to push and then it happened. I relived the miscarriage I had had when I was thirteen years old. It was exactly as if I were alone in my bathroom at 3589 Bridle Court. The pain, the gripping cramps, and the huge blood clot—I saw and felt it all.

It was the memory of how I got pregnant that my spirit, soul, and flesh fought drastically to keep buried. This was the beginning of the end of my time with Dr. Wilson. I was an emotional wreck when I returned home from the hospital. The switching of characters behind my mask caused serious headaches which caused me to be so confused. My racing thoughts and memories switched from when I was very young to my early teens. Some of the pictures seemed so evil and demonic. Maybe the Harrisons were correct; maybe I am filled with demons.

Once released from Charter, I remained in the day program for several weeks. Three of the other patients attending the program lived in a halfway house and saw a therapist named Janis Furtner, LCSW. I had no interest in switching counselors, but I knew I was not safe living at my house. I found myself hiding in my bedroom closet off and on all day. I had bruises all over me but had no clue as to why. I later discovered the cause of the wounds. My friend Dawn spent the night on my sofa one night when I felt especially unsafe. I lived in a split-level condo at the time. She told me I had fallen all the way down my steps around 2:00 a.m. She said it wasn't exactly like a fall, but more like I "rolled down the stairs" very fast. I then cried just like a small child, had no clue who Dawn was, became more frightened, and quickly crawled back up the steps.

The intense fear and flashbacks I was having had to do with someone coming to get me at night when I was very young, though I had no memory of this actually happening. I knew Ken had molested me when I was little, but nothing happened that would cause this much distress! I was unable to function at my job and was now on temporary disability. I desperately needed some type of support, structure, and accountability. I was very suicidal. If I had not had Cathy and a few of my other close friends, I do not think I would have survived. I still believed Christ loved me and that I would go to heaven, but I found it very difficult to believe that there could still be a purpose for my life. Would the war in my mind, the voices, the eating disorder, and the addiction to self-harm ever end? Certainly I would never have enough emotional health to not drain everyone around me, and I was sure I would never experience true joy! I made the tough decision to move out of my condo and into the halfway house just long enough to feel safe.

The halfway house was helpful; we were required to attend group sessions a few times a week and meet with the therapist assigned to us. Annis Roy, LPC, was the intern assigned to meet with me weekly. She was finishing her master's degree in counseling at the time. I still saw Dr. Wilson every week at her office, but the difference now was that I had additional support, accountability regarding my acting-out behavior, and there was a curfew. The option to flip my car, drive crazily, or engage in self-harm would now have consequences. The halfway house was set up within an apartment complex. We each had a roommate, and there were about ten other significantly wounded individuals living in the complex. There was a lot of support which helped immensely, but the greatest source of my will to survive and face the monsters in my nightmares was my assigned roommate, Lu.

She was several years older than I and had also been diagnosed with dissociative identity disorder. I knew Lu from group therapy at the Charter Peachford day program. She was the one who told me about Janis and the halfway house. The day I arrived to move in with Lu was the first day of my resolve to get well and fast. On that day, I discovered that very mentally ill individuals can appear emotionally stable out in the world, but if you live with them, it can be frightening.

The Lu who greeted me at her apartment door was not the same Lu I had met in our group counseling sessions! This Lu had an apartment with children's toys everywhere and posters of sea animals and puppies and kittens all over the walls. In a small child's voice, with mannerisms of an excited six-year-old, she showed me the bedroom she had created for me. The baby blue room had rainbows and stars painted on every wall, including the ceiling. It looked like one of the many stuffed rainbow ponies had thrown up all over the room. Next, she showed me her collection of Barbie dolls. She had names for all of her dolls, and each one had her own accessories and special living quarters within the huge doll castle in her bedroom. She literally held them as if they were real, and I quickly discovered she spent hours each day playing with her Barbie dolls. I was about thirty-three years old at the time while Lu was over forty. She invited me to play dolls with her almost every day. I didn't even play with Barbie dolls during my childhood; I surely wasn't going to start now!

Her strange behavior both perplexed and upset me. Was this how I appeared when someone else was in my window? Did I act like a baby one minute and then a perky teenager the next? Over the past six months, my own emotional stability seemed to be slipping from my hands like sand. Would I, like she, spend the rest of my life living from therapy session to therapy session? Would I lose hours of each day in a make-believe world? I guarantee no time would be spent with Barbie dolls, but I did have dozens of drawings, painted pictures, and writings all signed by different characters in my game. I'd wanted to help other children heal for as long as I could remember. How could I help them if I have decided to remain a child myself? The thought of my remaining "as is" frightened me tremendously, but also led me to ask God a thousand questions.

Lord, why did you make a way for me to complete my degree? Why did you not only help me pass that awful class, but even receive an "A" that I didn't deserve? Besides, now I'm in major debt from school loans, unable to work, and have even regressed to the point that I can barely take care of myself and remain safe. How will my education benefit me if all I'm ever going to do is sit around playing with dolls all day? Jesus, please help me? I hate Barbie dolls. Why did the visiting pastor speak your promises over my life at that conference? Also, what's up with Marie's vision last Sunday?

I attended the Grace Vineyard church at this point in my life. It took many years for me to feel totally safe in church. I often needed to flee the premises if the pastor began to sound more like a preacher than a teacher. Dr. Milton at First Baptist always sounded like a teacher, and the services were predictable. At the Vineyard, the services were often unpredictable and sometimes frightening to me. Remaining seated was very difficult when Scriptures were recited and worship included loud praise and enthusiasm. Holy Spirit activity was a huge trigger for me because of my mother's religious and sometimes dangerous psychosis.

During a recent Sunday morning service, I went up to the altar to ask for prayer. A sweet, older woman named Marie came over to pray for me. I was acquainted with her, but not enough that she would know anything about my background at this point. Marie was very close friends with June, one of my dearest friends at church. Marie taught many Bible studies at the church and was considered anointed. I trusted her, so I felt safe.

She began praying under her breath while her hand began to tremble. I had seen this strange phenomenon several times over the years and knew it was related to the Holy Spirit.

After the intense prayer she seemed to be having with God, she said, "Tammy, God showed me a vision of your journey. I see huge bundles of wheat in a field so far I can't see the end. The bundles of wheat are bound by huge and very strong chains locked tight. The Lord told me the wheat is your emotions, and He has kept them tight for you. Over time, as you are strong enough to handle it, He will loosen the chains slowly, so that the rage, guilt, shame, and depression, for example, will slip through at a pace you can handle. If He took the chains off too quickly, the large bundles of wheat would fall to the ground, and the seeds would dry up and be wasted. The harvester would not be able to use the wheat for His purposes."

I felt so defeated during that time in my life and could not imagine God still had plans for me. I had messed up everything. I had sinned way too much, had a very difficult time studying the Bible or even remaining in church services. My spiritual health was not great, but my emotional health was much worse. It felt like my emotional well-being was similar to someone with stage-four cancer. Something was slowly eating away at me which I had no control over. Even Dr. Wilson, a well-known and accomplished therapist in our community, could not help me. I was too fragmented, too far-gone, too corrupt, too manipulative, and way too needy to ever be used by God!

Surely God had given up on me by now. My dream had always been to help children heal who had also endured abuse. I wanted to open a special children's home to teach them, protect them, educate them, and love them.

So, who is this harvester in Marie's vision, and what's important about the seeds not blowing away? How does this relate to my life? I lived in an almost constant state of confusion.

For example, how did I end up in a nasty motel room in Harris, TX., and why is Dr. Wilson shouting my name? What boys is she telling me to stay away from, and why does she sound so frustrated with me? It often seemed she was already frustrated with me by the time I managed, or more truthfully, chose to get in the window. I could barely manage to make good or safe choices when she just felt frustrated with me. How would I ever handle her reaction to the evil dreams I was having or the disgusting things I saw myself do in the dreams? I felt like I was as evil as Lucifer in the Bible. Mother was correct to call me a "Laodicean witch." If Dr. Wilson ever knew about the secrets, she would surely despise me.

Dr. Wilson, unlike my new counselor, Annis, shared the same faith that I did, which was also the same faith as the Harrisons and Williams and many other unsafe places I stayed or people I knew. Dr. Wilson knew about demon possession; surely, she too would suggest I get the demons cast out. Would she be afraid to treat me or feel uncomfortable with me near her?

That's what happened with a very close friend of mine named Barbara. She and her husband were in leadership at the church I was attending. After several years, I trusted our friendship enough that I told her about my time living with Susan and George. The next time I saw Barbara, she was very nice, but said she did not want me to babysit Amy, her granddaughter, anymore.

Barbara went on to explain, "I know you wouldn't touch her, but do you think you are gay? I don't know how the spirits work, but if you have a spirit of homosexuality, you can understand my concern, right? What if those spirits in you jump onto her?"

By the time Annis entered my life, the hardest memories were already at the surface threatening to pop up. No mallet I held would be strong enough to keep those moles down much longer. My cutting and burning behavior became even more intense. I literally cut my female parts to the point that I had to be taken to the ER. Hating my body more than I can express, I severely mutilated any body part that was even remotely related to sexuality. I also put Comet and bleach in my bath water. The pain from my cuts took my breath away when I sat down in the bathtub.

Because I was terrified of Dr. Wilson's rejection, and because of the risk of losing even the tiniest amount of maternal love she might have for me, the option to disclose to her was nil. It was way too risky and actually felt "life threatening." Therefore, the characters in my game began telling Annis about my time at Ken's funeral home. I thought I already knew all that had happened there, just like I thought I remembered everything that had happened when he took me to Kansas and Missouri. I also thought he stayed a few nights with us when we returned from the trip and that I was never again alone with him after the trip. Characters that I had never heard of began drawing awful pictures that frightened me. They wrote things in my journal that just couldn't be true. No one would do such terrible things to a little child, and where did the other children come from? Why do I hear little children crying when I sleep? It felt like I was having an emotional stroke!

I changed and my life changed when Dr. Wilson said, "Tammy, you were pregnant, but it was not because of anything you did with Ricky."

The memories of my time in Kansas tumbled out over time. Based on the date, I then realized I had gotten pregnant while on the trip with Ken.

What I didn't understand was why did I hear voices and have thoughts such as, *I wonder which one got me pregnant. Do I need to contact him and will he pay child support?*

At one moment during the day, I knew it was 1997, and I was not currently pregnant. A few hours later, I might have horrendous flashbacks of being in motel rooms with men at thirteen years of age, and desperately trying to escape, but unable to move. I actually felt the pain of the rapes in my physical body, especially at night in my sleep. Then I would find notes in my journal where someone was trying to pick the name for her baby.

Please, God, just come get me now!

After a few months of having sessions with Annis, as part of the halfway house program, Dr. Wilson saw that I was becoming more and more unstable. She gave me an ultimatum: choose me or choose Annis. I was given one week to decide. Dr. Wilson believed my regression was due to Annis's inexperience as a counselor. Any therapist would have assumed the same. I tried to tell her about the strange memories that were coming up, but she did not believe me. Heck, half the time, I didn't believe me either!

To her credit, I now understand her skepticism. She had been meeting with me for five years; it's reasonable to assume the issue would have come up. One of the reasons it's so difficult to face childhood trauma is because it requires a temporary loss of control, and it's messy. The process reminds me of the pressure cooker Mother used to make chili when we were kids.

Dr. Wilson had also made a firm rule...that the characters in my game could no longer come to our sessions. I was now required to stay in the window during my time with her, but I often did not know what to say.

There's a little valve at the top to allow the steam to seep out slowly. During the memory recovery process, the fear is that the whole "pot" will eventually explode. This happened once with our pressure cooker. It started making a very loud and terrible noise. This was a childhood occasion when I was less than brave. I screamed, then ran into the living room, and put all the sofa cushions around me. My intense fear of things blowing up was very apparent that night. Mother put the "screaming" pot in the sink to run cold water on it, but within a minute or so, there was a loud boom. Chili covered the kitchen, especially the ceiling.

When I saw the damage and the mess, I thought, *Let's just move!*

I was actually Annis' first client after graduating from her master's degree program. Unfortunately for her, she entered into my healing process just as I was about to explode. I had no more strength to lift the mallet, no ability to keep the moles hidden any longer, so, the explosion would be very messy! Dr. Wilson had also made a firm rule several months prior to this that the characters in my game could no longer come to our sessions. I was now required to stay in the window during my time with her, but I often did not know what to say. Or was I too afraid to say it? I worked so hard during the week to keep the memories and feelings within the "pot," and now I had fifty minutes to let it seep out just a little, but not enough that an explosion would occur. The task seemed impossible and dangerous, especially when you took into account my level of confusion.

I was so spacey and so forgetful that simple tasks were becoming anything but. Making breakfast for myself could easily become too complicated to complete. One morning I found that I had left the carton of eggs in my freezer, and my favorite frying pan disappeared completely. How do you lose a frying pan? The moles were popping up too fast, and I was too terrified to tell Dr. Wilson, my friend Cathy, or anyone else I cared about. The risk was too great!

The week that I was to make my decision about which therapist to see was simply brutal and included nightmares, strange voices that scared me, lost time, diarrhea, vomiting, and so much more. I was physically and emotionally exhausted. My deadline was Friday. I was to call her answering machine and leave a message with my decision. I intended to call all week long; I even counted down the days. I imagined what I would say and then imagined her response, or what I wished her response would be.

"Tammy, I've been praying for you all week, and I want to continue being a part of your journey to heal. We've been through so much together and I love you."

To me, the decision was a "no-brainer"—I'd continue with Dr. Wilson. However, from the moment I received the ultimatum, a civil war broke out within me where it did not seem like there could be any victors. The casualties would NOT be numerous, just me. My fate actually seemed sealed at the point when Dr. Wilson required I attend all sessions rather than allowing the others inside to help me. The part of me named Amanda, who came when I was four to help me carry the pain of my grandmother's death was also the one who held most of the trust I had allowed myself to feel with Dr. Wilson. Amanda was the one brave enough to crawl out from under the desk at Oak Pines Hospital to meet with the new therapist.

I have no clue what happened that Friday except that I knew sleeping pills and laxatives had been taken. I woke up Saturday morning in a panic. Did I call Dr. Wilson? Oh gosh, what if I didn't call her? Nausea came over me almost immediately when I began sensing that I had NOT called her! I wasn't sure, but decided it would be best to leave her a message letting her know I intended to remain her client and would stop meeting with Annis. She returned my call, and I told her I definitely wanted to continue seeing her.

She then asked, "Do all of your parts want to see me?"

I later thought, *What a strange question; almost never do all my parts agree on anything!* We are all so different.

I had to confess; I wasn't positive that all of me wanted to continue with her, but I was making an executive decision.

"Dr. Wilson, I'm saying we will continue seeing you."

Then my worst nightmare actually occurred; it wasn't good enough. If I couldn't commit to being "all in" then it needed to be "all out." To say I was devastated feels similar to describing World War I as a disagreement between a few countries. Now I knew my deep and empty cavern would never be filled! I would never be able to get her to love me just like I was never able to get my own mother to love me. The next three weeks of my life were seriously fragile. I gave myself permission to commit suicide almost every day with a condition.

If you still want to commit suicide tomorrow, you can do it, but just wait till then.

In the meantime, God provided helpers, and of course, I used every coping skill, often the painful kind, to get me through the day. At that time, I felt more hatred towards myself than I had ever felt before.

The truth is I'm still very affected by the end of my relationship with Dr. Wilson. I dream about her more than I dream about anyone else I know. In every dream, I receive great comfort from her or sometimes painful rejection. The relationship in the dream is still maternal or has a nurturing feeling attached, and the emotions are very intense. I still battle shame in relation to her.

My thoughts in the dreams, with the associated feelings attached include, *I was too messed up, I'm unlovable, too weak, too ugly,* and on and on.

I understand in my head that the pain I still feel after all these years is due to transference, but understanding the reason does not fix the pain. Thankfully, the pain has lessened over time.

I sometimes wonder if this unhealed pain will remain with me for life similar to Paul's thorn in the flesh in the Bible. I do know one important fact: I have no power to heal myself! I must daily choose to walk closely with my heavenly Father and submit to His therapeutic program designed just for me.

In the five years I met with Dr. Wilson, I only remember crying one time. The pain coming up was not related to the abuse, but due to a family member accusing me of stealing from my paternal grandmother after her death. I had not! I can't count the number of hours I spent over the years fantasizing about Dr. Wilson holding me while I cried. After all, the intense desire for my own mother to hold me after every rape was bottled up tightly enough already. I envisioned the tears would one day come, and Dr. Wilson would hold me while I sobbed and grieved. I honestly would have chosen this fantasy to come true over winning a million dollar lottery; yet when the opportunity came, I couldn't allow it. She tried to hold me as I sobbed, but I turned from the very thing I longed for the most, someone to finally hold me when the pain surfaced. This is why I know I can't heal myself. Allowing her to hold me in that moment might have been one of the most healing hugs I would ever experience; yet, I refused. Why?

Just as I did not have the power to heal myself, I also <u>did not</u> have the power to cease my addiction to self-harm, lay down my eating disorder, control my emotions, recover the memories lost, or regulate the turmoil in

---

> *To me, the most amazing part of Father's therapeutic intervention and plan for my life is the fact that He had already begun the "good work" well over thirty years prior with my princess coat as a tangible sign that He was working on my behalf already. He knew my royal standing because He exchanged His royalty for my humanity.*

---

my mind that controlled my life. I <u>did have</u> the power to learn some self-soothing techniques and better coping skills, but I <u>did not</u> have the power to choose the healthier methods. I could "white knuckle" it temporarily, but I could not "be good" or "be healthy" for very long. I couldn't even choose my lifelong dream, the "ultimate hug!"

My inability to control much of anything around me, my feelings, my behaviors, etc., was terrifying. I'm not suggesting we have no control over anything we do. I'm simply saying that on my own, I had minimal control over much of my life. My healing and victory would require Father's power, provision, and love. To me, the most amazing part of Father's therapeutic intervention and plan for my life is the fact that He had already begun the "good work" well over thirty years prior with my princess coat as a tangible sign that He was working on my behalf already. He knew my royal standing because He exchanged His royalty for my humanity.

Philippians 1:6 (NIV) "being confident of this, that he who began a good work in you will carry it on to completion until the day of Christ Jesus."

To me, this basically says He already started helping me heal a long time ago and He won't stop until I'm whole. I'm not sure what my being "whole" will look like, but I'm thankful I have been His princess all along. He knew the sin, self-hatred, pride, selfishness, rebellion, and addictive behavior ahead; yet He wanted me to wear a Norma Kamali Princess coat. He even revealed through Marie's vision that my pain was so great, He has kept it stored in safe bundles, and He will loosen the chains over time, as I am able to handle it.

I wonder ... *If my heavenly Father knew I was a princess so many years ago, even though I was quite a mess, could He possibly have already had an amazing purpose for my life, even back then? Could this purpose be related to the reason for His intervention with the "A" in my Psychological Appraisals course?*

Unlike my earthly parents, my Father in heaven has continued to intercede during those times when, despite my best efforts, I could not have succeeded on my own.

Chapter 7

————◇◦⊂⟋⟍⊃◦◇————

MY DIVINE

TREATMENT PLAN

*S*he better not be talking about my journey!

That was my thought during one of my first Beth Moore Bible studies called Breaking Free. I sat with all the other women in my small group and was trying so hard to focus on the video. Beth's message was very engaging, but I struggled to stay in the moment. I knew the time was slipping away. In about an hour, we would be released to go home. It didn't matter for the most part where I was, it felt safer than being at home. *Samantha, my roommate, won't be home for another four hours; I guess I can go walk the mall.*

As I pondered about how to keep myself safe and emotionally intact for the next four hours, I heard something very strange, and frankly, mean! The statement was in Beth's voice, but I have no clue if it was part of her video series.

I heard, "It will get worse before it gets better."

How can she say this to all these people? How can she know our lives are about to get worse? What does worse mean? Is there a famine or war coming that no one else knows about?

It felt as if she were talking only to me. Surely she had to be talking to someone else because I was barely hanging on to this world.

Thanks for the warning, because it did get worse! The timing of Dr. Wilson's exit seemed so terrible at the time. Bible verses such as Romans 8:28 (NIV) which says, "And we know that in all things God works for the good of those who love him, who have been called according to his purpose," made me angry.

How could Dr. Wilson leave? *Doesn't God know how much I need her to love me? She has been very instrumental in helping me see that I had a right to set boundaries with my family, but I still needed help to actually do it.*

By this time, Mother was fifty-four years old, on disability, and fully intoxicated every minute of the day. She lived in a state of varying degrees of psychosis because she rarely took her anti-psychotic meds. Her physical health was as deteriorated as her mental health. Mother had cirrhosis in her liver, hepatitis, gallbladder issues, and malnutrition. Her skin was so jaundiced that it was hard to look at her, and she looked as though she were in her last trimester of pregnancy. She now had legitimate physical needs, and I'm the oldest child.

I was also the child who had been preached to the most, "Tammy, the Bible says, 'Honor your father and mother so that your days will be full.'"

She began pounding this verse into my head as a small child.

Mother felt the need to remind me of this verse often, so she left messages on my answering machine such as, "Tammy, your days are numbered! You are not honoring me. I told you I need money for my prescriptions. You won't live long if you can't even give forty dollars to your own mother."

She actually knew just about every verse in the Bible that would reflect my responsibility to care for her fully, "Tammy, you are to help the poor widows because they will always be with you."

Her version of scripture was simply that, her version, but she made it sound so authentic. Mother was not a widow, but who am I to argue such small matters with God.

Mother's ability to control me was very different from how my sisters responded to her neediness and manipulations. Rachael was able to distance herself both physically and emotionally.

Holly had no problem simply putting Mother in her place, "Mom, you're drunk. Go to bed."

Mother actually obeyed Holly for the most part. By the time Holly turned twelve years old, there was a complete parent to child role reversal. On the other hand I was so consumed by fear, guilt, and shame that Mother could usually control my actions and feelings simply by spewing out the right condemning Bible verses. Thankfully, because of our faith, Dr. Wilson was able to help me sort out my actual responsibilities regarding my mother, according to the Bible vs. Mother's expectations vs. my own perceived responsibilities. Dr. Wilson taught me that, yes, the Bible does say we are to honor our parents, but that does not mean I'm financially responsible to meet all of Mother's needs. The guilt I felt when I did not send money to my mother was miserable, but at least learning it was not an actual "sin," helped make the guilt more bearable.

At first, it wasn't enough for someone to give me permission to quit sending money to Mother, or take her to the doctor, or meet any of her other numerous needs. I needed someone to forbid it. My counseling sessions during the first year or so with Dr. Wilson were often spent dealing with the current trauma of Mother's behavior and verbal abuse. At some point in our work together, Dr. Wilson realized we would never fully delve into the childhood abuse as long as I was still in relationship with one of my abusers, my mother. Dr. Wilson then made a firm rule that I was not to send money to my mother, and I was only allowed to talk with her on a speakerphone while I was in a counseling session. The conversations with Mother during my sessions were usually very brief because it would only take a few minutes before Mother's manipulations and emotional abuse began. Dr. Wilson would then instruct me to "end the call right now."

I was unable to judge when my mother crossed each line; casual conversation turned to manipulation, which turned to verbal abuse, which then turned to emotional assault. If Mother had called screaming and cursing at me, and then threatened to kill me, it would have been much simpler. Instead, she sounded very loving and kind at the start of each conversation. She began the conversations with her concerns for my sisters. She knew the hook, my sisters! Once I was caught, she reeled me in with her tears and the litany of her endless needs. Mother almost always reported any recent "sins" my sisters committed or shared any grievances they had against me. Mother was a master at stirring us up against each other. She quoted bits and pieces of what was said and then placed herself as the advocate for the one she was manipulating. When I was the victim, Bible verses were thrown in to control my feelings and behaviors.

I'd be a millionaire if I had money each time one of my sisters called to fuss at me after I had been speaking with Mother just five minutes prior. The version of our conversation that Mother reported to my sisters had almost nothing to do with what we actually discussed. In fact, Mother was notorious for making a negative comment to one of us about the other sister and before we knew it, the author of the original comment was one of us rather than Mother. She was also great at exaggerating what was said.

Mother – "Holly has not gone to work in the last two days, and she owes me $148. Tammy, I just can't take the stress anymore. My light bill is seventy-nine dollars more now that she has moved back home, and my water bill is $129 higher."

Me – "You're the one who begged Holly to move back in with you, so that you'd have someone to help you with cooking and errands. Ask Holly when she will get her next pay check and see if she will begin making payments on the money she borrowed."

Next – Mother calls Holly.

Mother – "I just got off the phone with Tammy. She says you need to move out because you're causing me too much stress. Tammy says if you're not willing to go to work every day and pay me back all the money you owe me then you should move."

Next – Holly, who is now furious, calls me.

Holly – "What the hell! I wasn't on the schedule to work Monday or Tuesday because I worked two double shifts over the weekend. Why are you freakin' out over whether or not I go to work?"

Me – "I'm not the one upset. Mother called me about you not going to work and owing her money."

Holly – "If you're not upset then why are you telling Mom to kick me out? And what money? She's drunk. She bought two gallons of vodka on Friday and finished it off on Sunday. She sent $400 to her TV evangelist people. That's why she has no money!"

Holly had much better boundaries with our mother than I did and she tried to help me set boundaries as well. Even when Holly told me Mother was using the money I sent on alcohol rather than for her bills or medication, the guilt I felt was too overwhelming to just ignore Mother's pleas for help. Dr. Wilson was the only person in the world who had the power to help me break away from my mother's control. My love, or need for Dr. Wilson's acceptance, was thankfully stronger than the guilt and fear I felt regarding my mother.

Mother was also experiencing her own overwhelming feeling of guilt during the time I was seeing Dr. Wilson. She was often very suicidal and delusional.

On a Monday, she might leave a message such as, "I'm going to heaven tonight. I've already taken the pills," and would then leave me detailed information on how I was to execute her will.

On Wednesday, she might call back to say, "The angels didn't take me the other night because I had nicotine in my body. I'm not allowed to go to heaven with nicotine in my body, but I can go tonight because I'm to lay with the lion and the lamb."

The few years before Mother died, it seemed she was trying to get her affairs in order. Though I hated the messages back then, I'm grateful now that she not only left the messages, but that I wrote down what she said and how I felt about it. The messages she left validated some of my strangest puzzle pieces.

Mother called once to tell me that I bled a lot when Ken brought me back home.

She said, "Did you know you bled?"

Her unemotional tone sounded as if she was remembering it for the first time and felt very perplexed by the memory. I was stunned at first; panic then replaced the shock. At the point of this call, I still had very few memories of my abuse from Ken when I was little. I had lots of internal clues that something dark might have happened in early childhood. There were frightening pictures in my mind with no memory of being at the scene of the pictures. I had horrifying nightmares, knowledge about things, such as funeral home practices, with no idea how I knew what I knew, and a bizarre fear of benign things with no knowledge of why I was so afraid. Actually, I didn't have too many memories of my time with Ken in Kansas at age thirteen either.

As Mother began pounding me with questions about her memories of my bleeding, I tuned out much of what she was saying. She needed to know that whatever happened that caused me to bleed was not her fault. She needed to be let off the hook.

Instead of comforting her as usual, I focused on the blaring and frightening thought. *Did the bleeding occur after nights at the funeral home when I was two, three, four, five, or when Ken brought me home from Kansas at age thirteen? Why don't I remember? I did all the laundry by the time I was thirteen years old; if there was blood in my underwear, she'd never know. Oh God, please don't let this be true. It was when I was thirteen, right? I need it to be when I was thirteen!*

Whack, Whack, Whack – Don't feel it! Don't remember it! Don't think about it! I need my razor; I need pain now!

I have no clue if I told Dr. Wilson about the things my mother said regarding my time with Ken at the funeral home. Mother made many comments during this time that required me to quickly pull out my mallet to whack the ugly moles back down very fast. What I do know is there were many times when my conversation with Mother led to unbearable nightmares and severe self-harm. I'd lose large amounts of time and often left my condo in the middle of the night to find safety. I left "home" to find safety? Strange! I felt safer sleeping in my car in front of a friend's house or in the Waffle House parking lot than in my own home. This was a pattern in my life until my mid-thirties, but it was not until I began vomiting my strange nightmares onto my counselor, Annis Roy, that the answers surfaced.

As I write this, I can understand better why Dr. Wilson was so insistent that I not answer the phone when my mother called. Mother only called for three reasons. First, she called to alleviate some of the guilt she had been feeling over the years.

"Please forgive me for not sharing the money Henry has been sending over the years. It could have helped with all your medical bill debt."

Most messages included her plan for death, "Please forgive me for killing myself tonight and leaving you responsible for your sisters."

The worst message of all would be her declaration of deep love for me, "Don't you know I would give my life for you! I sacrificed everything to send you to Windward Academy."

Mother often felt the need to bring up everything she did for us in order to convince herself that she was a terrific and doting mother, "I paid for you to have majorette lessons, and you had an Atari before any of the other kids in the neighborhood had one. Your childhood could not have been that bad."

Second, she often called to ask advice regarding my sisters or to simply tell on them. Mother had an intense need to be the center of our attention and turning us against each other helped her keep secrets. A typical example would be when she called to ask for help with one of her bills, but then began telling me that my sisters were talking bad about me behind my back.

She'd say something like, "They said you didn't really have the flu over the weekend but just wanted attention from your friends. They think your friends spoil you, but I believe you."

If she managed to keep us upset with each other and out of contact, she could appear to be the "good guy," and we would not find out the truth. The truth in this instance was probably that mother was the one saying I wasn't really sick while my sisters might have agreed or simply nodded their heads. Part of her conscious or subconscious reason for this would be to prevent me from finding out that she was drinking again and had missed her last three counseling sessions. I learned in Al Anon that this is called splitting and occurs often in homes where someone is addicted to alcohol or another substance.

Third, Mother called to ask for help, especially financial assistance. I don't remember my mother ever calling to say, "How was your day?" or "I called to tell you I love you" or "Holly says you have a migraine; do you need anything?"

Even after I completed my Master's Degree in Community Counseling at Georgia State University, Mother never called to acknowledge my accomplishment or tell me she was proud.

My friends had very strong emotions about how I should be handling my family during this time. Bernetta hated my mother and could not understand why I ever spoke to her again. Rebecca said my mother was one of the sickest and most abusive mothers she'd had on her caseload at DFCS and thought I should have minimal, if any, contact.

My paternal grandmother shamed me for being so mean to my mother, "Don't you know blood is thicker than water?"

Church friends said, "Forgive your mother," and my sisters said, "You're bringing all this up for attention so that everyone will feel sorry for you."

I'm to act as if nothing bad happened in my childhood. I have a mental picture of my mother and my sisters sitting in front of me with a pocket watch in front of my face. I'm staring at the watch swing back and forth.

Rachael and Holly are saying, "The past was not that bad. You feel only happy feelings. You have no right to bring up the past or your pain. You feel only happy feelings."

My mother would be saying, "You had a wonderful childhood; you were spoiled rotten. My abuse was so much worse. Don't you remember being on the drill team in high school? I paid for your majorette lessons. You should feel only happy feelings."

Even when I hid my scars, put on a more acceptable mask, and tried to pretend we were a happy and healthy family, Mother wouldn't cooperate. There were times when I was diligent to let all calls go to voicemail. Mother had gotten wise and called from other numbers so I rarely answered the phone until I heard who was calling. She also wrote letters bringing up horrible memories, but skewed it to make the abuse my fault, her drinking my fault, her custody issues with my sisters my fault, and on and on.

Because Dr. Wilson and I shared the same faith, and because I trusted her, I was able to begin challenging the childhood teaching I had learned from Mother about my responsibility as her child according to God. Mother taught me that I basically owed her my life because God teaches us to take care of our parents. Mother took credit for just about everything I accomplished, but blamed me for her misfortune. Dr. Wilson taught me I had a right to care for myself and setting boundaries with my mother was not considered a "sin," but actually healthy. She also helped me challenge Mother's version of the Bible and reclaim some of my victories and accomplishments.

Graduation from high school, for example, was a huge accomplishment. When I was in the tenth grade, Mother told me I would be transferring to Windward Academy, a very expensive and difficult private school for eleventh and twelfth grade. She had always pushed for me to get a good education. Considering my home life, graduating from a typical high school would have been difficult enough. I'm grateful for the opportunities Mother provided, but her need for me to be well educated was a bit self-serving. Her desire to be in heaven with her own mother and brothers was a theme she spoke of often as we grew up, and my graduation day signified her freedom to leave this world and join her family.

On countless occasions, Mother told me, "I'm going to be with my Jesus once you graduate from high school. You'll be able to take care of your sisters with the insurance money."

I fully believed Mother would commit suicide on the very day I graduated leaving me with two sisters to care for, one seven years old and the other twelve.

As I shared the pain of my graduation day with Dr. Wilson, she began helping me see how often my mother robbed me of the typical joy many children experience during their life's milestones. I had already left home many months prior to graduation day. I appreciated the fact that Mother brought my sisters to the school for the ceremony, but I did not appreciate her insistence that my diploma belonged to her. Mother was emphatic that she was the one who earned it, not me. It was the long hours she spent at her second job, the stress over her mounting bills, and the transportation issues getting me to and from school that earned the diploma. Mother allowed me to hold the framed diploma long enough to get a picture taken with it, but she insisted it belonged to her. As we went our separate ways, Mother took the diploma home with her.

Dr. Wilson pointed out that it was my long nights of study trying to grasp the material, which I had never been exposed to at my public school, that earned the diploma. She pointed out what a miracle it was that I actually chose to finish school considering the circumstances of my life during those years. It was a testimony to my perseverance and strength.

In my therapy sessions, I was told strange points of view such as, "it was wrong of your mother to blame you for the cost of your education, unfair for her to expect you to take on the full responsibility of raising your sisters upon graduation, unfair for her to rob you of the feeling of accomplishment that that day signifies, and abusive for her to plan her death based on your completion of high school."

Dr. Wilson reminded me that most kids receive gifts and praise on graduation day. The graduate is recognized for her hard work, taken out for a special dinner with family, and often has a party to celebrate such a huge milestone.

Prior to my work with Dr. Wilson, I never knew anything my mother did would actually be considered abuse. I knew her schizophrenia and alcoholism put us in grave danger at times, but I thought the fact that she was an alcoholic, who was also mentally ill, excused what was done to us.

I thought, *It's not her fault; it's the alcohol.*

I even blamed some of the most brutal sexual abuse done to me on the fact that Mother was also molested. Whenever I brought up the abuse done to me, she immediately switched the topic to her own abuse. She would tell me the story once again about Mr. Gerald Freeman, a family friend, touching her when she was thirteen years old and the details of her brothers later beating him up. After Mother's first treatment program, she explained many times that alcoholism is a disease, it runs in families, and it's not her fault. If Mother made a decision while she was drunk, it couldn't possibly be her fault, right? The problem was, Mother was almost never sober!

It never dawned on me that my mother's expectations and treatment of me would be considered emotional abuse. Dr. Wilson actually considered Mother's continual threats of suicide to be abusive, as was her expectation that I be responsible to care for my sisters upon her upcoming death. I was shocked; how does one not know they are being abused? Dr. Wilson labeled so much of what my mother said and did as abusive. The strangest shift in my perspective occurred when I heard a tone of anger in Dr. Wilson's voice towards my mother when we spoke about the sexual abuse. This "shift" in the way I viewed my abuse occurred when I began revealing the details of the time I spent with Brian, my little sister's grandfather, when I was ten years old.

Even though Mother was in the process of trying to get a divorce from Charlie, she remained friends with his father. I have no clue why. It could not have been his looks, his personality, or character traits. He was much older than her and not someone she dated or spent much time with. This is one reason I was so shocked when he called to invite me to come spend a week with him. I hardly knew him but had enough experience with him to know I didn't want to be near him. The few times I had been to his home, he pulled me onto his lap, touched between my legs and kissed me very inappropriately. I hated the kisses most because he chewed tobacco, which tasted nasty. After the first time we went there, I told Mother why I never wanted to go to his trailer again.

She didn't express any anger towards him after my disclosure, but casually stated, "Ok, we won't go to his house again."

We did, however, go to his home again with her, but at the time of his current invitation, I had not seen him in about a year. After asking me to come and stay with him, he promised to take my sister and me fishing, swimming, and rafting.

"You will have so much fun and you can play with my hunting dogs." In spite of all the promises of fun, I panicked and tried to hand the phone to Mother. Putting my hand over the receiver, I begged her to tell him we could not go.

Mother was not willing to take the phone from my hand even though I reminded her, "He used to touch me wrong."

Mother simply replied, "Tell him Rachael is sick."

My sigh of relief should have been heard in China. I dodged the bullet as they say, or so I thought. I was frustrated that Mother would not get on the phone and tell him no.

I actually wanted her to say, "Hell no! You can't take my precious child anywhere. Don't you ever call our house again you #@*&%$&*#& pervert, and if you ever call here again, I'll hunt you down and shoot you myself!"

I wasn't even worth the effort for her to look away from her television show long enough to get on the phone to simply say no. At least she wasn't making me go.

I told Brian, "Rachael is very sick so Mother says we can't come with you."

This was a Sunday evening. Guess who showed up early Monday morning to pick us up? Mother had left for work at about 7:00 a.m. and Brian showed up about 9:00 a.m. As I saw him pull in the driveway, my head began spinning, and I couldn't figure out why he would drive over two hours to our house knowing our mother had already said no.

I immediately screamed at my little sister, "Go get in bed and pretend you're sick."

She was only five years old and had no clue what was going on. It was summer time, and we were home watching morning cartoons while Mother worked. Until Dr. Wilson pointed it out, it never dawned on me that most ten-year-olds are not in charge of their little sisters for the whole summer.

Thankfully, Rachael did what I asked and got back into bed while I called Mother. Brian, for whatever reason, felt very comfortable walking right through the front door which Mother had left unlocked. I immediately called Mother.

As the phone was ringing, I exclaimed, "Rachael is sick. We can't go!"

He immediately walked back to Rachael's bedroom while I waited for Mother to answer. Mother answered the phone after what felt like a billion rings.

I was getting more frantic and said, "Mother, he's here. Brian's here and he said he came to pick us up. I told you what he did to me. Please tell him we are not allowed to go with him. Please, Mother, I don't want to go!"

I'll never forget the next words that came out of her mouth.

How could a ten-year-old child forget her mother saying, "There's nothing I can do; you'll just have to go," when a perpetrator shows up at the front door?

I said, "Mother, how can there be nothing you can do? You're the mom; please call the police, talk to him, and tell him to leave."

Mother refused to speak with him on the phone and hung up. The dread in my gut was beyond description. I rushed to Rachael's bedroom hoping to explain the grave extent of her illness.

I'll simply explain, "She's too weak to travel; she might throw up in your jeep."

To my dismay, or should I say horror, Rachael and Brian were already packing our bags as they talked about the "fun things we would do."

Rachael innocently proclaimed, "I'm not really sick; Tammy just told me to say that."

To say the week with Brian was painful, barely seems to describe the horrendous abuse I endured every morning while we were there. He was in his late sixties and in poor health. He worked very hard to perform an act that he was barely able to complete at this point in his life. I guess he believed the problem was the small size of my body's entrance rather than his inability to perform. His anger and frustration showed through the violent ways he attempted to gain access.

Mother's words, "You'll just have to go," echoed in my mind.

Why did I have to go, and why doesn't Brian ever say, "Don't tell your mother what we are doing. It's a secret?"

I'm so grateful I had started my game long before this abuse! My little sister and I were never taken on a rafting or fishing trip. There was no swimming that week and the dogs he said we could play with were frightening. Brian, as the security guard, lived in an old trailer on a concrete production site. There were huge hills made of various colored dirt, rocks, and sand. The dogs were part of the security and not suitable for children. Rachael and I were extremely bored, and the heat was intense. With nothing to do, we climbed on the hills one day not knowing the temperature inside some of the sand hills was hot enough to cause our legs to get burned. Being heavier than my little sis, I sank deeper into the sand so the burns on my legs went almost up to my knees.

I would love to say, "I never saw him again after telling Mother what happened while we were there."

I would love to say, "Mother called the police and took me to a doctor once she found out what he did to me each morning."

I would love to say, "Mother took me to a counselor to help me heal and to address the fear and shame I felt."

I wish so many things . . . .

Why would a mother continue to send her child off with perpetrators? The shift in perspective that I learned under Dr. Wilson's care was that Mother was responsible for the abuse as much as Brian. I began to understand that Mother had many choices during my childhood that would have prevented most of the terror and abuse. Mother continued to rush into marriage as soon as the last husband left. She never chose to get marriage counseling or any type of restoration from her own wounding. Mother did not choose to continue attending the AA meetings recommended by the treatment center she attended. Most importantly, Mother was never willing to be honest with anyone who tried to help her.

In fact, about six months prior to Mother dying, I spoke with Mrs. Bell, the county mental health therapist who had been treating Mother for many years. Mother was required to meet with her at least twice a month in order to get her prescriptions filled. I called Mrs. Bell to tell her about Mother's current admission to another mental hospital and to ask if I could pick up Mother's anti-psychotic meds. As we spoke about Mother's medication, I also mentioned something Mother had recently said about her childhood abuse.

Mrs. Bell replied, "Are you saying your mother was molested as a child?"

I was astonished! During Mother's many years of counseling with her, she never mentioned any of the wounding she told me had occurred during her childhood in order to elicit my pity and compassion. I found out during my short conversation with Mrs. Bell that Mother had never divulged many important facts about her life: five marriages, sexual abuse, six years of extreme domestic violence, and so much more.

I eventually said, knowing she could not answer, "So what the hell do you talk about?"

I rarely "felt" my own anger, but on this day, I was mad. The strange thing was that I was mad at Mrs. Bell. I guess it was still not safe to feel anger towards my mother.

I began asking to see a therapist when I was in the eleventh grade, but Mother refused to pay for it. I knew I was losing control of much of my life. I could not focus on my schoolwork. To stay grounded, I needed to resort to self-harm almost daily, and my eating disorder was getting worse. I wanted counseling. Mother had the opportunity to get counseling so that someone could help her heal, and yet she never bothered to tell the truth. Instead, every time I expressed pain regarding my own sexual abuse, Mother brought up her own abuse by Mr. Freeman. I became Mother's therapist during late hours when I wanted to go to bed. If I showed even a small amount of anger towards her for not protecting me, she would begin crying hysterically about her own abuse and then came the guilt. If there is something called a "guilt trip," the one my mother sent me on was the trip of a lifetime, every time!

It seems like the following scenario occurred about a thousand times between my thirteenth and sixteenth birthday. Late at night, while Mother was very intoxicated, she would complain about everything in her life. She talked about her debt, the price of my school, the need for car repair, the stress from her job, her depression, and on and on. While my sisters would be asleep, Mother began talking about her will and what I was to do with her estate. Her level of intoxication predicted her progression of emotionality. By midnight or so, her mood could vacillate from hysterical crying to rage to a fear-producing laugh. At some point in the evening, Mother would basically pick a fight.

Mother – "You don't appreciate anything I do for you. Your school is costing me a fortune, and you can't even help me keep the house clean. "

Me – "Mother, how can you say that? I do all the laundry, clean the kitchen after school and clean both bathrooms. I clean all the time."

Mother – "You don't love me. You stopped loving me after Henry touched you. Why do you blame me for what others did?"

Me – "Mother, you know he did not just 'touch' me. You know he raped me, and you did nothing about it. He even told you he had sex with me because he loved me and wanted my "first" sexual experience to be with someone who loved me and would be gentle."

By the way, he was NOT gentle!

Mother – "I know how you feel. When Mr. Freeman touched me when I lost my nickel for the bus, I was terrified. After my brothers beat him up so badly, I felt guilty and did not want to think about it again."

Me – "Mother, you got touched! I got raped and not just one time but many times."

Mother – "Well, what did you want me to do, put my uncle in jail?"

Me – "Okay, then why did you make me go with Brian? He was not your uncle, cousin, friend, whatever! How do you explain away Ken and the guy with the sports car and the guy at the store and . . . ."

Then it came, the wailing!

Mother would begin her sobs. "You're right. I'm a terrible mother. You deserve a much better mother. You want my money anyway; that's all you want. Make sure you take care of your sisters; that's all I ask."

Mother would then either overdose on pills right in front of me, chasing it with vodka, or get her gun and leave for the night.

As she was getting her keys, I'd beg for her forgiveness. "I'm so sorry I said those things about you making me go when they hurt me. I'm sorry I blamed you. You're a good mother. You work hard to take care of us and provide a nice home. You take us to church, and you like to help others. You're a very good mother; please don't do this. I'm so sorry for what I said and it was not your fault that I got hurt. I love you, Mother, please don't leave!"

The above conversation occurred many times, and Mother overdosed more times than I can count. I called an ambulance a few times when she overdosed at home, but on many occasions, she took the pills or gun with her as she left. About a fourth of the time we went through this script, she either left physically, overdosed in front of me, or told me she was going to overdose and then went to her room and locked the door. She made sure I saw her pill bottles before locking the door. For obvious reasons, I was awake most of the night worrying about her, wondering if she would die that night, and imagining how I would be able to take on full responsibility of my sisters. Mother began this night drama when I was about twelve years old after she finally gained her divorce from Charlie. It began gradually and not often. But by the time I was fifteen, she needed my "counsel" and attention at least once a week. I'm not sure why, but our late night counseling sessions usually occurred on Sunday nights after significant amounts of alcohol over the weekend. The counseling sessions usually ended with either a fight or her wanting to commit suicide.

Even though it was she who picked the fight, I hated myself for being so mean and hurting her in the end. I now understand that she was saturated in guilt, and seeking a pardon from me, which I had no ability to give. In my early teens, it was simply too soon to be able to forgive her. She brought up her failures as a parent and then needed to explain it away, rationalize why she did it or allowed it, and then brought up all her attributes. After our fight, I'd go to bed and mentally rebuke myself for hurting her.

I should not have brought up the night she made me leave with her date at one in the morning. Maybe she really didn't know what he was going to do, but why did she tell me not to bother putting on shorts over my panties when I tried to

---

During my years of counseling with Dr. Wilson, she taught me that we all have choices.

---

get dressed? What does it mean that she angrily escorted me out the front door and insisted I get in the car with this stranger? Did she accidentally turn off the porch light? When did she think I was coming back home?

The stress was horrendous.

During my years of counseling with Dr. Wilson, she taught me that we all have choices. Mother had chosen to stay ill. The manipulative suicide games worked for her. It allowed her to get the attention and nurturance she needed but without having to actually look at her pain. Mother had chosen on many occasions to stop taking her anti-psychotic medication. She was told not to drink alcohol with this medication and to attend AA in order to help her stay sober. Because Mother often chose to stop taking her medications, she had many psychotic episodes during our childhood, which required her to be admitted to a behavioral health hospital. Mother's continual attempt to convince me that she was a helpless victim herself stopped working a few years into my therapy with Dr. Wilson.

Yes, the timing of Dr. Wilson's departure from my life seemed poor timing. Mother still had an endless need for my attention and care, but in actuality, Dr. Wilson's entrance and exit in my life was perfect timing. That's how my heavenly Father scheduled everything in my divine treatment plan. In the five years I was under Dr. Wilson's care, I learned so many valuable lessons, felt so many new feelings, and began understanding my childhood through healthier eyes. I didn't know the vast amount of progress I had already made by this time, or that our common faith kept me too afraid of rejection for us to progress through the deepest level.

Thankfully, I also did not know that the message I heard, "It will get worse before it gets better," during that Beth Moore Bible study would be very true. The warning was very helpful in many ways when the pain and fear did increase. First, it seemed Beth must have known how I felt and understood the typical progression of healing from trauma. My rebellious side then came forward, which caused a strange determination to continue in the fight. I was spiritually daring the enemy to try making anything worse.

I scoffed, "Only death would be worse than how I feel now. So Satan, you gonna try to kill me? Bring it on! Christ in me is bigger than anything you can do to hurt me! Besides, God says everything will work out for my good, and I've been called for His purposes, whatever that is!"

Lastly, the words, "it gets better," seemed to come from somewhere other than Beth. Like an echo, it remained in my mind, though I must admit there were long seasons of time when I did not believe I would survive!

Chapter 8

WHAT IF I DON'T SURVIVE THE MEMORIES?

Fall was a very difficult season for me each year as it arrived. The brisk cool air saddened me and caused a strange dread and fear inside. I experienced it each year but had never known why. One beautiful fall day when I was in my early thirties, I sat in my parked car looking at the changing leaves on the trees. I began having frightening flashbacks of some events that had occurred many years previously in the month of October. The fear and panic was so real! The visions and voices in my mind horrified me to the point that I gripped the steering wheel so hard that my hands hurt later.

In desperation I cried out, "Jesus, why did you let all that happen to me?"

In a very real sensation, I heard and felt these words wash over me, "Tammy, I cried every time!"

I was already "hanging on by a thread" when I needed to run away at sixteen to stop the sexual abuse from continuing. It must have been a different thread I gripped when Mother called to tell me my days were numbered, or when I had my first emotional breakdown leading to hospitalization. The thread I held in order to survive the sexual advances made towards me during my college years and the thread to help me survive the civil war inside regarding my food intake must have been very strong. At the point that I received Dr. Wilson's termination letter, I honestly thought I had lost my grasp on any sense of hope for my future. What I would eventually realize is that Father provided so many threads and wove each one in such a strategic way that, unbeknownst to me, it had become a rope for Him to pull me from a dark past and into an amazing future.

It would take a very strong rope to keep me on this side of sanity, at least that's how it felt. I'm not sure what triggered the hardest days of my life to begin. Was it the day I remembered my miscarriage, or did I get triggered in one of the group therapy sessions? Similar to when I tried to rescue the children in hell when I was in pre-school, I now needed someone with a long, strong rope to pull me out of my own hell. I needed friends to remind me that I actually wanted out, assure me that it's safe to come out, and yell at me when I refused to hold my hands up to catch the rope.

Peers in various treatment programs had demonstrated many advantages and strategies to staying stuck in the hole, which meant forever avoiding much of their memories and feelings of past pain.

Many of them talked about their last inpatient period as if it were a vacation from the current outpatient program. They knew the names of staff members at several different facilities, often seemed proud of not only knowing the routine at each place but also proud of knowing how to get away with as much as possible.

I heard statements such as, "Make sure you ask for Dr. Franklin because he gives the best meds."

"If you don't want to go to Mrs. Heather's group, just say you have cramps."

"The hardest part of the day at Stoneview is the feelings group run by Nurse Gina. Just slip out when she turns away; she never notices."

"If you want to cut on the unit, just ...."

"At lunch let me show you how we hide most of our food so they think we ate it."

The "attention" they received in the various hospital programs, plus the attention they received from their private therapist, seemed to fill enough of their empty cavern that they let go of the rope, thus resigning to a life stuck in the hole.

One of the strongest and most committed threads in my rope was my new therapist, Annis. During our first session, I brought up my faith and was hoping she too had the same spiritual beliefs. Hearing that her perspective was different saddened me, but I can't express how thankful I am now. During my life as a Christian, I heard so many people of faith assign my behaviors, motives, feelings, and beliefs to Satan or "evil forces of the darkness," as my mother would say. She started this line of reasoning when I was a very small child. If something was bad, it was demonic. If something was good, it was of God. There was no gray. I assumed every other person of the same faith had this belief as well. Surely, if I told someone about the horrifying pictures in my head, they too would believe that I was possessed with demons and in need of deliverance. I certainly loved Dr. Wilson way too much to risk these secrets with her.

I now believe one of the reasons I, and all of the characters that helped me play the game, felt comfortable telling Annis our secrets is because we were not emotionally attached to her in the same way as with Dr. Wilson. There was also not the risk of her assuming I was "entertaining demons" or playing "attention-seeking games," as my sisters angrily believed. I also know Annis arrived at the perfect time because Dr. Wilson had recently changed her method of treating individuals diagnosed with dissociative identity disorder when she joined another therapy practice. Her new rule during our sessions was that I must be "present" the whole time rather than allowing any "child parts" to come out. I would need to allow the memories they held to come through me, feel it head on, and then choose to live with that degree of pain for an indefinite amount of time. Impossible! There was no way I could face those memories without their help!

Because the parts of me who held the memories of my time at the funeral home with Ken were not allowed to meet with Dr. Wilson, they began telling Annis, the new lady, about the secret monsters. That day at Charter

---

I never considered myself to be strong, determined, bold, or a fighter. I saw myself as being very wimpy, weak, fragile, mentally ill, incapable, powerless, useless, guilty, and on and on. I am still shocked that the person I was then is the same person I am now. It took a few years of submitting to God's divine treatment plan before being able to acknowledge any type of positive attributes in myself.

Peachford was the beginning of the darkest days I would ever endure. The memory of the miscarriage began the process of letting the cat out of the bag, so to speak, except I had a multitude of cats. One might wonder, wasn't the actual abuse harder? Frankly, no! At least that was not my experience. I had developed some great coping skills early in life to help me distance myself from the emotional and physical pain. Of course more and more whack-a-mole type skills (alcohol, pills, cutting, burning, etc.) were necessary to cope as the years went on. The level of skills I had acquired or needed at this point was becoming very dangerous. This is one of the reasons I forced myself to live in the rainbow room at the halfway house surrounded by a hundred My Little Pony toys with a roommate who spent much of her day playing with Barbie and Ken. I hated living there but must have had an intense determination to survive.

I never considered myself to be strong, determined, bold, or a fighter. I saw myself as being very wimpy, weak, fragile, mentally ill, incapable, powerless, useless, guilty, and on and on. I am still shocked that the person I was then is the same person I am now. It took a few years of submitting to God's divine treatment plan before being able to acknowledge any type of positive attributes in myself. Thankfully, friends such as Cathy and my roommate Samantha gave me much needed support. They never gave up on me, always believed I would recover, and believed God had great plans for my future.

At the point when I officially became the high maintenance client of Annis Roy, LPC, at least that's how I saw it, my ability to stay grounded was almost non-existent. Grounded is a term used in therapy to mean centered or focused if used in regards to the typical client. When used in reference to someone with dissociative identity disorder such as myself, it meant having to force myself to remain in the "window" as required by Dr. Wilson, i.e. without allowing the characters in my game to come to the window. It meant not allowing myself to escape reality, for example by living in a world where everyone wants Ken for a boyfriend, but he is madly in love with Barbie who finally accepts his invitation to the beach party, as my roommate had chosen.

For me, staying grounded meant remaining outside my bedroom closet even though that is where my child-selves felt safest. It meant choosing coping skills, such as reading, cooking, or computer time in an attempt to keep the others in my game stuffed inside. The problem with the requirement was that the world held so many triggers that caused me to desperately want to retreat. Triggers can be an event, a person, a feeling, a memory, or anything that causes a person to feel acute pain. Often the trigger is mundane and the reason it causes pain is unclear. As a common example, while a recent widow is picking tomatoes from the garden she and her late husband had planted, a rush of emotion, grief and memories come flooding back with the same intensity of the original pain when he passed away.

When a child is abused over a long period of time, there can be triggers everywhere in the environment and with many people. Regarding my own trauma, it seemed hardly fair for me to be required to face the responsibilities of everyday life, taking a chance of getting triggered, while also being required to face our therapy sessions exclusively. For as long as I can remember, my self-assigned job required I remain separate from anything too painful because I was the one required to complete school, manage a career, and bring in the money to support everyone. All the characters in my game had different roles, memories, feelings, dreams, personalities, and abilities. Some of these parts of myself also interacted with the outside world, and though many of our friends were the same, some of us also had a few different friends and enjoyed different activities. Our calendar often had at least three different handwriting styles.

Karen, for example, was a powerful presence who came to live with us when, at seventeen years old, I began a search for my biological father.

I had not seen him since my tenth birthday when I told my mother, "All I want for my birthday is to see my 'real' father."

That visit occurred in a parking lot and was very brief. He gave me a small necklace and a kiss on the hand. He seemed like royalty to me, maybe because of the hand kiss, and I began imagining that I was a daughter of a king. Three years later, I got the nerve to call him.

So many awful things were going on in my life, and I had the thought, *If my real dad knew what was happening, he would come save me.*

So at thirteen, I did some research, made some calls and found him. It was a very short call.

He said, "I can't communicate with you until you're away from your mother. Call me when you're eighteen and on your own."

I tried to explain that Mother was the purpose of this call; I wanted to be away from her as soon as possible.

He replied, "I hate your mother and won't run the risk of having to be in contact with her again."

No rescue mission would be occurring that day, but I now had hope that in a few years, I'd be reunited with my father, and then I'd be safe and loved.

After moving in with Ms. Miller, and considered on my own, I did some searching and found my father again. I was so thrilled to discover he worked less than ten miles from where I lived. It took one phone call to my grandmother to learn his favorite cologne was Aramis, an expensive gift on a nanny's salary. On the Friday before Father's Day, I decided to take a chance and deliver the gift myself. The timing seemed miraculous. He was unlocking the door of a beautiful, new Mercedes when I arrived. The meeting seemed magical, and my heart danced when he recognized me immediately, smiled, and then kissed the back of my hand. I had dreamed so many times over the years about my father rescuing me, being proud of me, adoring me, and wanting me.

When I handed him the gift, he thanked me and said, "I've got a meeting now, but call me sometime."

I was so excited and told everyone I knew that I had seen my real father.

He wanted me in his life and would be spending time with me soon. He's so handsome, and he kissed the back of my hand."

I waited a week and called him.

Very excited butterflies were in my stomach during the initial chitchat and then he said something very unusual, "I'd like to start a relationship with you, but not until you've lost twenty-five pounds."

He went on to explain that he would teach me to ski out west in Vail or Breckenridge once I lost the weight. He also said he had a houseboat and would love for me to come meet his friends after, of course, I had lost the twenty-five pounds.

This is the point at which Karen came to live with us; the day I decided my biological father was actually "her" biological father.

She was a shy but very determined teen. Karen loved her father more than anyone else in the world, and she would have done anything for him! We all felt very sorry for her; poor thing, she had waited so many years to finally begin a relationship with her real dad. She was so sure he would be different from all the other men in her life up to this point. He would never touch her in bad ways and he would have protected her, but he simply didn't know about the abuse.

Karen thought, *Finally, I'm a princess and my real father will love me.*

No longer would she be a destitute and abandoned daughter of a king. She insisted we were no longer to be labeled, "evil sexual whore." Now she insisted we belonged to someone and the kiss from her father washed all the evil away. After all the many years of feeling filthy and unwanted, she finally felt clean and innocent. All she needed to do was get us to lose weight and fast. This is where the torturous dieting began which caused significant friction among the other characters in my game.

Karen was very perplexed by Ms. Miller's strange anger, actually rage, when she heard Karen's father had requested she lose weight before seeing her again. Karen had no feelings of anger. That was actually Velda's job. Karen was extremely excited because this meant she could control and predict her father's love. "Tammy's mother" as Karen thought of my mother, never had predictable love. She could love and hate you all in the same hour.

At least my dad will love me as long as I stay skinny, she thought.

Unfortunately, Karen had several supporters on her side of the anorexic fence. I had been a slim child until about the age of nine. I think that between one of my abusers telling me how much he loved my thin, tanned body and the stress of living in a very violent home, I gained about ten pounds. I vividly remember gorging on peanut butter sandwiches after school every day.

If I'm fat, they won't like my body.

Mother would often fuss about us going through a loaf of bread in three days, but she never questioned the reason for the disappearing bread. She simply bought more.

By the time I reached the age of seventeen, I was about thirty pounds overweight, had long stringy hair, rarely wore make-up, and either wore my nanny uniform or something else equally unattractive. Karen became very upset by how "ugly" we looked and began insisting we go on a fast. Five days of no food was the longest we ever lasted, but her determination to lose weight was fierce. She took money from my school savings and joined a gym close by and forbid us to eat most meals. I was furious when I discovered the missing money and the year contract in someone else's handwriting. When we became weak, I bought a liquid protein substance that tasted completely nasty, and none of us wanted to drink it. Karen was so desperate for her father to love and accept her that she willingly chugged it down each day for over a month.

A fringe benefit of having game characters living inside was that you could simply retreat far away from the window and avoid many things, events, or feelings. I honestly never tasted that nasty drink except for the first sip on that first day. However, I had the benefit of losing thirty pounds in one month. Yes, thirty pounds! How awesome except that poor Karen did not gain the fairytale life she expected. After losing the weight, plus five pounds more than her father had requested, she called him. He was a bit short on the phone again, but praised her for such a great accomplishment and for doing it so quickly.

He seemed proud, but then stated, "I'm flying out to Denver this week to ski, but let's talk when I get back." Click.

It was hard to continue keeping the weight off. Karen would become furious with me when I ate one of Ms. Miller's chocolate covered donuts.

I'd also snack on the special recipes I came up with for Adrienne. She was a picky eater so creativity was essential. It was trial and error. So what does one do with the leftovers? I've always hated to throw food away, so I took it upon myself to help the starving children in Africa by cleaning off the rest of her plate. This struggle with control over my food has been a huge challenge for most of my life. I either controlled my intake to the point of counting how many beans I was allowed to have, or binge and consume a billion calories within a few hours.

At the point that I began meeting with Annis Roy, LPC, exclusively, I was thirty-three years old, on long term disability from my job as a DFCS case manager, and almost totally incapable of managing my affairs, my health, my time, my relationships, and anything else that required thought, feelings or focus. My eating disorder was out of control, and we were all suffering from the civil war inside. Karen and a few others who desperately wanted to lose weight often punished those of us who had no self-control regarding food. She had three main supporters on her anorexic side of the fence: Crisco, Buffalo Butt and Lard Ass. These were nicknames Charlie, my stepfather, began calling me when I began gaining weight at nine years old. Unbeknownst to me, my nicknames became real characters in my game, but I did not discover this for many years.

On a typical day during civil war periods, internal voices would firmly say, "We will not eat anything today! No one will ever love us as long as we are fat. Dr. Wilson stopped loving you because you're so huge."

"But I'm hungry."

"If you eat that bagel, I'll cut right before you meet with Cathy. You're such a sloth!"

By the time I was thirty-four, our eating disorder took over to the point that we could not work on the issues caused by the childhood abuse. I was having very vivid flashbacks and many of them made no sense. I might recognize a piece of furniture, but not the person with me, or I might remember being in the car with someone at night, but have no idea where we were going and what happened there. The flashbacks usually occurred at night, and the power struggle over what we ate or did not eat was miserable by day. Annis realized shortly into our treatment that I needed more support than what she could provide. She had already insisted I attend either AA or OA (Overeaters Anonymous) meetings at least twice a week. A few months later, she added ANAD (Anorexia Nervosa and Associated Disorders) meetings to my schedule, as well as bi-monthly sessions with Paige Love, MS, RD, a well-known nutritionist who specializes in eating disorders.

Paige not only helped me create a healthy eating plan, but she was also very aware of how dissociation, sexual abuse, and eating disorders are often tied together. The problem with this "intervention" was that we didn't believe we had an eating disorder. Karen considered herself to be on a diet, but

---

The hope was that once we believed we had a serious eating disorder, we'd simply comply with the eating plan created for us. This is not what occurred. Instead, our obsession over calories, fat grams, number of items eaten, and so much more, became worse.

---

others felt no need to lose weight. In fact, Kerry, one of the ones in the window when the perpetrator told us how much he loved our tanned, thin body, had a huge desire to consume everything in sight. Her motto was, "Fatter is better," but I believe she was thinking, *Fatter is safer*.

While understanding that we were still at war internally with one another, even though we had a safe eating plan, Annis sought out a specialized therapist to convince us we actually had an eating disorder. We met with Evelyn Ross, LPC, a few times and attended some of the group therapy sessions she ran. The hope was that once we believed we had a serious eating disorder, we'd simply comply with the eating plan created for us. This is not what occurred. Instead, our obsession over calories, fat grams, number of items eaten, and so much more, became worse.

Annis was exhausted and running out of options to try. I had learned easier ways to purge while in group therapy with other women who had bulimia. Group therapy sessions can be very helpful, but required some major determination to heal. With half-hearted determination, you get worse! I found myself comparing my weight with everyone else in the group. I was jealous of the extremely thin girls because they seemed to get the most attention. They were able to curl up comfortably in their chairs, but the obese women like me were busting out of our seats. The one thing we had in common was the need to stay in control of our food and lives as much as possible, but we were failing miserably. Sometimes our behavior was similar to the rebellion you would witness in a two-year-old or a budding teenager who thinks she knows everything. Sometimes our desire to strictly control our intake began due to pressure from peers to remain thin in order to be accepted. For me, there were several impetuses that kept us stuck in the "cycle of insanity," as I called it. An episode of binging would lead to horrendous guilt, followed by a very painful session of self-punishment, such as burning my breasts by placing a knife on the hot coils of my stove and then placing it on my chest, followed by several days of minimal food, then feeling extremely powerful to the point of almost feeling high, and then excessive exercise. I can't count the times I worked out at the gym to the point of dizziness and then was asked to leave due to safety issues and liability.

There was one way I was different from the others in the group. I was living with separate parts of me that were either anorexic, bulimic, or a compulsive overeater. I had the extreme behaviors of all three depending on who was using the window that day. The stress was almost unbearable because it didn't matter which intake plan was followed on a particular day, either binging or starving, there would be many others inside who wanted to punish the others for not obeying their rules.

My poor body; I abused it in so many ways. It was during this time that I discovered I had hypothyroidism, which makes weight loss very difficult. Even after getting my thyroid levels corrected, I only lost a few pounds. The pattern of overeating and then starving myself had taken its toll on my metabolism. My body seemed to want to store everything I put in my mouth. I eventually ended up at 256 pounds, and I hated myself more than I can describe. A retreat leader from my church gave us the assignment to go home and stand in front of the mirror. We were to say affirmations to ourselves, so that we learned to love ourselves as God loves us. It was the most dangerous homework ever given to me!

I faithfully tried, hoping to relieve some of the venom I felt towards myself. I borrowed some examples of positive statements to say because I could not think of one thing about myself that I believed was good or of value. Nothing! As I stood there taking the time to actually look at my face, something I avoided as much as possible, rage came forward with an intensity I can't describe. I grabbed my face, dug in hard, and scratched it from top to bottom as deeply as I could with all ten fingernails. I wish I could say this was the end of my self-destructive session, but the truth is, my roommate had to rush me to the emergency room that day to stop all the bleeding from various parts of my body. My private area was bleeding as well.

In my experience, eating disorders are partially the result of self-hatred. How do you learn to love yourself? It seemed impossible, but my heavenly Father had so many circumstances ahead to help me heal, but it would take a few more years. Even after acknowledging that I actually had an eating disorder, I still had too many characters in my game that had very different reasons for wanting to be in control of what we ate. Unfortunately, I was unaware that many of the characters existed.

The last pieces of the puzzle called "me" were the hardest. At this stage of my healing, it was time to face the worst memories. My eating disorder held many clues to my past, and helped me whack the memories and feelings that surfaced back down. I certainly had many reasons to have issues over food. Not only did many of my abusers make remarks about my body size, my mother did as well. She wanted me to lose weight enough that at fourteen years old, she began buying street drugs from some guy to "help" me. I remember each drug had a strange name such as speckle birds or pink footballs. The substance was basically an amphetamine, also known as speed. She kept the baggie of pills in the butter slot of our refrigerator.

To speed up my weight loss, I decided to begin taking jazzercise classes after school. I put together an outfit and came out to model for her. I was excited and assumed she would say something positive and encouraging. I put on my gym shorts, which were the school colors, red with white trim. I had a blue shirt that was very comfortable so I made that the top. I had not thought about the colors resembling our national colors, red, white, and blue. When I came into the living room, I fully expected a morsel of praise. She had just gotten home from work and was sober at this point.

It seemed reasonable to ask her opinion, but imagine my surprise when she flatly said, "You look like a fat Wonder Woman!"

I know in my head that it must have hurt, but I didn't feel much of the pain. A teen girl "mysteriously" named Wonder Girl, came to live with us at that moment. She sadly looked like a fat version of the television character, Wonder Woman.

One of the others inside remarked, "Poor thing. Her mother is so cruel."

It was years before I discovered Wonder Girl was living with us and hated to eat, along with many other characters that were hidden from me. It was essential to my sanity and ability to function to be left in the dark, so to speak, when it came to many memories and feelings. I had always remembered Mother's comment, but had absolutely no feeling about it.

Annis realized that as long as I was so dissociated from my internal world, recovering from our eating disorders would be almost impossible. The next step included another hospitalization. I hated being in the hospital, but at least this time I would be going on a volunteer basis rather than due to a crisis. Annis did some research and found McLean Hospital in Boston that had a unit specializing in the treatment of women diagnosed with a dissociative disorder. I was there for a five-week, much-needed nightmare. If it were not for my faith, I would have given up on the hope of recovering long before this point. After at least six inpatient hospitalizations, it was hard to believe I could one day have a fear-free life without lost periods of time. So many circumstances occurred over the years that led me to believe my Father in heaven was watching over and helping me.

During this hospitalization, what looked like unfortunate circumstances, the primary therapist assigned to me being out of town for the holidays, turned out to be one of the factors that helped. Strangely, having an individual therapist would have helped me keep my past in the past. Up until this point in my recovery, I fought the memories of what happened when I was very small, and much of what occurred when I was thirteen with Ken. Though my mother, aunt, and Joyce (Mom's friend) had verified a few strange memories, I was still able to convince myself that most of the flashbacks could not have happened, or were distorted or made up somehow.

While at this hospital, we attended many group therapy sessions. There were about eight other patients in the program, all with the diagnosis of dissociative identity disorder. Three of the women had experienced sexual abuse by members of a cult and I felt very sad for them. They each had an eating disorder, used self-harm as a way to cope, had a fear of someone coming to get them at night, and some other strange similarities. I was still able to convince myself that the sexual abuse I endured was minimal compared to them, and that my abuse was the typical kind, which was difficult enough! I think the hardest part and the reason I fought believing what had been surfacing over the last year was not because of the nature of the abuse by Ken, but that something bad happened to me that I did not remember fully. It was the missing puzzle pieces that distressed me the most.

Group therapy sessions, where all the women are dissociative, can be quite interesting, difficult to follow, and of course, never dull. Most of the women brought a blanket or stuffed animal to hold and often spoke in very child-like voices. I had a very difficult time remembering the names of my peers in the first place, but trying to remember the names of all their characters and their roles was impossible. While Grace's four-year-old character named Twyla shared about missing her daddy after the divorce, Carry's angry eight-year-old, Heidi, would come out and rage about how much she hated her daddy. Random giggling occurred during the rare quiet moments when everyone was either too nervous, too ill due to migraines, or simply too exhausted to speak.

The rule for group sessions was that we were not allowed to share specific details of our abuse so that the others would not get triggered, but we could share the feelings regarding the abuse. I said nothing during group for the first two weeks after admission. I was still in shock by all the grown women talking, playing, and singing as if they were four, six, or eight years old. I, on the other hand, worked extremely hard to stay grounded, meaning not allowing the characters in my game to come to the window. I obsessed over controlling my food intake in order to help me keep everything stuffed down until a particularly traumatizing experience occurred during a group session in which I lost all control.

It was in one of our group sessions the second week I was there that the puzzle pieces began to come together, and I didn't like the picture it created! Susan, the patient sitting beside me, often had a rebellious teen named Cindy in her window who cussed, made crude comments, and was very angry. She was also very funny. I enjoyed the time I spent with her on the unit when she came to her window. During this particular group session, I heard a voice beside me that was neither Susan nor Cindy. Evidently, someone younger in their game got triggered and began quoting Bible verses and singing a song very quietly. This voice caused loud noises in my head and horrendous anxiety, enough that I felt myself struggling to stay in my own window. I tuned into the group to see who was talking so that I could shut her up in order to make the little girl beside me stop her chanting. Instantly, I was consumed by a volcanic rage and felt the need to rip someone apart.

Molly was the patient who had begun sharing her feelings about her stepfather and the abuse, but then began crying loudly and appeared to be seeing something none of us could see. She looked absolutely terrified. It became obvious that my friend sitting beside me, not sure what name to call her, had left her window, and it was now a young child sitting beside me. The young voice began quoting a religious chant under her breath. I was not fazed by Molly's outburst; I had had many flashbacks myself over the years, so I felt nothing but compassion. Flashbacks are so real and often unpredictable. By this time in the session, I had actually checked out of group and was in my head. I was very good at retreating mentally from the things going on around me, a very necessary skill for my survival. However, the soft voice of the child chanting beside me caused an internal breakdown that rattled me to the core.

I had heard those "verses" before, and what wrecked me was that I could finish her sentences. I knew her abuse was due to her parent's cult involvement as a child, but we had not talked specifically about her abuse. How could I possibly know some of the lyrics she was softly repeating? I became very distraught myself and began seeing pictures in my mind of Ken with some other men, and the setting was the funeral home. I had absolutely no memory of the pictures I was seeing, and why did I know this song? Within five minutes, the flashbacks became so vivid and the body memories so real that I could not stay grounded. I had tried very hard for almost two weeks to appear sane and as in control as possible, but I was now losing the battle.

Unfortunately for me, the staff and other patients were focused on Sarah who was still crying. No one noticed that I was falling apart at the seams. I felt myself running out of the room, and had no power to choose to stay. The next thing I remembered was dinner four hours later and vomit in my bathroom sink. The fact that time seemed to play tricks on me was not the stressful part on that day; this phenomenon had occurred most of my life. The frightening part was the welts all over my arms and legs and the horrendous pain in my private area. I discovered later that the pain between my legs was called a body memory. What I knew at this point was that I was hurting "down there," and the pain seemed familiar. Actually, the pain felt similar to how my body felt after being raped by Mother's boyfriends. At one point, I remember needing to "pee" really bad but was afraid to go because, "it's gonna burn really bad, and it hurts me!" I felt like I was three or four years old. The chatter I heard in my mind sounded like several very small, frightened children. The way they enunciated their words was strange and yet seemed so familiar, similar to how one vaguely remembers a dream.

The "daymare" after group began occurring often throughout the day. The urge to allow the others to take over the window was almost unbearable. By the third week, I relented at night when everyone else was asleep. I'm not sure which "children" came out, but I do remember a night staff member who talked with them each night. The reason I remember this is because I was so horrified and embarrassed each time I was close enough to the window to hear them.

Oh no, now I'm talking like a little kid. How humiliating!

Thankfully, two of my close friends, Pam and Cathy flew to Boston for a visit. Counting down the days until they arrived helped me focus on something positive. I also needed a few familiar and unhealthy coping skills to help distract me from the new memories, actually pictures, surfacing.

Within a few days of arriving at my new "home" in Boston, I began partially restricting food in order to stay in control. At the point when I began having daymares, I began restricting almost completely. From past experience, I knew how to eat just enough to stay functional but restrict enough to help me survive, at least that's how it felt. The reason I'm thankful that my assigned therapist was on vacation much of my time there is because I needed to finally face the truth and not be numbed by drugs. I had been able to remain separate from the memories of early childhood abuse for over thirty years; it was time to peek back at my past, so that I could have a future. In order for me to feel safe enough to remember, I needed to be home. I needed to return to my therapist Annis, who already knew some of what had happened during the time I spent with Ken. I needed to feel safe in my own city with the many houses I was welcome to enter when I needed to run away from my own home. I needed to live with my safe roommate, Samantha. She watched over me and reported pertinent information back to Annis. For example, she gladly held me accountable regarding self-harm and food intake. She should get an award for all I put her through, yet I know God handpicked her to help me. Lastly, I needed my other close friends and church to help me feel safe. Even with all these resources, feeling totally safe would not occur for almost two more years.

After returning home, I discovered I had lost fifteen pounds in the five weeks I was away. My body ached; I had strange physical pains that could not be explained; and I felt weak and exhausted. The positive side was that I had become more determined than ever to face what was lying just below the surface. Once again, similar to my response after rooming with Lu, I absolutely was not willing to stay stuck as a person who suddenly began acting like a little girl. While away, the characters in my game wrote a running commentary in my journal about their observations on the unit, their memories, and feelings. Without being in a safe place and with someone I trusted, I knew I could not keep myself safe if I read it. What I now fully knew upon returning home was that something much more sinister had occurred during my childhood. The frightening pictures in my mind, the painful body memories, the knowledge of cult practices, such as the chants, and of course, the gripping new fear that made no sense, forced me to admit I had been running from actual "monsters" most of my life. Thankfully, not only did Annis know much of the reason I was having such a hard time, she also had more knowledge than the average therapist about how to treat individuals who had been abused by a religious group. Janis, her practicum supervisor, had many years of experience treating survivors of cult abuse. Annis was determined to cheer me on to the finish line, if there is one.

Annis and my friends created a safe living arrangement, so that I was not alone for too long during the time frames that memories were coming. I gave up efforts to prevent game characters who knew about the cult abuse from coming to the window. I had not been all that successful anyway. There are several thoughts and methods of treating individuals diagnosed with a dissociative disorder. Annis and Janis, her previous supervisor, believed it was important to work with whoever showed up during a session. I was expected to stay near the window as much as possible during sessions and learn to communicate better with the characters in my game. They also created ways for me to be accountable for my actions. I had to admit that as time went on, I had more and more control over my ability to stay grounded, and was more aware of my memories and surroundings. I also had to admit there were times I engaged in self-harm or eating disorder behavior when I could have tried harder to use a safe coping mechanism. I also had to admit I engaged in self-harm and eating disorder behavior to gain attention rather than just to escape emotional pain. Truthfully, I hate the "admitting" part of growth!

I can't tell you it was easy or that there were not a few more crises ahead. It was a slow process partially due to my many physical ailments. I once read a book called *The Body Bears the Burden: Trauma, Dissociation, and Disease* by Robert Scaer which helped me understand why I had so many autoimmune disorders and other physical issues such as migraines, bladder issues, hypothyroidism, digestive issues, Barrett's esophagus, and irritable bowel disorder, just to name a few.[1] Even chronic stress can compromise the immune system and lead to autoimmune diseases.

When abuse is chronic and occurs during the formative years, it changes the brain in ways that cause a hyper-vigilant stance towards life that twists reality into danger. When this happens, one gets so overwhelmed with unbearable body feelings that the thinking part of the brain just goes off-line. It becomes extremely difficult to use reason in evaluating a situation or in finding ways to soothe one's self. On many occasions during recovery, the body sensations were just as anxiety and fear producing as it would be if I had been forced to stand on a train track as the train approached and had no power to move. Self-injury, though maladaptive, actually changes a person's physiology in a way that helps them calm down. I could focus on my physical pain in order to get a footing on my reality.

Annis was willing to do a few unconventional things to help me believe my memories. Raven and Nevar, important characters in my game, were about thirteen years old and held a lot of the memories from my trip to Kansas and Missouri with Ken. I do not believe Dr. Wilson ever met them even though I was in treatment with her for several years. There were parts of me way too terrified to ever let someone know those secrets. Many of the parts of me believed the cult could still hurt them if we told. Raven, Nevar and some of the children who helped me cope when I was young, like Misty who was four, had begun telling Annis more information about the strange religious stuff that had occurred. Some of them also believed whole-heartedly that the "church people" were still in the same location and expected them to return, or they would be in trouble. They also believed the church people were actively looking for us. This explains my life on the run. For as long as I can remember, I never felt safe where ever "home" was, so I often spent the night at other peoples' houses. I also kept spare clothes in the trunk of my car, a blanket, toiletries, etc.

So many people during those years said, "How do you do it, live out of your car?"

At one time, I had at least five different places that I could spend the night whenever I needed to feel safe. The thought, *No one can find me here repeated in my head a zillion times.*

Many of the other characters, including me, had no memory of that abuse by the church people except for occasional flashbacks and snapshot type pictures. I think no one wanted to know! Pedophiles are so devious and can do many things to force a child to cooperate. In Isaiah 32:7 (NIV) the Bible says, "Scoundrels use wicked methods, they make up evil schemes to destroy the poor with lies, even when the plea of the needy is just." Children are poor; they own nothing of their own and must dependent on adults for basic physical and emotional needs. Pedophiles use lies to trick them. Many of the "wicked methods" used by cults are for the purpose of keeping their evil deeds a secret. One of the wicked methods may be having someone who is wearing a police uniform to abuse them, thus causing them to be afraid of police officers. I was thirty-four when I learned of this tactic.

Many of the children holding the memories and feelings of our time with Ken had unusual fears, and many of them were related to food. Annis took "them" to restaurants to help them see food as safe. During the dinner, Misty was trying to find the courage to eat more of her dinner when a police officer entered the establishment. Annis said Misty's face transformed from content to terror in seconds, she froze and then vomited all over the table. She began shaking and staring at the police officer as if he were about to rip her apart. This incident was one of many where Annis spent time with them in outside settings and learned very quickly what would have taken years to learn in an office setting.

I was extremely fortunate to have this extra help. There are many reasons, including liability, that therapists are not allowed to do this. She risked losing her license. As my treatment was approaching the end, I asked her why she took such a risk. Her reply shocked me. "During the six months you were in the partial program, Janis and I were astounded with your determination to heal, your desire to be honest, and your level of insight. We both knew you were one of the rare clients who desperately needed unconventional help, but would actually benefit from it." She then said something strange to me, "Spending this much time with a client would almost always do more harm than good."

Simple cruelty is another example of the evil schemes abusers use to control their victim. Many of the missing puzzle pieces of my childhood came unexpectedly and were very traumatic; some occurred through simple dialogue. Annis and Misty were headed to the park one day when they passed a subdivision entrance with many colorful flowers planted in large beds.

Misty stated, "Drive faster, that's where the dead people are!"

This was a clue, but to what?

During another therapy session, Misty was explaining that she needed to return to the church people because "they're waiting." Annis tried to convince her that many years had passed, so the church people were probably not there anymore. Misty insisted she would be leaving to find them, or else her punishment would be worse. This is when Annis made a deal with her that they would go together to find the church people. During the next therapy session, held on a Saturday, one of my game characters named Hope gave directions to Annis which led them to a funeral home about an hour away from her office. The name and exterior of the funeral home had changed, but it was still there. Annis said Hope was very confused but insisted on going in.

As I look at these events now, I am amazed at God's faithfulness to help me know the truth, face it, and then heal. The Bible says in John 8:32 (NIV), "Then you will know the truth, and the truth will set you free." I knew as long as I ignored my pain, refused to look at my memories, or deny the truth in any way, I would be chained or bound to the wound. Part of this understanding came while I completed an inner healing program called Elijah House being offered through my church. Annis, too, was determined to help us face the truth just as Dr. Wilson had previously done regarding the miscarriage at thirteen.

Mr. Sampson, the owner of the funeral home, greeted Annis and Hope as they walked in. Hope looked around as Annis had a conversation with the owner. Hope became upset and began pointing to all the differences in the current building. Windows were moved, an addition was built onto the property, and walls were changed. She also pointed out a hidden door that led to a basement area, which no one would know about unless they had spent significant time there. Mr. Sampson was surprised she knew so much about the changes, especially about the hidden door. Hope began explaining some of what she remembered, and Mr. Sampson remarked that he knew Ken personally and bought the facility directly from him. He also insinuated he was not fond of Ken and had found some rather unusual and disturbing items downstairs.

Hope began unloading her memories and wanted to know if the church people were now at the "graveyard." She described the cemetery and crematorium located about another hour away where she and some of the others spent significant time. Surprisingly, Mr. Sampson knew of the facility, but stated he didn't think the crematorium was used any more. Hope insisted on going there, and Annis complied with the expectation that if the characters holding my fears and memories of the abuse by the church people learned

---

When the children of Israel began their forty-year journey in the desert they did not know the trials, the fears, and the pain would get worse before it got better. Job did not know that God had every intention of restoring everything the enemy had taken away.

---

the truth, they would begin to heal. Their healing of course, actually meant my healing. One of the most precious clues Father gave me was confirmation about the strange items in the basement. My mother had spoken of Ken's closet of body parts. I had pictures in my head of what was done with the body parts, and now a total stranger is sharing the details of what they found after buying the property.

When Annis and Hope arrived at the cemetery, which was now overgrown, Hope became even more confused and began reliving some of her memories. She pointed out the building where they burned the bodies and so much more.

At one point, one of the young characters of me named Rachel came out and began crying hysterically, "Why am I back here? I thought you said we're safe now!"

It was a traumatic day, but very helpful. A lot of my confusion regarding our strange environmental fears was addressed in one day. Another blessing that came from this intense pain was the validation I felt. *So I'm not crazy!*

This thought must have repeated in my mind at least one hundred times in the months to come. There were several people in my life, mostly family, who minimized my abuse, shamed me for still suffering from it, and believed I was blowing my abuse way out of proportion to seek attention. I now knew that I was not crazy. Regarding my need for so many hospitalizations, discovering the secrets I kept, even from myself, made healing from my past possible. However, remembering what happened and experiencing the pain that accompanied the abuse made self-care very difficult. Unfortunately, I did not know at the time that I was actually speeding towards recovery and that the pain would one day be mostly gone. In such a kind way, Father had let me know that it was going to get worse before it got better.

When the children of Israel began their forty-year journey in the desert they did not know the trials, the fears, and the pain would get worse before it got better. Job did not know that God had every intention of restoring everything the enemy had taken away. There were so many days when I was positive that I would not survive the memories, the intense flashbacks, the horrendous fear, the financial setbacks, the rejection from family members, the fierce need to express my rage onto my own body, or the various physical ailments. I did, however, know that there were people who cared about me and who were not giving up hope that I would one day be restored to my original whole self, Tammy, the one whom God loves.

Chapter 9

———⟶◦⟨⟨⟨⟩◦⟵———

WHAT'S LOVE GOT

TO DO WITH IT?

EVERYTHING

A close friend, also diagnosed with dissociative identity disorder, once asked me, "How did you integrate and become one person? Did all your child parts have to leave?" I chuckle to myself when I'm asked these types of questions. I imagine myself in my final therapy session, and I tell everyone inside, "Ok guys, pack your bags, it's time for you to leave. I simply don't need you anymore." A few moments later, hordes of angry children run crying and screaming from the therapy office never to be seen again.

This question is actually very difficult to answer and everyone's journey to wholeness will be different. I never made a rule or plan inside myself that the child parts had to "leave." During the years of my divine treatment plan, the need to escape reality and retreat inside myself lessened over time, as did the need to hurt myself. I had to give up my rights to many decisions and choose a higher (much healthier) road, but Father greeted me with His assistance each time I took His path. His main requirement was simply, actually not simple at all, to make the choice to love: love others, love and appreciate myself, and allow God's love to permeate my pain, which would require a very different relationship with Him than the one I had.

My journey seemed to take an eternity, but I've learned not to carry shame regarding how long it took or what mistakes I made along the way. In the movie *The Wizard of Oz*, Dorothy discovered that the power to get back home had been within her from the moment Glinda placed the ruby red slippers on her feet., Unfortunately, Dorothy had a powerful enemy who lied to her. The wicked witch maintained that the slippers, meaning the power Glinda had given Dorothy, belonged to her instead. The witch's plan was to take Dorothy's power even though that meant destroying her. Doesn't that sound like what Satan has planned for us? To help Dorothy survive, Glinda directed her to a yellow brick road, the path that would ultimately heal Dorothy by helping her discover the power she already had.

I had a lot to discover on my own path, and I needed to see it and experience it myself. It was not enough for therapists and friends to simply say, "You're loved, especially by God" or "The abuse was not your fault." Dorothy needed Glinda, the good witch, to make sure she met the necessary people to guide, love, and protect her on the journey. Dorothy had to experience the safe relationships, the times Glinda intervened to save her, and the pain of missing her home. Strangely, Dorothy also needed the wicked witch to challenge her with painful circumstances and trials, which ultimately made her stronger, less self-centered, more determined, and wiser. To discover the power and strength Dorothy had within her, Glinda made sure Dorothy walked through specific circumstances, some being difficult, frightening, and painful. During the journey, Dorothy learned many vital lessons, such as we all suffer pain and adversity, we all have many gifts and talents, there are times when we need to ask for help (Scarecrow), the importance of facing our fears (Cowardly Lion), and love has the power to heal, but also has the power to cause very intense pain (Tin Man). After her long, exhausting journey when there were times she didn't think she could go on, Dorothy discovered her inner ability, with the help of Glinda, to fight for what she wanted: to return to a safe place where she experienced joy, safety, and love. For Dorothy, it was her childhood home.

For me, it obviously was not my childhood home! My Oz would be an internal place where I felt loved, safe, and valuable. It would be a place where I experience joy and peace instead of nightmares, flashbacks, and self-hate. I desperately wanted to find a place where I wouldn't be so starved for love that I was willing to destroy myself to get it. It would be a beautiful place where I would not be addicted to anything in order to fill a void or escape pain. I would be able to pour from my love cup into others with the sole purpose of helping to relieve their pain until they are able to trust their own Glinda. During the long and very agonizing journey to my Oz, I'm positive God watched over me just as Glinda watched over Dorothy. For example, God never needed to send snow to wake me up in a poppy field, but there were many times He either sent awesome blessings or allowed the enemy to cause significant pain in order to help me wake up from my contentment to emotionally and mentally sleep through my life. I had to have the strong desire to run through my poppies to get to the palace. Isn't it just like Satan to lead us into what appears to be a beautiful field of flowers, later to discover it's actually a trap? He shows us an image that appears to offer good feelings and happiness; yet, he laces it with something that will actually destroy us by causing us to check out of life forever. Satan's purpose in trapping us in his cruel lair is to prevent us from ever reaching our final destination.

When I think about my journey down the yellow brick road, love is the first word that comes to mind regarding my integration, or living life without needing to exist in separate puzzle pieces to face each day. One of the biggest obstacles to reaching my Oz (wholeness) was the extreme self-hate that controlled so much of my life and the inability to love others in a healthy way. "Healthy" meaning safe boundaries, the ability to see the pain in others, the willingness to allow God to heal my empty love tank which was painful at times, and the willingness to move forward rather than become content somewhere along the yellow brick road. I'll give an example. During my days of being in and out of psychiatric hospitals and treatments programs, I met a lot of wounded people. Many of them, like me, had found enough coping skills to exist and even have moments of joy. Some had actually become proud of their disease. The anorexic patients loved to compare new purging methods, new diet pills, the newest weight loss strategies, and their latest success in deceiving the staff regarding their treatment and intake. They complained about the pain of having no muscle but also seemed filled with pride at their small frame and ability to stay in control. They seemed to feel superior to the overweight patients, who in their estimation, had no self-control!

This is very similar to my days in treatment with others who had been diagnosed with DID (Dissociative Identity Disorder). It seemed as if they had embraced their extreme ability to dissociate with a strange pride.

Their dialog included sentiments such as,

"How many alters do you have?"

"Have you been to McLean Hospital yet?"

"What meds are you on?"

"Does your therapist allow your parts to come to the session?"

"Have you met the new girl on the unit? She's a singleton."

Singleton is a word they use to separate themselves from those whose abuse must have been minimal. In one hospital, there was a group of women on the unit who rarely socialized with the other patients. They believed the singletons, and the multiples could not understand their level of pain because their abuse was inflicted by a cult. They ate with each other, did their crafts together, and remained attached to each other on the unit during free time. Sadly, I was qualified to hang out with most of the cliques: eating disorder patients, multiples, cutters, addicts, and cult survivors, during my hospitalizations. When I look back now, I recognize the lies we hung onto so tightly. Imagine feeling pride for being one of the sickest or most abused patients. The higher the level of abuse, the more one felt entitled to extra attention, special status, different rules on the unit, or more privileges.

To reach my final destination, I would also be required to obey that "still small voice" which mostly told me to let go of my rights and trust God. Thankfully, that still small voice was loud and clear! Similar to Glinda telling Dorothy to go back for the witch's broomstick, God required me to go back and face the wickedness in my past. By this, I mean facing the memories and allowing the pain to surface. The long process was agonizing, but just as an infected wound needs to be lanced and cleaned out, so does an emotional wound. I consider Satan to be the wicked witch in my life, and he sent his little minions to steal my power by telling me lies. Dorothy's power was in her shoes; my power was and is, in my mind.

Similar to Glinda telling Dorothy to go back for the witch's broomstick, God required me to go back and face the wickedness in my past.

I remember as a child being very frightened during the movie when the witch's monkeys came down to capture Dorothy and take her to a very scary place where she couldn't escape. The feeling of being captured and taken to a frightening place was very familiar every time I watched *The Wizard of Oz*, though I did not always remember why. For many, the best part of the movie is when Dorothy clicks her shiny, red shoes and says, "There's no place like home." She is then transported back to her place of safety and love, her home. For me, my favorite moment was when her three friends risked their lives to rescue Dorothy. My least favorite portion of the movie was when she was saying goodbye to her friends. That scene caused me to ache; I wanted her to stay there, maybe because I could not relate to her desire to return home. Dorothy's friends faced their own fears because of the love they had for her. Glinda watched over her and loved her as well. It was this great love that ultimately saved her life and returned her to where she was intended to be all along!

In the book of Matthew, Jesus was asked which law is most important. His answer was very simple, yet impossible. I'm to love God with all my heart and love those around me with a pure and unselfish love. I began discovering that most of my "love" was self-centered, poured out or withheld based on my own needs, and conditional. Ouch! I was not aware at the time that my own needs and pain trumped my ability to put others first. I was simply starving and though I tried to be a loving friend, a good sister, and a faithful Christian, I had very little to pour into others, and what I did have, I spent mostly on myself. Like the woman at the well in the book of John, I needed the living water that Christ offered. To me, living water represents the emotional nourishment that I learned, over time, could only come from my faith in God. In AA, the recovering alcoholics learn they are powerless over their addiction and pain, but that there is a higher power that is able to bring about complete restoration. Not only is faith required, but also a difficult twelve-step journey requiring the addicts to face their past, admit their faults, look and feel the pain inside, choose forgiveness, and then be willing to let go of the guilt! I was not an alcoholic, but I needed the same painful journey. I was addicted to negative thinking, self-harm, carbohydrates, and people whom I thought should meet my needs and refill my empty love tank over and over again. There was one person that for years, I simply could not forgive. I could not let her off the hook—me!

My broken soul prevented me from feeling and trusting God's love just for me, my friends' love, and from feeling even an ounce of self-worth. Every drop of love, esteem, and respect poured into me, leaked right back out causing me to desperately seek a refill. I had no power to stop the pain or develop a self-love that would ultimately help me stop hurting and hating myself. Over time, I found three keys that opened the door to an amazing life filled with fun, freedom, and peace. Upon owning all three keys, I found myself in the center of God's will and calling on my life. The first decision was to learn to love others. The love I'm describing looks nothing like the "love" I typically see all around me.

Loving Others

The act of loving others seemed to be the opposite of what I would have guessed God would use to help me heal. I was the empty cavern. I was the one with the third-degree burns that needed immediate attention. I'm the one who had been sexually abused. Shouldn't the world be sad for me, want to make it up to me, want to take care of me? Didn't I deserve extra kindness, extra portions of love, forgiveness, and grace? I was raised by an alcoholic parent, so I never learned how to set boundaries. I was sexually abused so I never learned I had a right to set a boundary. Why should others be allowed to set boundaries around themselves? Don't they all know I have needs?

Love is a choice, not a feeling. I've heard this many times but discovering it to be true was powerful. I was sitting in church one Sunday many years ago feeling absolutely miserable. There were many reasons why I had a hard time sitting through church services. First, of course, were the triggers such as Bible verses being quoted and communion. Second, I found church at that time to be the loneliest place I endured each week. It was not that I didn't have friends there, but they all had families to go home to, whereas I felt orphaned. Throughout life, my own parents were unavailable emotionally and later physically as well. They both died while in their mid-fifties. I have never been married and have no children. My church friends had families and love and happiness, and I have nothing, or so I thought. To avoid the triggers and sadness, most of my time within the church was spent caring for everyone's children. I've always loved children.

On this particular Sunday, I was in the service looking around at all the people. I hate to admit it, but I was having a huge pity party, which was not unusual. My definition of a pity party is when I allow myself to compare my life and pain with my perception of other people's pain and rate myself as being more wounded and more entitled to feel miserable. In the service, everyone looked so happy, so in love with Jesus, and so beautiful. I was very numb in my faith, and I was positive that no one could ever honestly call me "beautiful."

I sat judging people in my head, *They don't care about me. Not a single person came to visit me while I was in Charter* and sadly, so many other ugly thoughts.

I knew the Bible tells us in many places that we are to love others. It felt like God was asking me to pour from my empty love tank into their full tanks.

Visitation from your pastor, another church leader, or even your church friends is a fairly reasonable expectation, unless you consider the fact that I rarely told anyone that I had been admitted yet again into another treatment facility.

No one even notices when I'm gone for weeks at a time. I could be dead for years and no one would know or care.

This huge pity party lasted throughout the service until the end when I heard, *Are you loving them?*

Yikes.

I argued for a few minutes, *Well, I take care of their children in the nursery almost every week, besides, what do they need? See how happy they look; their lives are perfect.*

Once again, God's still, small voice asked, "Are you loving them?"

I knew the Bible tells us in many places that we are to love others. It felt like God was asking me to pour from my empty love tank into their full tanks.

I thought, *What the heck is He thinking; doesn't He know how much I need others to pour into me? I'm the one with the painful childhood. I'm the one with no parents, and I'm the one in so much emotional pain that I cut myself to feel better.*

Once again, "Are you loving them?" This seemed like a cruel expectation and impossible! Although I had no expectation of this assignment helping me in any way, I was good at playing the martyr role.

Jesus loved everybody and then He died. I guess that's how my life will be. Once again, like my childhood, I take care of everybody else, get minimal in return and then I'll die. Maybe I'll get a mansion in heaven with a pool or something as a reward for helping others.

I then began thinking of all the perks I should get in heaven for doing the next right thing. As soon as the service ended, I looked around the auditorium and noticed an attractive woman sitting a few aisles over who sat alone.

Okay, Lord, I'll go "minister" to that lady over there, but I better get a pool and sauna in heaven.

I didn't know her, but I assumed she couldn't be in any real pain; she was thin. I'm not kidding. I fully believed most thin people were happy and had a great life. The exception would be the emaciated women in my eating disorders group. I've heard them describe their body pain many times, but I still would have preferred horrendous body pain over being fat. Regardless, I approached her with a smile and said, "My name is Tammy; I've seen you here many times, but I don't believe we've met."

Her name was Cindy, and she greeted me warmly. Our church had a café, and we decided to have lunch together. We sat chatting for hours, and I learned a few lessons just from our time together that day. Over the next few years, I discovered she was in a very loveless marriage and it had been that way for many years. Her husband Brent was an angry man who gave 150% to his work as the vice president of a large company, but only gave minimal portions of passion and time to his family. This meant they were very wealthy, but he had a strong need to control the money she spent. He, of course, spent huge sums of money on his hobbies, such as golf and travel.

Cindy had two children whom she adored. Brent loved his children but had no clue how to show it if love meant having emotions. Instead of showing love in a tangible way, he was very hard on the children expecting them to excel in everything they did: school, sports, etc. Unfortunately, his involvement in the children's activities caused them more stress than feelings of being loved. Sadly, he was especially hard on his son who was becoming an angry teenager. Unfortunately, Cindy had no way to prevent what was happening around her. Even a divorce would not have kept Brent's authoritarian nature from wounding his children. Brent's father had had the same need to control his family's lives rather than embrace them unconditionally. There was no affection and no affirmation, which meant no joy in the home and minimal laughter.

Looking at Cindy's family from an outsider's perspective, it looked picture perfect. It looked to me that she was blessed abundantly leading me to believe her own childhood home was filled with activities such as baking with her mother or sitting in her father's lap. Her children were always dressed nicely in church, were polite, and they all smiled as if nothing was amiss. She drove a very nice car, and their large well-manicured lawn would imply happiness. The mat at the front door said "Welcome," yet they rarely invited anyone into their home. Over the course of our friendship, I was one of the privileged few. Prior to being let into her world, I judged them to be happy, yet their lives were a miserable existence. The emotional temperature in the home relied on the mood of Brent when he arrived home from work. When he did arrive, everyone walked on eggshells to prevent a harsh rebuke.

I also discovered that Cindy too had been molested as a child. Knowing that wounded people are usually attracted to other wounded people, this explained her willingness to marry an unaffectionate man who would take care of her financial and physical needs, but who had nothing to give emotionally. At the point of getting married, she had nothing to give emotionally either because she was still able to keep her moles whacked down and unaddressed. Over the years, as God, her children, and others poured love into her empty love tank, she began to heal emotionally. There came a point when she desired this same intimacy with her husband, but he was content with his fence up and his feelings stuffed. One of the facts I learned in my relationship with Cindy was that enduring childhood abuse is hard enough on its own, but then living the rest of your life in a cold relationship is much worse.

Over the course of our friendship, it was becoming much harder to hold on to my victim role mentality as I had to acknowledge the deep pain in others. I began feeling so much compassion for her that I longed to do anything I could to make her life more bearable. What I did not know is that as I focused on helping her, I was feeling much better about my situation. The whining in my head and negative self-talk lessened over time. I felt better about myself as I saw that I had the ability to help someone else with no expectations in return. Additionally, Cindy was a precious woman of faith who poured into me as well, so the benefits were very mutual. God's expectation that I love others was an unexpected balm on my own pain. This was my first lesson on agape love; many more were to come.

Discovering Cindy's pain was insightful because she was one of the women in our church that I judged to be happy, blessed, and whole. I was learning that as I judged others, my estimations were usually wrong or incomplete, preventing me from being able to truly love them. Because of my life circumstances and insecurities, before giving my friends or those around me a chance to reveal the truth, I was very quick to judge their motives, circumstances, and behaviors in a negative light. Even when the truth was revealed, because my self-esteem was pitifully low and my love tank so empty, it was much easier to believe the lies in my head such as, *She didn't call back because she doesn't really care about me, or I wasn't invited because I'm boring; they only hang out with their fun friends.* I could have prevented so much unnecessary pain for myself if I had learned not to judge people's motives and behavior.

Part of my divine life lessons regarding how to love others occurred many years ago when I took an inner healing course offered by Elijah House. After we examined the scripture, Matt. 7:1 (AMP) – "Do not judge and criticize and condemn others, so that you may not be judged and criticized and condemned yourselves," our leader asked us to examine our hearts to see if there was anyone in our past whom we had not forgiven.

I immediately pictured my mother and began explaining to God, *In case you haven't been paying attention, I have a right to judge my mother, even hate her. Her "choice" to drink alcohol has ruined my life.*

I gave God plenty of examples of how her drinking and refusal to get treatment caused her to make some very poor parenting decisions, some life threatening. Then it happened again. The Holy Spirit has a way of illuminating the truth so specifically that it's difficult to argue!

As I recited a list of all the ways my mother's alcohol addiction had caused my sisters and me so much pain, I heard, "How is your mother's addiction to alcohol any different from your addiction to sugar?"

What did God just say? My sugar, that's very different. Why would being fat affect anyone else? It's not like you can get a EUI (Eating Under the Influence) for eating a dozen donuts while driving. Fat people are not dangerous and don't embarrass others. They might be embarrassed themselves, but no one else gets hurt.

As I pondered all these thoughts, I began thinking about the various vows I made to myself just about every morning: I won't eat any sugar today,

I won't ask Samantha, my roommate, to bring home the leftover pastries from La Madeleine today, I won't eat carbs today, I will not eat today, I will fast until Friday, etc. I usually broke every declaration by 10:00 a.m. Sadly, at the moment of placing a morsel of food into my mouth, the feelings of failure, hopelessness, depression, and self-hate grew to the point of indulging all day to fight or numb the guilty feelings from the first bite that morning. It was an ugly and very painful cycle every day. Did my mother also fight and fail each day? Did she too experience this same shame, guilt, and self-loathing? Light bulb moment, mother's addiction to alcohol was just as, if not more, painful and out of control as my food and self-harm addiction. In addition, she had to battle it while being responsible for three children.

As I pondered on these questions and compared my life and weaknesses to my mother's own obstacles, I realized I was very much like my mother. OUCH! Usually, this realization would cause someone to feel devastated. Instead, a fresh download of compassion and love for my mother washed over me with the same power a waterfall would have on muddy feet. I thought of feet because I realized how much shame and guilt I had attempted to impose on my mother when I had the same faults she did. I realized Jesus adores her just as He adores me. At that point, I imagined myself washing her feet and telling her how much I understood her pain.

I wanted to say, "I'm so sorry for the pride and unforgiveness I've carried."

Over the years, so many mean sentiments had occupied space in my heart such as, *At least I'm not an alcoholic like my mother.* How humbling to know Jesus still loved me and had a plan for my life even though I had cast stones at her for the very thing I had been doing for years.

I also began imagining myself as a parent. I thought about my panic when I couldn't get to my razors or carbs or even alcohol at times to avoid the pain and memories just under the surface. I imagined my mood swings, anger, and depression, especially if I was not able to play my game. How well does one care for children when extreme insomnia prevents sleep and rest?

Also, how would I be a good parent if my child greeted a different mommy each morning depending on what I needed to do that day, how I felt, or what memories I was fighting to whack down?

I immediately began to understand why God tells us not to judge others. I knew that people, simply because of my obesity, could easily judge me as lazy and without any self-control. They would be wrong. I controlled most every part of my life down to how many peas I'm allowed eat. No one who knows me would ever call me lazy. Because of my many long-term visits to psychiatric hospitals, people could judge me to be permanently disabled, mentally incapacitated, or attention seeking. My co-workers at DFCS could have easily judged, "She just doesn't want to come to work." They had to cover my caseload on many occasions when their own caseloads were already close to being unmanageable. Many judgments could have been made during those recovering years regarding my character, behavior, motives, and future that would turn out not to be true.

Learning to choose to respond to people with pure agape love is difficult and painful, but very rewarding. To help me with this, God put an amazing couple, Mark and Maria Goldstein, in my life to help me discover some of the areas where I was sabotaging myself, my relationship with others, and not loving from an emotionally healthy place. The Goldsteins needed a live-in helper to care for Grammy, Mark's elderly mother, because his company required they live bi-coastal for months at a time. A mutual friend recommended me for the position and though we had attended the same church for many years, I had never met them. I would not have been willing to move in if it meant living in a home full-time where a man lived. I still harbored much distrust and judgment against men. I had trusted too many untrustworthy men who ended up hurting me that I was not willing to let down my guard. I "knew" what really went on in the homes of couples around me, even from our church. I "knew" men controlled their families and with harsh methods. I "knew" men flirted with other women and cheated." I "knew" too much to ever trust Mark, so I managed to stay away as much as possible during their time back at home. However, over the years of living in their home and watching their relationship, I realized I had judged the whole male population based on my experience with the men my mother chose to be around. God knew what I needed for further healing, so He placed me in a family that I couldn't run from because I needed a place to live and financial assistance. He also knew the personality, temperament, and level of integrity it would require for me to ever trust a man wholeheartedly. Living with this amazing couple helped me see God's original intention when He created marriage and family.

It was in my relationship with Maria that I learned the most about healthy relationships, communication, and so much more. One of the first lessons I learned was that I did not fully understand the concept of judging others and that I still often did it. I thought judging was when I felt pride if I saw others doing something wrong and then looked down on them for

---

I learned from Maria that judging others includes the times I judge the motives, thoughts, and feelings of others.

---

making wrong choices. I had already learned statements such as "I would never...," or "I always..." often reflect a judgment being made. I had already been working on catching myself when I had those type thoughts, so I assumed I wasn't someone who judged others very often. I guess I had pride for not being prideful. However, I learned from Maria that judging others encompasses so much more and includes the times I judge the motives, thoughts, and feelings of others. For example, if she was not meeting my needs or responding to me in a way that I believed she was, as my friend, responsible to do, I judged her as not caring about me, forgetful or even angry. I was especially quick to believe someone was mad at me, which is what I feared most.

The belief system I learned as a child, common when raised by an alcoholic, was: love comes and goes unexpectedly, nothing is as it seems, people will ultimately hurt me, especially people who proclaim to care, and rarely do people tell the truth, especially relating to how they actually feel about me. I believed if I was not meeting someone's needs, I had no value to that person and no power to make them stay. This meant I volunteered to do anything possible for those I cared about in order to keep them in my life. I volunteered to clean their house, do their errands, keep their kids, and I even gave huge amounts of money to friends and family that I cared about to control whether or not they loved me.

The problem with this was that I never actually believed anyone loved me because I unconsciously judged his or her feelings as conditional. I got burned many times due to my un-wholeness. I once had a very close friend from church named Sadie whom I spent a lot of time with, even holidays. We had many common interests, such as our faith and quickly became close friends. Due to the maternal "love" she offered, it was a no-brainer when my precious friend lost her job and entered into a season of financial crisis for me to "rescue" her. I completely trusted Sadie and when she said, "I promise I'll pay you back," I absolutely believed her, even at the point when she easily owed me ten thousand dollars. "Love" really is blind when it comes to wounded people!

Prior to my ever loaning my friend money, I already knew she had forged my name on an application for a school loan. Thankfully, the loan center sends out statements to co-signers as well. I knew nothing about the loan, and it was for a substantial amount of money.

I was in such shock, though not angry, and asked, "How could you do this?"

She explained her financial situation and said she was desperate. She apologized, and I easily let it go. I would have done anything to help her and because of my own un-wholeness, I did! When her dryer broke, I bought her a new one. When her car was totaled, I bought her a used one, and on and on. My desire or need for maternal love was a driving force in my willingness to bail her out of financial trouble over and over again. Even when I saw her buy unnecessary items instead of making a payment, I still looked the other way. I made excuses in my mind to hold onto the feeling that she really loved me.

It was after my ten-week mission trip to Ghana when I was living with the Goldsteins that Maria insisted I confront Sadie regarding the money she owed me. While I was in Africa, I had given Sadie access to my bank account in order to make it easier for me to access the donations that came in. Upon return, I discovered Sadie had chosen to deposit some of my mission's money into her own bank account.

When I questioned her about the money, she said, "I thought I could put the money back into your account before you came home; I promise to pay you back."

I fully believed her. It was Maria's wisdom that turned on the lights in my relationship with my friend, whom I still love very much. Thankfully, my love is now from a much healthier perspective.

Maria confronted me firmly and said, "What your friend did was stealing, and you need to confront her with that truth!"

I resisted initially, but figured once Sadie gains employment she would happily pay me back, and maybe with interest.

My thought was, *Maria will then see that my friend loves me very much, and my instincts about her are correct.*

Being as loving and forgiving as possible, I did as Maria requested and confronted Sadie about the money she owed me thus far. I even made myself use the word "stole" once in the conversation. Sadie was very sweet, acknowledged that she owed me at least ten thousand dollars and insisted she would pay me back. She was very upset that I would frame what she did as stealing because she would be paying me back eventually. Even after she won a very large settlement, eventually has still never come!

This conversation occurred very close to Thanksgiving, and we had plans for me to again spend that day with her and her grown sons. When we hung up the phone, I fully expected everything to remain the same.

We're still very close. Though it might be in very small increments over a long period of time, she'll eventually pay me back. All is well with us.

I was completely in the dark and am so thankful Maria helped light my way. The day before Thanksgiving, I received a letter from Sadie stating I was not invited to Thanksgiving dinner, she was very hurt and angry that I would

---

One humbling example taught me a very valuable lesson: think the best of others before assuming the negative.

---

accuse her of stealing, and that I was emotionally too unhealthy to be her friend. I have never heard from her since the day I received the letter. Unless she allows God to heal her wounds as well, I will probably never hear from her again, but I pray for her. I know some things about her life and the wounds she's tried so hard to ignore. This knowledge makes it very easy for me to forgive her.

I learned so much through my relationship with Sadie and similar to Dorothy, I needed to walk through the painful experience in order to address some of the ways my early wounding was still causing me pain and preventing me from loving others in a healthy way.

A friend said, "How can you still love Sadie even though she hurt you so much?" My thought, *How can I judge her; she was correct in her assessment. My actions were partially driven from a place of "need" rather than "love."*

If I had loved her from a healthy heart, I would have addressed the forgery issue very differently at the beginning of our friendship. I basically chose to ignore it out of fear that she would be upset with me and emotionally "leave." Next, I would have sought wise counsel regarding the best ways to help her. I've learned it is not wise to loan money. Best practice is to give freely, but only what I can afford, and if it's a large amount, do it with wise counsel.

Another lesson I learned is that yes, she owes me money which should be paid back, but she has every right to choose with whom she spends her time just as I have the same right. We are to love others and treat them with kindness, but that does not necessarily require us to spend time with them. I will never fully know how much my wounding has caused harm and pain to others. The main lessons I learned were that meeting someone's needs does not guarantee they will love me; my need to get my love tank filled was still causing me to remain in unhealthy relationships; people are not all good or all bad. We often make decisions based on our previous pain, experiences, and faulty belief systems. We believe the enemy's lies, and our vision is often very distorted. Thankfully, God provided Maria to teach me many lessons about God's perfect love.

At the same time that I was learning about unhealthy relationships, Maria and several of my other friends were modeling very healthy love, which must include boundaries, complete honesty, and the willingness to be humble. I have found it impossible to love perfectly without the power of Christ strengthening me, healing me, and placing people around me, such as the Goldsteins, to model forgiveness, patience, kindness, and self-control. The last one is a never-ending battle, brutal to learn, and never fully accomplished!

I've learned so much about how to love in a healthy manner; sometimes the only way to learn such a lesson is by doing it wrong in the first place. One humbling example taught me a very valuable lesson: think the best of others before assuming the negative. For this lesson, Maria was the chisel Father used to help me love more like Him. She and I were in her kitchen one day while I was still living in their home, and I noted a new picture on the counter of Maria and some of our friends from church.

I casually asked, "What was this for?"

She responded, "Some of the women from church came over last Saturday for prayer, lunch, and just fellowship."

Though I had not been home the previous Saturday, I was very hurt for not being included. I did not choose to share my pain with her at that point, a big mistake. Regrettably, it ate at me for weeks.

Thoughts such as, *She doesn't really consider me one of her inner circle friends. She just spends time with me occasionally because I help take care of Grammy. How can she lie to me! Maria tells me mushy stuff like, 'I love you to the moon and back,' but then doesn't include me when the important people at church come over.*

I noticed that our pastor's wife, the assistant pastor's wife, and other women in leadership were in the picture. I've been at our church for over fifteen years, even longer than Mark and Maria, but I guess I'm still not important enough to be included.

Previously, without checking out the truth, I ran from relationships when there was pain, confrontation, or any sign that I was about to be rejected. I bolted to avoid the pain I thought was headed my way when the rejection came. My motto was, "Leave them before they leave me." There have been many times in my relationship with Maria that I believed, "She'll definitely leave me now!"

There were also times when I tested her; *I'm not calling her back. If she really cares, she'll call to check on me. If she really cares, she'll come downstairs to check on me; she knows I'm sick.*

I wouldn't call Maria or share my expectation; I'd simply wait to see if she "really cared." It's so embarrassing to admit this kind of childish behavior still existed in me after so many years of counseling and ministry.

Part of the un-wholeness still within me was due to my lack of experience within a healthy family. At this point in my relationship with Maria, my emotional skin burn had decreased from a third-degree to a first-degree burn, so I managed to stay in the friendship physically, but continued to keep my heart at a distance. It was a few months before I brought up the pain. During this time, I had allowed my mind to judge her and focus on the times she had let me down. It was as if my brain now had a strange filter that distorted even positive encounters with her as negative. The thoughts were often unfair and a lie based on my faulty belief system built upon past wounding.

She's mad at me because I forgot to wipe down the counters. She didn't even say goodnight Monday night. She's like my dad; she talks to me about eating healthy because she would love me more if I were skinny. She says I'm family, but I've never been invited on one of their family vacations, maybe if I lose weight?

My list of her "faults" grew and my expectations of her did not allow or consider that she might need quiet or alone time, or that she simply might be in a bad mood, be tired, sad, or forgetful. The expectations I had for her didn't filter through any sort of thought process but just seemed to exist. I wasn't even aware that I imposed these thoughts and expectations on her.

By the time I brought up the "offense" to Maria, my anger and hurt had grown in size to the point that I spoke to her with blame in my tone. I shared how much I was hurt that she chose not to invite me to the church luncheon on a Saturday a few months back. Maria was shocked and in disbelief at my accusation, partly because I had held my hurt in for so long without telling her about my wound. In spite of all the evidence I had over the last year that she loved me, I had never considered there might be a good reason I was not invited. Sadly, I had also chosen to focus on all the ways she had failed me rather than to remind myself of all she had done for me. In this incidence, the reason I wasn't invited was because the women in leadership at our church had planned this prayer event and asked Maria to host it in her home. Maria had no input as to who was invited. Our discussion that day was very painful, humbling, and wonderful. I learned that I was still easily offended, struggled with jealousy, had chosen to hold unforgiveness in my heart, and hadn't chosen to think the best of her until I asked for clarification. The best part of this incident is that I began questioning how often I judge someone to have harsh or unloving sentiments towards me yet I would be totally wrong. As Maria shined the light on the lies I believed, it seemed like the cracks and holes in my love tank were continuing to heal quite nicely.

I feel so sad when I see others lash out at someone else because they totally misjudge the incident. One day at the mall, I was standing in a long line while the lady in front of me was holding a large bundle of children's

---

When people are abused, whether as an adult or child, they will grow to be easily offended. Some will express their rage outward and some, like me, will express their rage inwards.

---

clothes in her arms. She was also trying to manage her three small children, and I felt so sorry for her. As is typical of children, one headed west from the line and another decided to explore the east side of the store. The poor woman could barely see over all the clothes piled up in her arms, so she bumped into another shopper. From the reaction of the woman bumped, you would think she had just been beaten, robbed, and her identity stolen. I had never seen someone get so angry and so fast.

The expletives coming out of her mouth included all sorts of ill motives and everyone around was thinking, "What's her problem?"

When people are abused, whether as an adult or child, they will grow to be easily offended. Some will express their rage outward and some, like me, will express their rage inwards.

Mark and Maria were so gentle and loving during the times I needed guidance in healthy relationships. One of the huge hurdles I needed to jump over was the need to learn what the Goldsteins called "Buy-In." I had expectations of others and made assumptions that the other person or people had not agreed to. For example, not only had I never expressed my expectation that I should be invited to the social events that occurred in the Goldsteins' home, they had not agreed to fulfill my expectations. Until discussing this with them, I didn't think of what I was doing as having an expectation, but after thinking about it, I realized several things: they don't get hurt when I don't invite them to functions I attend, they don't hold anger in their heart when I disappoint them or when there has been a misunderstanding, and I've never seen signs of them being jealous of others but instead, glad when they see others move forward.

Obviously there are no perfect people, and the Goldsteins would be the first to admit they are far from it. They are, however, a great example of the type of people God placed around me to teach me about healthy love and healthy relationships. Another friend, whom I've called, My Buddy for over twenty years, prays for me often and occasionally calls me during her early morning quiet time to share a Bible verse she has read. Her intimate, early morning time with Jesus has been a wonderful influence on how I spend my mornings.

Over time, I've gotten to a point of emotional wellness that I'm able to release offenses much easier and give grace instead of blame. I learned that if I really love someone, I'd often choose to focus on that person's needs rather than constantly placing my broken vessel in their face for a refill. This required me to become very intentional in controlling my thoughts about others and myself. I chose to worship when I felt numb in my faith. I chose to pray for people whom I would have rather cursed. For example, I knew the Bible tells us to love our enemies. Though at times I might have prayed through gritted teeth, I obeyed God and prayed for each man who had molested me. I only knew the name of twelve of my abusers, but I decided not to pray the typical prayer, "God bless ... and God bless..." Instead, I prayed for each one as if he were my best friend. I prayed for God to heal them, heal their family members, bless their finances, and forgive them for what they had done to me. Yes, I prayed for God to forgive them.

When I began praying for those who wounded me, including my mother, a strange and unexpected phenomenon began to occur almost immediately. Huge blessings began pouring out upon me. I got a large "refund" that I had no idea I was eligible for. People started treating me with favor when it didn't make sense, my boss chose me for a special assignment, and so much more. Not only did some of my tangible circumstances improve, the best transformation began to manifest in my heart and spirit. For example, over time, forgiving others became very easy. I gained an internal understanding that people hurt others because they are wounded and starving to fill their natural need for love. God created us to desperately desire love. If we are not allowing Him to be our main source, we are running to each other, fighting to get filled up. I now have so much compassion and grace for others. Throughout most of my life, I experienced unimaginable pain until I learned to go to the only water source capable of filling me to the point that I never thirst again. As I chose to find ways to love others purely, flickers of joy began showing up in my heart while the bitterness and self-loathing began to dissipate. I'm now so filled with the love of Jesus that I easily spill over onto others.

Chapter 10

———————————⟶o⟨⟨⟨⟨⟩⟩o⟵———————————

I LOVE ME—I LOVE

ME NOT!

For me, learning to love others was essential to learning to love and appreciate myself. One of my biggest issues was that I labeled the feeling of 'need' as the feeling of 'love.' I wanted those I care about to depend on or need me. I attempted to manipulate their feelings towards me, giving me a false sense of control. I could easily assess all the ways my friends might need me, turn myself into a pretzel to meet that need, and then I was guaranteed 'love' for a while longer. If that didn't work, I helped them in various ways financially to keep them wanting a relationship with me. This is similar to being happy when my father said, "If you lose twenty-five pounds, I'll begin spending time with you."

Awesome, I thought, *He will love me as long as I'm a certain weight; I can control his love.*

The main problem with my strategy was that, except for a few fleeting moments, I never actually felt loved. I settled for feeling needed, which sadly, did nothing to restore my soul, the empty love cup that had caused me so much pain for as long as I could remember.

> [4] Love is very patient and kind, never jealous or envious, never boastful or proud, [5] never haughty or selfish or rude. Love does not demand its own way. It is not irritable or touchy. It does not hold grudges and will hardly even notice when others do it wrong. [6] It is never glad about injustice, but rejoices whenever truth wins out. [7] If you love someone, you will be loyal to him no matter what the cost. (emphasis mine) You will always believe in him, always expect the best of him, and always stand your ground in defending him (*The Living Bible*, I Cor. 13:4-7).

Most of us have heard these verses from the Bible, but how much of it do we actually accomplish? It seems to me that humans either have a tendency to esteem themselves too highly or depreciate themselves to a point of self-loathing. It is impossible to feel and demonstrate pure love for others if our primary goal is to decrease our own pain. Our low self-esteem, guilt, and shame can cause us to feel the need to control the emotions and behaviors of others.

Regarding the divine water or love source we have in Christ, it often comes through other people. Unfortunately, because Satan keeps promoting messages such as "Just Do It," "It's my way or the highway," "Revenge is sweet," or "We let you have it your way," we continue to fall deeper and deeper into sin and selfishness. We are also victims of the selfishness and rage in others. The enemy knows that when he causes us to suffer, our pain, when mixed with our pride, has the potential to bring out the very worst in us! We wound each other in the most destructive ways.

Alternatively, I've met many people who have gone through insurmountable pain, rejection, or difficult circumstances; yet seem to have an ability to love more deeply than most others. I desperately wish there was a pill that instantly caused all things to work together for our good like it says in the Bible. I've always loved reading success stories, testimonies of restoration, and stories of accomplishments after major trials. I wish I had a dollar for every success story I studied, yes studied, in either my Weight Watchers or Fitness magazines. I longed to have a 'Before and After' story! Weight loss always seemed like climbing Mt. Everest. I worked so hard to get a few feet higher only to fall back down lower than I started. Why does suffering sometimes cause some people to achieve dreams and accomplishments that they would never have experienced without their pain? Why does even the smallest setback sometimes cause people to destroy their own lives? Why does abuse in childhood either lead someone to rage, hate, and act violently, or have deep compassion, more patience, and the ability to have mercy for others? There are a billion books written on the topic of suffering. What does this topic have to do with me learning to love myself?

I believe the reason I don't get angry or hold grudges easily is because of love. I believe the reason I rarely demand my own way and enjoy finding new ways to bless others rather than seeking my own gain is because of love. I believe the reason I'm patient regarding most things and look for the best in others before jumping to the easiest negative conclusion is because of love.

I've met many people who have gone through insurmountable pain, rejection, or difficult circumstances; yet seem to have an ability to love more deeply than most others.

I believe the reason I am not quick to judge others is because I learned firsthand that God did not send Jesus into the world to judge me but to love and rescue me.

For most of my transformation years, I had no clue there would be a "before and after." The changes in me occurred slowly over time with no scale to measure my spiritual flesh loss. Fat loss is measured by numbers and easily monitored. If a scale to measure my flesh loss existed, some of the variables to monitor my progress would be:

Self-centeredness: focuses on herself 82% of her day with 79% of those thoughts being negative.

Two years later

Self-centeredness: focuses on herself 61% of the day with 60% of those thoughts being negative.

Seven years later

Self-centeredness: focuses on herself 29% of the day with 14% of those thoughts being negative.

Congratulations on your flesh loss, Ms. Kennedy!

Judgments: hates mother and abusers 100%, willingness to pray for enemies 0%

Two years later

Judgements: hates mother and abusers 72%, willingness to pray for enemies 71%

Seven years later

Judgements: hates mother and abusers 0%, willingness to pray for enemies 100%

Congratulations on your flesh loss, Ms. Kennedy

Love: demands her needs be met 84%, envies others at 93% (dangerous level)

Two years later

Love: demands her needs be met 49%, envies other at 76% (still concerning)

Seven years later

Love: demands own needs be met 26%, envies others 18%

Congratulation, Ms. Kennedy! You have a miraculous level of flesh loss.

For your own benefit, for the wellbeing of others, and for the glory of God, we suggest you keep the weight off!

Learning to love and accept myself required a major repair in my soul. Jeremiah 18:4 (ESV) says, "The vessel he was making of clay was spoiled in the potter's hand, and he reworked it into another vessel, as it seemed good to the potter to do." I can relate to the feeling of being spoiled or damaged and needing to be reworked or reformed by the loving hands of a potter. To begin considering myself as someone with value, I needed to believe others value me, believe God values me, and acknowledge the lies I believe about myself are simply that—lies!

I'd love to begin this paragraph with, "God revealed knowledge to me regarding humans' inability to love one another during an anointed dream." The truth about my discovery is that I was flipping channels one day and stopped at the Maury show. I saw all these people fighting but also using the word 'Love' to describe how they felt towards each other. Their tone was mean, the first girlfriend was very jealous of the second girlfriend, the second girlfriend hated the first girlfriend, and the guy who had impregnated both women was arrogant and rude. Each person demanded their own way and made decisions based on their own needs rather than what would be best for the children involved. The "guests" rehearsed and repeated every wrongdoing the others had done, and there was no glimpse of forgiveness on anyone's horizon. In fact, revenge was considered the right and fair thing to do. You cheated on me, so I have every right to cheat on you, even if it means I get pregnant by someone else or I get someone else pregnant. Isn't that a perfect example of, "I'll cut my nose off to punish you?"

I don't think humans are capable of loving each other with absolutely no expectations in return. What I so easily saw was that the guests and even the audience considered what was being offered or retrieved as love. When their expectations were not met, a wrath came out that could in no way be called love. It's so tempting to blame everything on the cheating husband, wife, boyfriend, etc., but the truth is none of the guests had a clue about how to genuinely love someone. Even the ability to love their born or unborn child enough to choose forgiveness, patience, kindness, and humility was nonexistent.

For much of my life, I thought most people love well, but that I either had a problem picking the ones who know how to love or I was just too unlovable. I guess I wanted to believe real love is probable and predictable as soon as I figured out the key to unlocking it in others. Instead, I saw pictures in my mind regarding how people try to meet their own need for love, respect, value, etc.

Some people are constantly <u>performing</u> for others. Their song and dance personality says, "Look at me" or "Pay attention to me" in hopes of <u>earning</u> a few drops of love from others. People controlled by shame feel very undeserving of love, so they become like chameleons, changing themselves into anything they perceive someone might want or need. This includes starving themselves to be skinny, enduring plastic surgery to attain more beauty, pursuing vast wealth, or submitting to peer pressure in exchange for a moment of "love." If the shame they feel is substantial, the person might allow various types of abuse, engage in illegal activity, or allow others to completely control them. All this for a few drops of love poured into their broken cup that will not hold anything for very long; thus requiring a constant refill.

When I was so dissociative and playing my game, it felt like each of us took turns holding out the cup to get a drink and passed it to the next stating, "Here, you go try to get us some love; it's your turn."

Sadly, there are also people who, instead of trying to earn or beg for love, feel very entitled and believe they have a right to demand love, respect, and attention from everyone around them. I went to high school with some kids who came from very wealthy families. There were many times I noted my classmates had an inability to appreciate much that was given to them and though what they owned would have been considered by me to be beyond my wildest dreams, was something they expected and felt a "right" to own. By being friends with some of my classmates in this situation, it helped me have compassion and less judgment for them. If you are given filet mignon every day, you never truly know the joy of eating a hot dog. In fact, only the food considered "better" than a filet could make you happy. Yes, a strange analogy, but it is very easy to see that people with a lot of money, or who have star status are usually very unhappy. In extreme cases of being indulged, a person can develop a narcissistic personality, be very cruel, controlling, and abusive. They feel entitled to have others fill their love cup as often as needed with no expectation of ever giving anything back. Will they ever get to enjoy the feeling of being loved? No. They might get performance, obedience, or lip service, but their soul will not feel loved and valued.

Lastly, I saw wounded individuals who have given up on getting love from others. Having no faith or trust in people, they pour alcohol, drugs, sex, and many other behaviors or substances into their own cups as a substitute for the love they crave. I then saw a picture of me. I was running from person to person begging for water. I did all of the above behaviors because I was soaked to my core in shame. Then I saw something strange that I had never known about myself before. My own hand was covering the top of my cup. I begged and pleaded and manipulated and twisted and performed, all for a few drops. Then, just as the drops approached, I quickly placed my hand over the cup, but why?

The Tin Man in *The Wizard of Oz* discovered love has the power to cause great pain. I certainly learned that to be true by the time I was in first grade. However, I eventually learned that love, when healthy, also has the amazing power to heal my wounded heart. The deep self-hate I carried most of my life would be the most difficult obstacle to my return to Oz, a place where I'd experience joy, safety, and love again. I first needed to understand that I was blocking the very thing that would help me heal the most. It always mystified me that on the only occasion when I actually cried "real" tears in

Dr. Wilson's office, I turned away to prevent her from holding me.

She even pleaded, "Turn around; let me hold you."

You have no idea how much I wish I could go back and redo that day. I'm not sure why, but I still long for that hug from her. "Real" tears are still very rare for me, but I know Jesus is keeping them in a bottle for me, and if or when He sees the need for me to express them, I'm sure they will be available.

I had imagined and dreamed of that moment occurring so many times. I deeply longed for the feeling of being held by her while I cried, so why would I not allow it? Unfortunately, I had cut off my ability to cry tears when I was very young. Instead, to this very day, I get a migraine headache the moment I feel real tears approaching. I'd rather cry now! Why was I too terrified to feel the very thing I wanted most, her love and comfort? It took another fifteen years to find the answer and in a very unexpected way, through my foot.

I had lived with the Goldsteins for about two years when a giant light bulb illuminated a very dark place inside me. They were having some friends over for dinner, and we were all seated tightly at the kitchen table. Mark was asking his usual questions to stir up some interesting conversation. Due to the small space, Maria and I were seated very close. I had my left, shoeless foot propped up on my right knee under the table. About halfway through the sharing time, Maria took hold of my foot and did not let go. No one else knew about this endearing sign of love or the instant battle in my head. The flashing short circuit in my brain was a clue that something very huge was occurring. I felt sudden panic and the thought, *Don't feel it*, resounded over and over in my mind. Her hand squeezing my foot downloaded a warm feeling of being truly loved. Fear almost immobilized me, and I felt an immense need to dissociate as fast as possible and put my foot far from her reach. Unfortunately, or fortunately, much healing had occurred by now and my ability to totally shut off my feelings had long passed. The ability to be numb and check out immediately had helped save my life, but was now preventing me from entering into a depth of relationship that would ultimately help me heal.

Numb, even if only partially, had been safe because most things in my life growing up were very unsafe, especially people. Imagine the pain a child would endure if she continued to expect her mother to hold her if she came home crying after being raped. It didn't take me too long to quit having that expectation as a child, and it didn't take long to shut off the desire. To me, this is why transference sucks? All that desire and need (cruelest feeling ever) is stored up over all the years and then the moment you get into a relationship where you begin to trust, those pesky feelings and pain start bursting forth without much control to suck it back in!

Numb allowed me the power to walk away from a relationship without being devastated. Numb made life bearable, not only when Mother failed to comfort me after the abuse, but also expected me to comfort her, take care

---

Over time, I learned that every coping skill I learned to help me survive the pain in my childhood was now blocking me from the healing I so desperately desired.

---

of my sisters, and pretend I was happy with no needs. I actually cannot remember one time when I received comfort or any sign of compassion after abuse, except from school officials the time I was raped on school property. Numb made life bearable when someone says, "You're my child now," but then offers you up to her husband for sexual purposes. Numb makes life possible when close loved ones are unable to be part of your support system, and when close friends say, "You are entertaining demons by allowing them to dwell in you," because of my need to compartmentalize everything that had happened in childhood. It seems I could write a whole book about the advantages of emotional numbness. However, over time, I learned that every coping skill I learned to help me survive the pain in my childhood was now blocking me from the healing I so desperately desired. That night, while Maria sweetly held my foot under the table, remaining numb seemed almost impossible!

I was forced to make a huge and very difficult decision. I wanted to feel the specialness and intimacy of the friendship she offered, but felt so afraid. Maria had boatloads of friends and had no <u>need</u> for me. She could easily hire someone else to care for Grammy, so I truly had nothing to offer her, or so I perceived.

My mind began to battle, *Don't let her in. Don't feel it. Put your foot back down on the floor now! This feels so special; maybe she can be trusted with my heart. It's a set up; she'll eventually leave. They all do.*

The thought, *It's a set up was especially loud.* The dialog back and forth went on for the rest of the dinner and she continued holding my foot. I continued to allow it. I knew this sign of affection was completely innocent. I had never seen a married couple so in love, and after thirty years of marriage. I knew this was nothing like what happened with Susan, and I knew she had no expectation of anything in return. The dilemma was very difficult but so worth the stress!

Before dinner was completely over, I sat there allowing myself to feel and acknowledge her great love for me. The truth was, until she took hold of my foot that night, I wasn't aware that I had kept a steel gate around my heart. I felt a deep love for her, but due to fear, I had not allowed myself to <u>feel</u> her love for me. Instead, I stored it as head knowledge instead. Maria and I are morning people, so most of our sweetest times were early in the morning. I don't think I got much sleep that night as I weighed the pros and cons. The next morning, I told her about my experience during dinner the night before. It was so monumental to me because I had made the decision to "let her in," which simply meant feel her love for me. Feeling the love offered by others is a huge risk, and I was still very worried that I had made a mistake.

Maria, with a huge smile on her face, lovingly questioned, "Don't you know by now that you're never getting rid of me?"

I believed her, and I still do.

Once I began allowing myself to really feel the love Maria and my other friends had for me, I then needed to learn that love really could be unconditional even when circumstances seemed otherwise. In a book I read many years ago called *The Five Love Languages*, written by Gary Chapman, I learned that humans have a preferred way of receiving and acknowledging love.[3] If a person's first love language is physical touch, yet they have a history that causes them to fear anger and confrontation, it's easy to see why someone would submit to emotional, physical, and sexual abuse in order to be held or touched. Over time, not only was my broken love cup fusing back together, but I also began to discover people have so many ways they show love depending on their childhood, personality, temperament, and other life experiences. By learning to look for signs of endearment and love, even if it did not manifest in a way I would have wanted or expected, I was able to protect my love cup from further breaks.

For example, I had never considered that love could look like anger. I returned home early from my ten-week mission trip to Ghana because I was ill most of the time I'd been there. Upon returning, I found out I needed my gallbladder removed. The night I came home after the surgery, Maria was bringing in fluids for me to drink and asked if I had urinated since the morning surgery. I said, "No," but was not concerned. Maria began pushing as many fluids as possible to "wake up" my bladder after being sedated. As the evening progressed, she became more and more concerned saying this could be dangerous and that I needed to go to the emergency room to be catheterized. Her concern did not manifest in a loving tone that I would label as love. Considering the fact that I was super sensitive to anger, her concern felt harsh and uncaring.

When I panicked and expressed my fear of being catheterized due to the abuse in my childhood, she replied, "If you need to call your therapist, do it right now because we are leaving!"

Where was the "Oh honey, I know this is scary, but I'll be right there with you?" There was no touchy-feely kind of voice that soothed my fear. I read her as being agitated and on the verge of outright anger if I did not either pee or head to the car immediately. Thankfully, during this time, Maria's cousin Katherine, who practices homeopathic medicine, also lived with us. Katherine tried to calm Maria down and assured her I was not in danger yet and would be okay. They actually argued and Maria gave Katherine thirty minutes to get me to pee or I'd be headed to the emergency room. Katherine put a small pill under my tongue and we waited.

During the first twenty minutes, I was not only very stressed, but also positive Maria was furious with me. Furious with me meant the absence of love! I seriously did not think the two emotions could ever exist together.

> *If my idea or definition of love looks like a red circle, anyone offering his or her blue square or green star shape of love would be unrecognizable to me.*

The assumption that Maria was furious with me was due to the tone in her voice, the lack of affirmation, and the loud noise she was creating in the kitchen. I have no idea what she was doing to cause so much noise, but it reminded me of the loud noises I heard as a child when Mother and Charlie were fighting. I'm sure my own fear caused me to read everything as more extreme than what was actually occurring. However, everything changed in just one moment.

As I lay there, more afraid of losing her love than the actual procedure of being catheterized, I had a thought, *What if her stress and passion mean she loves me?*

This had not seemed a possibility until that point.

What if the banging in the kitchen means she's so worried about me that it's coming out physically and frantically?

I started looking for evidence that this could be true. I immediately thought of so many examples of times she had reacted in a similar way with her children, other family members, and especially with Mark, whom she adores. How could I have been so blind? She was frantic because she loves me so much. Due to that epiphany, I realized that I often discounted the love offerings of others because it did not look or feel like my definition of what love should be. I was reminded of those yellow plastic toy boxes given to toddlers to help them learn their shapes. If my idea or definition of love looks like a red circle, anyone offering his or her blue square or green star shape of love would be unrecognizable to me. I would need to turn my yellow box around to allow that shape to enter. We each want love presented to us in a particular way. By choosing to think the best of others and choosing not to react immediately to a behavior or tone that wasn't what I wanted or expected, I opened myself up to receive even more love. By looking for possible alternatives to why a friend had not lived up to my hope or expectation, I often found my expectations were unreasonable and did not allow for grace. It took practice and felt very uncomfortable at first because I expected rejection and any boundary felt like rejection. Actually, I seemed to read clues of rejection in most interactions with others and unless they were giving me their undivided attention with lavish doses of overt love, I was sure I was being rejected. By allowing myself to consider Maria's reaction might be love instead of anger or rejection, it allowed me to open my heart and eyes to see how much others loved me as well.

As I sat in church, many years prior to this event, and the Lord kept asking me, "Are you loving them?" I was indignant that He expected me to attempt to pour into the "full love cup" my peers enjoyed from the "empty cup" I thought I held. Without understanding His reasoning, I obeyed, over and over again. I eventually discovered what God already knew, that in learning and <u>choosing</u> to love others, my own cracked, and leaky love cup would begin to heal. I did not have the power to love or accept myself. During the years of abuse, it was not safe to be angry with the people in my life who were hurting me. Combining that with all the lies I believed such as "I'm dirty, I'm ugly, It was my fault, I'm bad," etc., the rage and anger inside were directed towards me rather than outwards towards others. I couldn't find anything to love about myself, so it seemed impossible that anyone else could either.

There had never been a time when I was able to describe something I liked about myself. I could not control how I <u>felt</u> about myself, but over time, I had more and more control over my <u>behavior</u> and <u>choices</u>. Just like choosing to intentionally love others, I took small steps towards learning to value myself. These small steps included many behavioral hospitalizations, many nights sitting in 12-Step meetings, many therapy sessions, many hours of studying while completing inner healing courses, such as Elijah House, many hours of listening to Bible teachers, such as Beth Moore, and choosing to remain in safe relationships with close friends even when I wanted to run. It also required obedience when I heard the small or loud voice telling me what step to take next. I can't imagine how different my life would have been if I had not obeyed God in several key moments. The more I obeyed, the more He lead and the more I healed.

Making these choices day after day was very difficult, but there were many bright spots mixed in the process. There were many times I needed to be confronted with a truth I did not want to hear. It was so hard to remain in a place of humility instead of pride when I felt embarrassment after needing to be remolded in a particular area. It seemed every area of my pot needed refashioning. Most of my life, it felt as if everyone else was innately more valuable and relatively flawless compared to me. I discovered that acknowledging the humanness in others and then offering them mercy and forgiveness, helped me find mercy and forgiveness for myself. These "discoveries," and then the acts of obedience to follow, were necessary in order for me to reach my place of restoration, joy, and wholeness, otherwise known as my Oz.

Glinda in *The Wizard of Oz* guided Dorothy to a path where she would meet the three friends who would assist her in the journey. They loved, taught, and protected her. Glinda watched over them in the journey and provided help when necessary. I absolutely know God set me on the very path that would lead to the people and circumstances He chose in order for me to heal. I made so many mistakes and poor decisions on my journey, but God adores me. There were times I intentionally walked into what the world calls sinful behavior in order to get a few drops for my love cup, but God has always been willing to turn my own sin and the sins of others done against me to work out for my good as long as I continued to love Him (Romans 8:28). Remember, love is not a feeling necessarily but a choice. I can tell my best friend that I love her a thousand times a month, but if I act jealously and become angry when she spends time with other friends, talk bad about her to mutual friends, or expect her to pay for lunch because she makes more money than I do, then I'm not loving her. I learned I was not "loving" God until I chose to treat Him differently. If my love for Him is conditional, if I compare how it seems He "blesses" others compared to me, if I choose to do my own thing, go by my own rules, or live according to my feelings rather than His wisdom, I'm not loving Him. The awesome part is He knows my past wounding, life experiences, genetic makeup, IQ, and so much more. As humans, we are brutal in our estimations of each other! God alone is able to judge me accurately and He says I'm carefully and wonderfully made. (Ps. 139:14)

The saying, "Hindsight is 20/20" makes more sense to me now than ever before. The truth that the abuse didn't make me a bad person, gross, ugly, dirty, defective, unlovable, or worthless is so clear to me now, but why didn't I see it before? There is a profound discussion at the end of the movie, *The Wizard of Oz,* which illustrates this revelation very well. Professor Marvel had just flown away in the hot air balloon because he didn't know how it worked. Dorothy suddenly loses hope that she can ever go home, but, of course, Glinda returns in her bubble.

DOROTHY: Will you help me? Can you help me?

GLINDA: You don't need to be helped any longer. You've always had the power to go back to Kansas.

DOROTHY: I have?

SCARECROW: Then why didn't you tell her before?

GLINDA: Because she wouldn't have believed me. She had to learn it for herself.

TIN MAN: What have you learned, Dorothy?

DOROTHY: Well, I think it wasn't enough to just want to see Uncle Henry and Auntie Em. If I ever go look for my heart's desire again, I won't look any further than my own backyard because if it isn't there, I never really lost it to begin with. Is that right?

GLINDA: That's all it is.

SCARECROW: But that's so easy. I should have thought of it for you.

TIN MAN: I should have felt it in my heart.

GLINDA: No, she had to find it out for herself (Metro-Goldwyn-Meyer).

God, in the very beginning, provided all we needed to remain in a safe place where we had food to eat, the ability to create a family for emotional support, and where we felt valued and loved. Because of our sin nature, we've had to take a lot of journeys to discover the very thing that should have been so easy. This ultimate discovery requires us to follow the path He designed for our life and obey when He says, "Don't eat the apples" or "Go back and face your enemy." We must seek intimacy with Him above all others and rely on His wisdom rather than our own understanding. So what is this "ultimate discovery?" What is it that humans long for more than anything? What knowledge does Satan work so hard to hide from us? What is so amazing and so astounding that we even need the Holy Spirit to help us comprehend?

Without the next chapter, I would never have made my most glorious discovery!

Chapter II

SO AM I REALLY

A PRINCESS?

It seems I would have "discovered" God's full love for me the moment I saw Jesus in the sky at four years old, or when I saw the hem of His garment and felt His kiss on my head that difficult day in church. There are zillions of times I should have acknowledged the vast love God has just for me. At age forty-four, it wasn't that I didn't know God loved me; duh, He loves all His children here on earth. By this time, I hadn't needed formal counseling in a few years and other than some difficult health issues was content. I had no way of knowing that God would be sending me to Ghana, Africa for the last few steps in reaching my final destination, Oz on earth. Who would guess that God would take me so far away to discover my royalty and the abundant and never-ending love He has just for me? Head knowledge moves to the heart!

I had moved from the Goldstein's home and was teaching children placed in a self-contained classroom in the public school system. My precious students taught me so many valuable lessons, especially about love, during the time I was supposed to be teaching them. Some were severely autistic, and others had Down's syndrome, but in many ways, they were brilliant. Unfortunately, the stress of teaching, along with the many years of stress while working as a primary case manager for the Department of Children's Services, took a toll on my health. It was spring of 2009, and I had barely survived the massive paperwork expected of teachers, especially special education teachers. I knew I would not be able to teach another year and had been asking God to show me what I was to do in the fall. He answered firmly and in a Ghanaian voice.

One Saturday afternoon, the Goldsteins invited me to lunch to meet Maxine, a missionary they supported, and Theophilus(Theo), the Ghanaian Pastor, who traveled with her. Maxine founded Village Medicine, an amazing ministry made up of faithful and precious board members, Ghanaian doctors, and other personnel to bring medical supplies and care to unreached villages who don't have access to medical care. Maxine, an American, raised funds in the states for the supplies, used her medical training from the U.S. to teach the Ghanaian doctors more effective treatments, and had been living in Ghana for several years. The ministry she founded, and the sacrifice she put into it is inspiring. I was excited to meet them but had no expectation of ever seeing them again, much less living with them! During lunch, we all chatted for a while, and then I noticed Maxine and Theo nudging each other. They told me stories about the Ghanaian people and their life there. Most of Maxine's stories included snakes, some very big snakes. It became obvious at some point that they believed I was the person they had prayed for to come help with a special project in Ghana.

I told Maxine, "If snakes are part of your travel itinerary, I'm not interested. I hate snakes!"

I also explained that I have an extreme sensitivity to heat and other health issues. Clearly, they were wrong in their assumption of my being an answer to their prayer!

The Goldsteins were getting a little miffed at their insistence, but they were farther down the table and in conversation with other people they had invited. Mark and Maria knew me; they really knew me! I think they were even more positive than I was that God would not be "calling" me to Ghana.

However, about midway through lunch, another friend asked, "Tammy, if you're not planning to teach next year, what will you be doing?"

I replied, "For as long as I can remember, my ultimate dream has been to help children heal from sexual abuse and eventually open a home specifically for their recovery. I have no clue how this will ever happen."

As I described my lifelong dream, Maxine's and Theo's eyes opened wide and mouths dropped. They had not told me yet why they wanted me to come to Ghana. All I knew was they were positive I was the person to come. It's very hot there, and snakes would be part of my future if I went. I know I mentioned that already!

Theo and Maxine continued to pressure me into agreeing to come to Ghana. They explained the purpose of my trip would be to help them design and direct a children's home currently under construction. At this point, Maxine's stories changed and now included the terrible ways children are being abused in the villages. I had already heard some very sad stories because the Goldsteins had gone to Ghana previously and brought back the sad pictures with the stories to match. I had no desire ever to go somewhere far away. I had always been the person in the church pew, listening to missionaries share their testimony of all they will be doing and thinking, *God bless you; here's a hundred dollars. Go save the world, I'll just stay here and "pray."* Even after Maxine told me about the hurting children, I replied, "I'm not the one to go. There are snakes, and I hate the heat, but I'll give you some money."

After giving my firm and final "not me," Theo, the pastor, raised his hand towards me and in a very firm, passionate voice, said, "You will come to Ghana; God will give you peace!" I'll never forget that moment!

This is when the Ghana miracles started. First, I had a very real and intense dream that night, and I rarely remember my dreams. I was in the tomb where Indiana Jones, from the movie, had stood, and black snakes were everywhere. I could feel them crawling on my feet; I was too terrified to move. Then I saw the most beautiful dark skinned baby about twenty feet in front of me. In the dream, I had the most intense maternal feeling I'd ever had, and I desperately wanted to hold the baby. That meant walking forward through the snakes. I trembled but my thought over and over was, *I have to hold the baby*. The love I felt was the most intense feeling I'd ever experienced. As I began slowly putting one foot in front of the other. It seemed to take forever, but I eventually approached the baby and reached out to hold her. When I woke up, I had real tears streaming down the sides of my face. I had no clue it was possible to cry in your sleep. It was seriously powerful!

This dream happened on a Sunday morning. As I woke up, I prayed, *Father, if You're calling me to Africa, You need to make this very clear because I can't go without Your anointing, power, and provision. Actually, Lord, You will need to make me go!*

> *I had asked God for a very clear and undeniable sign that I was to fly to Africa to face snakes and extreme heat. The Holy Spirit telling this woman "Remember Africa" in front of my rocks on Stone Mountain could not have been a clearer sign.*

During the altar call at church, I went forward to request prayer, hoping someone would say, "Tammy, you're not being called to Africa. Go sit back down!" Instead, two women came up behind me to pray; both were on the prayer team and considered anointed in our church. After they prayed silently for a few minutes, one of them asked if I wanted prayer for something specific. I shared a tiny bit of what had occurred the day before and asked for them to pray about my "calling to Africa."

The moment I said the word Africa, one of them began trembling and repeatedly said, "It was about you. All day it was about you."

It took her a few minutes to calm down, but she then explained what had occurred the day before. She had taken her children to climb Stone Mountain, and as she approached a huge rock formation at the top, she began trembling and heard the Holy Spirit say, "Remember Africa" over and over. Even the shape of the huge boulders looked like the continent of Africa to her, and she said the feeling was intense. After playing on top of the mountain, she and her children headed back down the steep trail. While passing the same rocks, she began trembling again and continued to hear "Remember Africa" off and on all day.

I had asked God for a very clear and undeniable sign that I was to fly to Africa to face snakes and extreme heat. The Holy Spirit telling this woman "Remember Africa" in front of my rocks on Stone Mountain could not have been a clearer sign. I was so humbled and awed at her experience that I was not able to share at that point why this sign was a very clear answer. She had no way of knowing how sentimental those boulders were to my sisters and me. Shortly after I ran away, the Department of Family and Children's Services removed my sisters and placed them in a children's shelter. After I had run away, I had no control over their protection, so it was only a matter of time before a crisis occurred that required police intervention. If I had known running away would be the key to being rescued, I would have run away the day I took my first step!

My sisters and I were very close, so the separation had been difficult for all three of us. To ease the pain, their DFCS case manager allowed me, at seventeen years old, to pick them up from the shelter for an adventure to Stone Mountain. I always bought a bucket of Kentucky Fried Chicken for us to eat after we finally ascended the steep mountain trail. We usually sang all the way up, ate our chicken on the huge formation of boulders near the top of the mountain, and laughed a lot! How could my praying friend know that the exact place where the Holy Spirit shook her and repeated "Remember Africa" was the same place I spent many happy days with my sisters? It was our safe place, so what did this mean? Oh no, not the snakes! My friend was having this divine moment the same time Maxine and Theo were telling me I was to come to Africa. Just like us humans, I continued to ask God for more verification. Even the Goldsteins thought their divine choice was way off. I actually hoped the Goldsteins were correct until God began making the financial and emotional "provisions." Though our human mind and faith scoffed at my mission assignment, God knew why He was sending me to Africa; it had nothing to do with me being qualified.

During the preparation months, while getting ready for my huge "calling," several people, some barely knowing me, approached and said, "Your mission to Ghana is about your healing, not about you helping their ministry."

One church member firmly said, "Your healing will be completed in Ghana."

I was a little annoyed by their sentiment. I thought, *Of course, I can help them, I taught special education. My Master's degree in counseling will surely come in handy, and I worked as a DFCS case manager for fifteen years. Why do I still need healing? I'm fine now!"*

Describing the miracles in Ghana and the pain, feels impossible. How does someone condense the ten weeks I spent there into a few paragraphs? I experienced so much: major rejection, painful physical illness, excommunication, disappointments, intense insomnia, very frightening spiritual warfare, and the end of a dream. However, I also experienced precious times of joyful play, major breakthroughs, multiple speaking engagements to help others heal from sexual abuse, the blessing of teaching behavior modification techniques to staff at a home for abandoned children, many miracles, an ocean vacation, the acknowledgement of my royalty, extravagant love, and the beginning of a new dream.

On my first visit to one of the remote villages where Maxine and Theo brought medicine and the message of God's love, I had an intense encounter with one of the children there. A beautiful little girl, who looked about three to four years old, stood in front of me with a huge grin. Time seemed to stand still and at that moment, it felt as if she and I were alone with no activity around us. I stared as intently at her as she did me. Though she was wearing a dirty little dress two sizes too big, I felt as if she were royalty. I actually trembled as I reached out in an effort to touch her hand. The sense was that I was standing on holy ground, so I seriously wanted to drop to my knees.

In my spirit, I heard the words, "She is the least of these and one that I adore."

The little girl wanted to touch me as much as I wanted to touch her. Wow, my next thought was life changing. *I must be one of the least of these, just like this little brown princess.* She and I had experienced suffering, yet we were considered one of God's least of these, whom He loves lavishly.

Little Brown Princess

Your eyes are sad, because you don't know. Bought with a
price and He loves you so.

Frail, thin arms and dirty face; but precious to your Father
who offers His Grace.

Hard work ahead and just to survive. Children in other
countries; play and thrive.

My heart adores you, I see in your eyes; pain of hunger,
but He hears your cries.

I too have felt it, couldn't escape the pain. Nights of darkness and days of rain.

Bringing you hope, extending His love; Jesus to hold you,
my arms sent from above.

*Abundance of love, wealth of joy He will bring; Me sent to
Royalty; your father is a King.*

Written on 9/7/09, the day I met the brown little princess.

**The Lord replies, "I have seen violence done to the
helpless, and I have heard the groans of the poor. Now
I will rise up to rescue them, as they have longed for
me to do." (Psalms 12:5 New Living Translation)**

During my ten weeks in Ghana, I witnessed so many examples of God's love for His children living there. They have almost no possessions, certainly nothing we would consider valuable; yet, they appeared to be much happier than most Americans. The children played with sticks, broken toys, and rocks. They laughed and smiled as if they owned the newest electronic gaming system. I think I saw God in the wind playing with some little girls in a field one day while traveling to Theo's church. The dirt road was very flat, so it was easy to see three small children playing with a little black bag far in the distance. The child running ahead of the others would throw the plastic bag up, and the wind would take it up just above their heads. The bag would tease them by dropping just low enough for them to try catching it, but looped back up just out of reach. When one of the children finally caught the bag, they would toss it in the air again. It appeared as if the Holy Spirit was playing the game Keep Away, but occasionally allowed them to catch it just like a parent would do with a child. The smile and joy on their little faces were profound, and I began to remember all the times my Heavenly Father helped me in the midst of my pain. He NEVER left me, and His plan for my life was that I NEVER be abused. John 10:10 (NIV) says, "The thief comes only to steal and kill and destroy; I have come that they may have life, and have it to the full." Satan is the thief and master deceiver. He began lying to us in the Garden of Eden, and we are still listening to his lies.

The dynamics of how all this works reminds me of the story *Sleeping Beauty*. Maleficent, a powerful, evil figure, appears uninvited at the celebration of baby Aurora's birth.[4] She announces her intention to kill the princess on her sixteenth birthday, death by the prick of a spinning wheel. After Maleficent's departure, Merryweather, the passionate fairy Godmother, canceled the curse of death and changed the course of Aurora's future. Instead of death, a Prince would come, kiss her, and take her to his royal palace living happily ever after.

We are Father's children. He loves us more than we will ever be able to comprehend. In the Garden of Eden, Satan's ability to deceive us allowed him access to our circumstances here on earth. He can and does cause tremendous suffering. Jesus said in John 16:33 (TLB), *"I have told you all this so that you will have peace of heart and mind. Here on earth you will have many trials and sorrows; but cheer up, for I have overcome the world."* Jesus holds the ultimate key to our future and His plans for us are spectacular. Jeremiah 29:11 (NIV) says, "For I know the plans I have for you," declares the Lord, "plans to prosper you and not to harm you, plans to give you hope and a future." I equate our life on earth with Aurora's sixteen years of sleep while she waits for her prince. Life while waiting for our redeemer is sometimes good, marginal, or a nightmare; however, our Prince is coming to take us home, and He chooses all of us!

Regarding His choosing all of us, I learned a very interesting detail about the verse in Matthew 22:14 (AMP) that says, "For many are called (invited and summoned), but few are chosen." In this parable, the king was preparing a wedding banquet for his son. He sent servants out to the ones on his invitation list, but they refused to come. Then the king sent even more servants to tell them the oxen and cattle have been butchered; it's all ready. Please come to my home, enjoy the free food, and the party. Some of the guests chose to do their own thing and opted to miss the party. Some of the other guests chose anger, beat up and then killed the messenger. The king then became angry, sent his army to kill the murderers, and then updated his invitation list.

The phrase, "but few are chosen" never seemed fair to me until I began to understand the significance of the offer. The king ended up inviting local street people and those living all the way to the end of the country. In verse Matt. 22:10, it says the king invited both the good and bad. In a nutshell, the king invited everyone, but it was the humble, the poor, the lost, the broken, the wounded, and the ones who desire to eat from the king's table that eventually enjoyed the buffet. It seems that the people most likely to appreciate the huge gift are the ones who ultimately choose to be chosen. Think of it this way. The next time you feel slighted because you can't afford a new car like the Joneses, be thankful. The next time you feel inferior to your friend because she has 4189 friends on Facebook compared to your 289, be thankful. And, during your journey on the yellow brick road, be thankful. Why?

Most people who are wealthy, popular, famous, spoiled, or adored have a very hard time choosing to attend the King's buffet. Why? They don't feel

---

Most people who are wealthy, popular, famous, spoiled, or adored have a very hard time choosing to attend the King's buffet.

---

a need for a relationship with Him. I think this explains the issue about why rich people can't go through the eye of a needle in the Bible.

I've been thinking about this King's party parable for a long time because I want so much to understand why some people who go through extreme trauma come out stronger and even more resilient. Conversely, why do some people seem to have a very low threshold of pain and crumble when life throws them a few small challenges? What variables go into the decision to choose the banquet table while others run from it? I decided to write my own modern day parable to see if I could make sense of this riddle.

Three Sons are Chosen but Who Will Go?

Mr. and Mrs. Leverette, a successful and loving couple, had three sons: Steve, Frank, and Jake, whom they adored. Their sons attended the same school in their county, enjoyed team sports throughout their high school years, and as a graduation gift, were given the opportunity to travel to a destination of their choice with a friend. The Leverettes had worked hard to create a very lucrative company to be handed down to their children at the right time. Being wise parents, they required the boys to live on a fixed income while attending college in order to learn the joy of hard work and money management skills. Upon graduation, they would then be required to complete a two-year internship within the company to demonstrate their ability to lead others fairly and with compassion.

After spending the summer in France, Steve returned home and started college. His classes were challenging to say the least, but he was willing to work hard. Steve trusted his parents, knew they had his best interest at heart, and of course, looked forward to the reward of running a profitable company. During his four years away at the University, Steve experienced some quite difficult circumstances. For example, Steve was mugged one day in the school parking deck and received a nasty beating. Thankfully, his parents provided the best possible medical care, and they made the crisis as bearable as possible. Despite the hardships while at college, Steve experienced peace of mind during his time away.

The next year, the Leverettes' second born son, Frank, traveled to Switzerland and while there, met other young people who were avid skiers. Though he knew the conditions his parents set for him in order to be given a portion of his father's company, Frank decided to stay in Switzerland for a while. He loved the relaxed atmosphere, the pretty girls, and life with minimal responsibilities. College and work, he figured, could wait until he experienced all the fun Switzerland had to offer. His decision – I'm turning down the invitation, but just for now. I'll give my parents some of my time in a few years when I'm too old to have fun. I'll let them influence my choices, ethics, and all that mature stuff when I'm older. They'll always love me!

Lastly, Jake the youngest son, decided to travel to a city called Gomorrah in the country of Sodom. Throughout high school, he had chosen to hang out with some exchange students from Gomorrah. He never introduced his friends to his family because he knew they would not approve. Jake's parents were very protective, set firm boundaries, and desired complete success for each son. The Leverettes' definition of success was not necessarily wealth, but the true contentment that comes from hard work, close family ties, and the joy of accomplishing a goal.

During high school, Jake and his Gomorrian friends had no desire to make good grades. They chose to skip school often in order to have fun. It was during these teen years that Jake learned to make excuses, tell lies, and manipulate others. He wasn't a bad kid, but at this point, simply wanted to do things that felt good. That's the reason for his decision to travel to Gomorrah after he graduated from high school. Mr. and Mrs. Leverette gave him their blessing when Jake left for the summer but became very concerned when he did not return in the fall.

Jake enjoyed when his parents called, but he was very good at establishing reasons why it wouldn't be possible to return at that time. Either he was too busy to call for flight arrangements, didn't want to offend his friends by returning home so soon, or he explained that his latest girlfriend just might be the one for marriage. Jake just needed "a little more time," which spread out to several years. He knew how to pacify his parents' concerns.

Soon after arriving in Gomorrah, Jake reported to his family that he found a wonderful church and hated to miss services. He knew his parents would be pleased to know he was attending a church regularly. What Jake failed to tell them was that the churches in Gomorrah serve a very different god from the one he knew as a child. Though Jake never intended to leave his childhood home permanently, or his parents, and his faith, the longer he stayed in the country of Sodom, the deeper his indoctrination became.

In my parable, the three sons were all loved the same. Steve, the oldest son, followed the rules his parents set, even when he did not understand why the rule was important. He worked hard in school to have the necessary skills to run his father's company. His decision – I choose to be chosen!

Frank, the middle son, had the attitude, "I want to follow the rules and work hard in school, but not yet. I'll enjoy sowing my wild oats first and experience all that life has to give. I know my parents don't approve of my lifestyle and choices, but I'll come back later. His decision – I don't want to be chosen right now.

Jake, the youngest son, loved living far beyond his parents' reach. He felt ready to make his own decisions, rules, and schedule. He loved his new friends, enjoyed his immoral life, and had no desire to return to his parents. Jake even made fun of anyone associated with his parents' company. Occasionally, however, he had moments of guilt for the things he was doing, knowing his parents would say his behavior was either wrong or self-destructive. Jake simply acquired various substances or engaged in even more perverted behavior to bury his feelings of guilt and shame. He did not chose to be chosen. His decision - I don't need to go to the King's buffet. I have everything I need right here!

In my parable, the parents represent God. He loves all of us so much and desires great things for our lives. Though I was very responsible like the oldest son, I blamed God for so many things in my life, but mostly I blamed myself. I felt so unworthy of Father's blessings that I kept myself numb. I didn't run from God like Frank and Jake to "enjoy the pleasures of life." I found very little pleasure in anything, but only because I thought the pain was all I deserved. I had the head knowledge that God loved me, but I hated myself too much to actually have heart knowledge of His love. What I call heart knowledge of God's love is probably the best feeling I've ever experienced.

As is His nature towards all His children, God never stopped calling my name, and He never gave up on me. I can see the crystal ball that the wicked witch showed Dorothy with Auntie Em frantically calling, "Dorothy, where are you?" Our heavenly Father never stops calling us to come back home. He still wanted me to have that wonderful future where I would experience peace, my Oz on earth. There was only one obstacle in my way – me!

Thankfully, God not only showed me His heart, but He also helped me understand why my heart was still aching – I believed a lot of lies.

Reflecting back to the story in the Bible about the woman at the well who meets Jesus, He asked her for water and started a conversation. He let her know that He already knew about her sin, and He was not rejecting her. She got so excited that she ran back to her own town and began telling them about her sin. Where were her shame and guilt? Why was she willing to tell everyone about her sin in order to point the way to Jesus? Why wasn't she full of self-hate and an intense need to be punished? Why didn't she run back home, break out the old wineskins, and then call one of her old lovers to come hang out?

If the old me had met Jesus at the well when Jesus began acknowledging my sin, I'm not sure I would have been able to chat long enough to discover His true heart towards me. I would have assumed His next words would be some form of rejection. My head would have dropped, the feeling of shame would permeate even more within my soul, and then the self-incriminating thoughts and accusations would begin resonating in my mind. Running as far away as possible would have felt like my only option. Since physically running away has not always been possible, I simply closed my heart to protect myself. I expected rejection. Because I would have hated myself even more, I'd begin to punish myself verbally and physically. I would have used whatever means necessary to numb my pain and guilt: excess food, alcohol, cutting, strict diets, etc.

If the woman at the well had chosen to live in shame, she would not have been able to feel the healing love Jesus had for her. She would have run home feeling worse and probably sinned even more to numb her pain. She would not have brought the good news of the living water to the people in her hometown. She would have missed out on all the wonderful things God had planned for her future. In the story about the three sons, if Frank and Jake had decided to return home, their parents would have done anything possible to help them have the wonderful future they had planned for them at their birth. The two brothers would simply have a later start than their older brother Steve, who by then, would be running the company and own much of the stock.

What I discovered over time – my heavenly Father does not get ruffled when I disobey. He already knows I'm going to mess up big time. The problem with sin is that we allow shame and guilt to enter in and take root

---

As long as we listen to the master deceiver's lies in our head, he is able to keep us from the King, the living water that will sustain us.

---

in our soul. Then we keep hiding from God, which will prevents us from getting the very power we need from Him to fight the temptation of the sin in the first place. It also keeps us wearing those scratchy fig leaves that really chaff.

As long as we listen to the master deceiver's lies in our head, he is able to keep us from the King, the living water that will sustain us. Satan had already robbed me of my childhood and teen years by taking over the minds of my abusers, which they allowed. He then robbed me of my young adult years by keeping me in a constant state of shame, guilt, and self-loathing which I allowed for a time. All along, I had a choice to listen and believe God, or to listen and believe the father of all lies. In Romans 6, it says we have the choice to be a slave to sin or a slave to obedience. I'm sure Steve made a lot of mistakes during his preparation years to take over his father's company. He probably failed a few tests, stayed out too late, drank too much with his college buddies, and sometimes chose outright rebellion. In my parable, Steve's parents knew and expected him to walk out his preparation years imperfectly, making a lot of mistakes that he can choose to learn from. When he made mistakes, his parents were there with open arms. I wish all parents were like the Leverettes, but that would have required them to have parents just like the Leverettes as well. There is too much evil and wounding in this world for a set of Leverette parents to exist, but we have a God who is a gazillion bazillion times better!

He knows everything about me: my talents, gifts, temperament, personality, and genetic make-up, such as IQ. Because He knows every wound, and He understands my limitations due to having a sin nature, God's ability to show me grace is beyond what I can understand. However, He can't give me the bright future He has planned for my life until I've done my part of the work to get prepared. Steve had to discipline himself in many ways to be prepared to take over his father's company. He had to study hard, memorize facts for the tests, choose self-control in many areas, and submit to his parents' authority in order to learn humility. All great leaders have learned to be humble first. During all the mistakes along the way, Steve's parents desired to help him reach his calling and receive his inheritance. They were willing to help in any way and at any point.

This is what I've learned about God's love and my royalty. My Father in heaven never wanted me to be used and abused. He did not want me to be raised in a home with a very mentally ill mother, a domestic abuser, an absent father, and a host of pedophiles in and out. He never wanted my abusers to be wounded in their childhood either. Father also never wanted me to punish myself for the abuse, and He never stopped helping me heal.

I couldn't see what was happening in Father's realm and certainly could not comprehend His plans. Similarly, in the movie *The Wizard of Oz*, Glinda watched over Dorothy after sending her down a difficult path to help her find her "heart's desire." I can look back and easily see that God walked with me during my journey to Oz, my inner place of peace, joy, and contentment.

During the first twenty-five years of my life, I could easily describe myself as the Cowardly Lion since I was terrified of so many monsters, both real and imaginary. I had so much insecurity, shame, and fearfulness that I was often stunned when someone actually wanted to be my friend. One of my favorite lines in the movie was said by the Cowardly Lion, "Well, wouldn't you feel degraded to be in the company of a cowardly lion? I would!" This is how I felt most of the time, especially in high school and college. It felt as if others were taking a blow to their reputation if they were seen with or befriended me.

Other times during my life, I would have described myself as being similar to the Tin Man. I was numb as if I had no heart, but I could act as if I felt all the typical emotions everyone else felt. Now that I no longer need to play "my game," and have chosen to face all the feelings I once learned to ignore, I've learned like the Tin Man that feelings can be very painful. However, once I moved past the painful memories and feelings from childhood, new and wonderful feelings began to seep in. I'm now thankful to have a heart!

During my journey, I needed my insides replaced like the Scarecrow. The old coping skills have been replaced with healthy ways to deal with pain and stress when it comes my way. My mind needed to be renewed by the power of the Holy Spirit. I know not to let angry and self-destructive thoughts repeat in my mind. I don't journey this road without mistakes, but when one is made, I forgive others and myself easily. It would be a tragedy to ever allow Satan the power to control me again. I focus on the prize, the day I get to live in the real Oz with the one true King, who never stops loving His children.

Epilogue

Isaiah 61:7 (NIV) says, "Instead of your shame you will receive a double portion, and instead of disgrace you will rejoice in your inheritance. And so you will inherit a double portion in your land, and everlasting joy will be yours."

I got a late start running my Father's company, King's Treasure Box Ministries, but I have no regrets. He helped me step out of the guilt and shame and without needing sparkly red shoes! He has doubled my inheritance and tripled my "everlasting joy." It's never too late to get back on the yellow brick road.

Notes

1. Scaer, R. C. (2001). *The Body Bears The Burden: Trauma, Dissociation, and Disease.* Binghamton, New York: Haworth Medical Press.

2. LeRoy, M. (Producer), & Fleming, V. (Director). (1939). *The Wizard of Oz* [Motion picture]. United States: Metro-Goldwyn-Mayer (MGM).

3. Chapman, G. (1995). *The Five Love Languages: The Secret to Love That Lasts.* Chicago, Illinois: Northfield Publishing.

4. Geronimi, C. (Director). (1959). *Sleeping Beauty* [animated Motion picture]. United States: Walt Disney Company.

For more information, helpful resources, and how you can get involved in helping people recover from sexual abuse, visit:

the kingstreasurebox.org

CPSIA information can be obtained at www.ICGtesting.com
Printed in the USA
LVOW10s0617220915

455193LV00001B/1/P